Mark Shand (1951–2014) was a travel writer with a playboy past which he exchanged for the life of a fund-raising conservationist. His travel books include *River Dog: A Journey down the Brahmaputra, Queen of the Elephants, Skullduggery* (a journey he undertook with his friend Don McCullin) and *Travels On My Elephant* for which he received the Travel Writer of the Year award. The latter journey directly led to his foundation of Elephant Family—a charity specifically established to protect the environment of the Asian elephant, tiger and orangutan, and is engaged in the creation and acquisition of jungle corridors that connect together the various different forest reserves.

TRAVELS *On My* ELEPHANT

An Indian Journey

Mark Shand

SPEAKING TIGER

SPEAKING TIGER PUBLISHING PVT. LTD
4381/4 Ansari Road, Daryaganj,
New Delhi–110002, India

First published by Jonathan Cape 1991
Published in the UK by Eland Publishing Limited 2012
Published as a paperback in India by Speaking Tiger 2018

ISBN: 978-93-87693-08-1
eISBN: 978-93-87693-09-8

10 9 8 7 6 5 4 3 2 1

For sale in South Asia only

Text set by Nick Randall
Printed at Shree Maitrey Printech Pvt. Ltd., Noida

For Clio and Tara, one small, one big, both loved

This reprint is dedicated to my wonderful daughter Ayesha

Contents

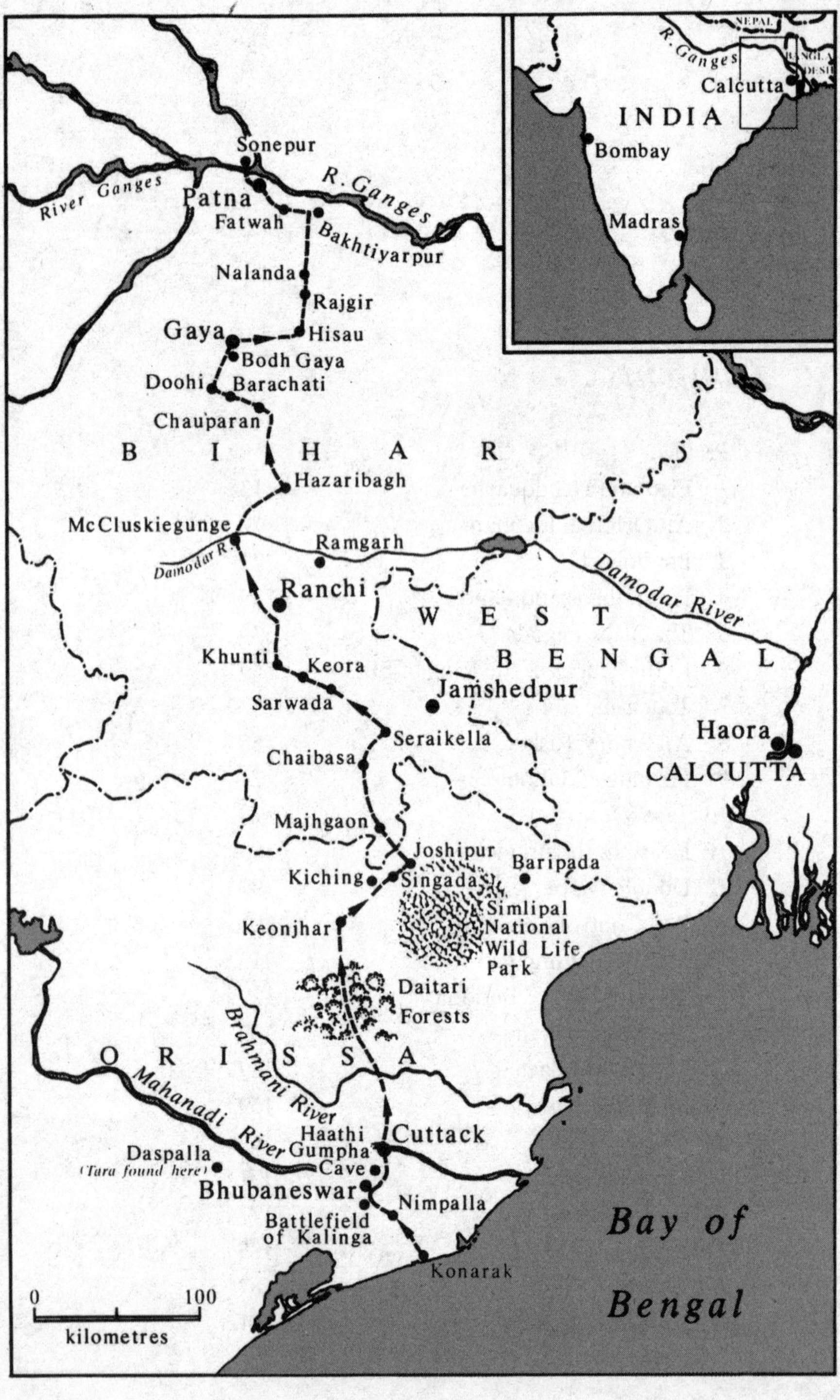
NEPAL
R. Ganges
BANGLADESH
Calcutta
INDIA
Bombay
Madras
Sonepur
River Ganges
R. Ganges
Patna
Fatwah
Bakhtiyarpur
Nalanda
Rajgir
Gaya
Hisau
Bodh Gaya
Doohi
Barachati
Chauparan
B I H A R
Hazaribagh
McCluskiegunge
Damodar R.
Ramgarh
Ranchi
Damodar River
W E S T
B E N G A L
Khunti
Keora
Jamshedpur
Sarwada
Seraikella
Haora
CALCUTTA
Chaibasa
Majhgaon
Joshipur
Baripada
Kiching
Singada
Simlipal National Wild Life Park
Keonjhar
Daitari Forests
Brahmani River
O R I S S A
Mahanadi River
Haathi Gumpha Cave
Cuttack
Daspalla
(Tara found here)
Bhubaneswar
Nimpalla
Battlefield of Kalinga
Bay of Bengal
Konarak
0
100
kilometres

Prologue

'AM I RIGHT in assuming that you want to buy an elephant?' the voice from New Delhi shouted down the telephone to me in London. Even through the hiss and static of the long-distance connection I could detect the apprehension in the voice.

'Yes,' I shouted back.

I was restless again. The last time I had been restless, I ended up being pursued by cannibals in Indonesia. This time, I had decided on a quiet jaunt across India on an elephant. This idea evolved from a drawing I had discovered while clearing out my grandmother's house after she had died. The drawing was of an infuriated male elephant about to charge a little Indian mahout or elephant driver. I took it with me and forgot about it – at least I thought I had.

A few days later I opened a book on India. Staring jovially at me from the page was a bewhiskered gentleman, wearing a dashing plumed hat, sitting nonchalantly astride an elephant. It was Tom Coryat, the eccentric Englishman who travelled to India overland in 1615, on foot, on twopence a day. When he reached the court of the great Moghul Emperor Jahangir, he wrote: 'I have rid upon an elephant since I came to this court, determining one day (by God's leave) to have my picture expressed in my next booke sitting upon an elephant.' I was now obsessed. With or without God's leave I was determined to have my picture expressed in my next book sitting upon an elephant.

I rushed to the library where I read a few classics on elephants. From the notebooks of Leonardo da Vinci, I received sound information:

> The great elephant has by nature qualities which rarely occur among men, namely probity, prudence and a sense of justice. They are mild in disposition and are conscious of dangers. If one of them should come upon a man alone who has lost his way, he puts him back peacefully in the path from which he

> has wandered. It is so peaceable that its nature does not allow it willingly to injure creatures less powerful than itself. If it should chance to meet a drove or flock of sheep, it puts them aside with its trunk so as to avoid trampling upon them with its feet; and it never injures others unless it is provoked. They have a great dread of the grunting of pigs and they delight in rivers. They hate rats. Flies are much attracted by their smell and as they settle on their backs they wrinkle up their skin deepening its tight folds and so kill them.

How could I go wrong? It seemed I had chosen a most practical and agreeable travelling companion.

Now I was telephoning a friend in New Delhi. 'Yes, I want to buy an elephant,' I shouted to him, as if this was the most usual of requests.

'You must be mad,' his voice echoed. 'Still, I suppose it's possible. India is full of elephants, but what are you going to do with it when you leave? I don't see your parents taking kindly to it residing in Sussex. Think of their beautiful garden. Why don't you rent an elephant?'

'Rent one?' I yelled. 'It's not a car.'

'All right, I'll see what I can do.' I could hear the resignation in his voice. 'Meanwhile I suggest you contact Pepita. I think she has an elephant.'

'Thank you so much. Goodbye.'

'Mark,' he shouted frantically. 'There's just one other thing. Where are you going to go on it?'

'Well, um … er …' I stuttered feebly. 'To be frank, I haven't really given it much thought yet.' In fact, I had not thought about it at all. I just imagined myself climbing aboard and setting off.

Pepita Seth is an unconventional English woman, married to one of India's finest actors. A scholar and talented photographer, she spent ten years in Kerala documenting the religious rituals of southern India. There she became obsessed with the elephant that so enriches Kerala's ceremonies and festivals. Now she lives in Delhi. I wrote asking if I could buy her elephant. Pepita replied promptly. Her writing paper 'ELEPHANT OWNERS' ASSOCIATION' announced what surely must be the most exclusive club in the world: No, I could not buy her elephant, she wrote indignantly. 'On the other hand I know where you can get one. The Sonepur Mela in Bihar, the world's largest animal fair. Elephants, cattle and horses have been sold there for centuries. I went three years ago and must have seen three hundred elephants. It happens sometime at the end of November, depending on the full moon.'

It was now the beginning of August and the Mela was not for another four months. I couldn't wait that long. I decided to leave for India immediately certain that I would find an elephant once I got there. After all, I now had a goal – a place to sell it. I just had to find one and ride to the fair.

I

Elephant Headquarters

INDIA SHOWS WHAT she wants to show, as if her secrets are guarded by a wall of infinite height. You try to climb the wall – you fall; you fetch a ladder – it is too short; but if you are patient a brick will loosen and then another. Once through, India embraces you, but that was something I had yet to learn.

When I arrived in Delhi it was my ladder that was too short. I wanted everything immediately. The monsoons had broken. Black, swollen clouds brought the usual rain, humidity and chaos. Roads were awash, taxis broke down, peacocks screamed. I perspired, worried and developed prickly heat – and I had only been there a few days.

Inevitably I consulted a fortune-teller. 'You are married, yes,' he stated wisely.

'No,' I replied.

'But you are having a companion, I think.'

'Yes.'

'You are most fortunate, sir. Soon you will be having another one. I am seeing many problems. But do not worry, sir,' he added brightly. 'They will only be getting worse.'

With characteristic generosity my friend had put his house at my disposal. It was to become 'elephant headquarters' and the mantle of co-ordinator had settled, however unwillingly, upon his shoulders. In the following week his elegant dining-room was converted into an operations area fit for a world war. Maps and papers littered the table, kit bags, medical supplies, mosquito nets, tents and food rations occupied corners. People dropped in and out. The telephone never stopped ringing and his staff worked overtime producing a continuous chain of refreshments. Game wardens, wildlife officials and forest officers, retired shikaris, politicians, journalists, government servants, ministers and just plain friends were contacted – all important people with tight schedules who went out of their way to help. Undeservedly, however, the bricks had already been loosened for me.

'Everybody's so kind,' I remarked to my friend incredulously.

'It is not you that they're worried about, it's the elephant.'

In this merry-go-round of madness I sloshed from office to office pestering people. I spent a morning discussing the reproduction cycles of the gharial, the Indian freshwater crocodile, and another looking at slides of seabirds. I was offered a camel and found myself buying a jade green parrot from a mobile bird seller, which promptly bit me. I listened carefully to mercurial advice on ancient routes and less carefully to lectures about pilgrimages and migrations affected by lunar and solar cycles. I heard about the great temples and festivals I would see, the jungles I would travel through and the tribals that I would encounter. 'And elephants?' I would eventually enquire hopefully.

'India is like an elephant,' I was told. 'She moves slowly.'

At last a vital brick fell out. Through my friend I met an important bureaucrat who had a deep knowledge of wildlife and, more important, was an expert on elephants.

'Orissa, the old kingdom of Kalinga,' he said, studying the map I had spread before him, 'is where you should go. For centuries the rulers paid their tributes in elephants. They were known as Gajpati, the Lords of Elephants. In fact,' he continued, 'you will almost certainly be retracing some ancient elephant route. You tell me that you are ending the journey at the Sonepur Mela in Bihar.'

'It was just an idea ...'

'Well, where did those elephant tributes go? To Pataliputra, the old capital of India, or Patna as it is known today. Sonepur is a few miles north of Patna, across the Ganga. Now,' he paused for a moment. 'In India every great pilgrimage or journey begins or ends at a temple or place of worship.' He smiled. 'In your case particularly an auspicious start would be of great importance. You might consider the great Sun temple at Konarak, the Black Pagoda. The main structure is supported by a carved frieze of two thousand elephants and the north side is guarded by two colossal war elephants which are so lifelike that, on moonlit nights, visitors often mistake them for the real thing.'

I now had a complete journey more or less mapped out, but still no vehicle. 'And an elephant, sir?' I enquired with diffidence.

'Your best bet is the zoo. I'll give you a letter of introduction to the director of the Nandankanan Biological Park. He's a helpful man and runs one of our better establishments. If anyone can find you an elephant, he will. Now, whatever you do, don't buy a Muckna.'

'Of course not,' I replied firmly, assuming more knowledge than I possessed. Obviously he did not believe me. He explained that a Muckna is a male elephant without tusks that suffers from a kind of inferiority complex and is usually exceedingly dangerous.

'Like a sort of eunuch,' I suggested brightly.

'Well, yes,' he replied, looking at me oddly. 'I suppose that's one way of looking at it. Of course, you will need a mahout and a charkaatiya.'

I must have looked perplexed.

'A charkaatiya,' he explained patiently, 'is a man who cuts fodder for the elephant. Its daily consumption can be as much as two hundred kilos. In certain areas, fodder will not be available, so you will have to buy it. It will be expensive. And,' he continued, 'it might be a good idea to get hold of a jeep. You can probably hire one in Orissa. You'll need back up.'

I swallowed hard. My entourage was growing. The idea of climbing on and setting off vanished. I would now command a small army.

His information was limitless. He advised me on the different types of howdahs, the price of elephants, their feeding habits, medical care, emergency tactics, mahouts and elephant commands (alarmingly there were eighty-four of them). Before I left, he gave me the letter and told me that when one is buying an elephant, there are five points to look for that one doesn't look for when buying a wife, and vice versa. Unfortunately, he could not remember what they were.

Back at the house I found my friend pacing the garden nervously.

'I'm off to Orissa,' I announced happily.

'I know,' he sighed. He was born in Orissa and had spent his childhood there.

'Well, don't look so miserable. You are about to get rid of me. Anyway you should be happy I am going to visit your home.'

'That's what I am worried about,' he retorted testily. 'You are bound to get into trouble, or else get lost. You must take somebody with you. What about the language? How on earth are you going to understand anything?'

I had become so obsessed with finding an elephant that I had not given this a thought. Two or three months of sign language could become confusing, in fact, unbearable. 'What should I do?' I asked anxiously.

'I think I know a man. He is a photographer. This kind of folly will appeal to him.'

'When can I meet him?'

'In about ten minutes,' he announced smugly. 'I have invited him for lunch.'

Ten minutes later a distinguished, well-built man, sporting a full moustache and wearing Rayban sunglasses, loped into the garden. He took off his glasses. 'You!' he barked fiercely. Puzzled I looked around me. The garden was empty. He then roared with laughter and held out his hand. 'I'm Aditya Patankar. We have met before – at Holi. But I do not think that you would remember me.'

I cringed at the mention of the Spring Festival of Holi, a wild, bacchanalian affair where people smear each other with coloured powders. Pulverised by traditional opium concoctions I had passed out in a fountain. He won't want to come, I thought.

'I don't know much about elephants,' Aditya said, to my surprise. 'As a child I was taken by my father to see the elephants in the stables at my cousin's palace in Gwalior. These elephants were used for ceremonial occasions and for the tiger shoots. About one hundred years ago the ruling Maharaja hoisted two of the great beasts on to the roof of the palace to ensure that the ceiling would withstand the stupendous weight of two Venetian chandeliers he wished to install. But tell me about your journey ...'

Over lunch I weaved a beguiling tale of a well-planned expedition.

'I don't believe a word of it,' he said with a smile, 'but I will come. There is another reason. You see I'm a Maratha – my ancestors, of whom I'm intensely proud, formed a superb fighting force, and were reputed to have invented guerrilla warfare. Their barbaric reputation alone was enough to strike terror into the heart of India. Both Orissa and Bihar suffered from their swords. It will be interesting to retrace some of their exploits.'

I realised I was extremely fortunate. Already I liked this straightforward man with his loud voice and laughing eyes. We were an unlikely pair, I thought to myself – an Indian nobleman and an errant Englishman, thrown together by a whim, like some mad nineteenth-century expedition, except the quest was not for a lost city or a hidden treasure, but for an elephant.

Two days later we flew to Bhubaneshwar, the capital of Orissa.

2

An Original Elephant

THE LONG ARM of coincidence, in which travellers are often held, found the director of the zoo – the very man for whom I had been given a letter of introduction – travelling on the same flight. There were no elephants that he knew of for sale in Orissa, he told us sympathetically. In fact he himself was looking for elephants both for his own establishment and for a temple. He then suggested we try Madras. 'In the meantime visit my zoo. See the white tigers and the kangaroos that have just arrived from Australia.'

'Well that's that,' I said glumly after we returned to our seats. 'We might as well catch the next flight back to Delhi.' I turned to Aditya, trying to stay calm. 'What on earth are we going to do?' He was fast asleep.

Bhubaneshwar – the city of a thousand temples – was draped in thick black cloud, glistening from the wet kiss of the monsoons. A steamy heat hung in the air. Even the sparrows, those lively occupants of Indian airports, were silent, wilting on top of the announcement speakers.

At the hotel the receptionist asked politely, 'Sands, that is your good name?'

'No, it's Shand.'

'Welcome to the Prachi Hotel, Mr Sands. How long will you be staying?'

'Until I find an elephant.'

'First class,' he said encouragingly, with a slight inclination of his head.

We had barely reached the stairs when a room-boy approached us. 'You are looking for elephants, sir? I have one friend who has many. All sizes. Shall I call him?'

A few moments later there came a knock at my door, which I flung open to the surprise of an elderly man wearing a smart two-piece polyester safari suit. Behind him the room-boy struggled with a large suitcase.

'My name is Fakir Charan Tripathy,' the man said recovering his composure, 'I have elephants.'

'When can we see them?'

'Now, of course, sirs,' the man replied, opening the suitcase. Inside were rows of elephants made from ivory, ebony and sandalwood.

'Please be making a selection. Finest quality. Most reasonable.'

Aditya camouflaged his mouth by pulling on his moustache and explained that these would not meet our requirements. The man seemed confused. Then an expression of wonder crept across his face. 'Aah! You are wanting an o-r-i-g-i-n-a-l elephant.'

The room-boy said suddenly, 'I've seen many elephants.'

'Where?'

'Outside my house, sir. Often they are passing. My children love to see them.' He looked down at his hands in shame. 'I try to keep my family inside. We are very poor and I cannot afford to give away money or food. Only last week three ...'

'Saddhus!' Aditya exclaimed. 'They must be saddhus, and they can't have gone far. They will be stopping at every village and it shouldn't be difficult to follow their route.' He turned to me. 'You see, Mark, the elephant is revered in most parts of India. It represents the elephant-headed deity, Ganesh, our Hindu God of Protection. These elephants are usually ridden by con men masquerading as saddhus, or holy men – a powerful and very lucrative combination. They criss-cross the country, begging, living off the consciences of people much worse off than themselves. Now, you are to stay here. If they see that face of yours the price of an elephant will double. Mr Tripathy, will you come with me?'

'With pleasure. For a small fee. But there is just one other thing. Why is the gentleman wanting an elephant?'

Aditya whispered something into his ear. With a broad smile Mr Tripathy shook my hand before leaving the room.

'What did you tell him?' I demanded crossly.

'That you are an Englishman.'

'Well, so what?'

'Everybody knows that the English are mad.'

At three o'clock in the morning Aditya returned, tired but elated. They had located the elephants about sixty miles west of Bhubaneshwar in a small town called Daspalla. They were indeed begging elephants owned by saddhus.

'Did they want to sell?' I asked anxiously.

'We can take our pick. There are two females and one tusker. The tusker comes from Nepal and is a good elephant, or so they tell me. But what the hell do we know about elephants? We must get some expert advice ...'

'What were they like?'

'Oh, devious buggers, they ...'

'No, no, not the saddhus, the elephants.'

'Big. Like any elephant. I didn't really see them properly. Now let's get some sleep. You'll have plenty of time to look at them tomorrow.'

I found I couldn't sleep. All night everything I looked at became an elephant – the shadow of a swaying branch, the moon-filled clouds or even the television set. My obsession had indeed turned to madness.

It took most of the day to locate the zoo director who kindly agreed to lend the services of his chief mahout, Bhim. Our party had grown. There were now four of us. Myself, Aditya, Mr Tripathy, with his suitcase of elephants, and a young taxi driver called Indrajit, who had impressed Aditya with his driving skills the previous night. He was a handsome, courteous young man, who radiated energy and had dark fierce eyes – the kind of eyes that remain fierce even in jest. But I wasn't thinking about a chauffeur, I was eagerly waiting to set eyes on my first mahout.

In Delhi I had been lent a book on elephants entitled *The Elephant-Lore of the Hindus*, which had detailed the essential qualities required in an elephant driver:

> The supervisor of elephants should be intelligent, king-like, righteous, devoted to his Lord, pure, true to his undertakings, free from vice, controlling his senses, well behaved, vigorous, tried by practice, delighting in kind words, his science learnt from a good teacher, clever, firm, affording protection, renowned for curing disease, fearless, all-knowing.

The mahout was waiting at the gates of the zoo. Bhim was a man of indeterminate age, the colour of a walnut, bandy-legged and carried himself like a wounded soldier. As we got out of the car he executed a shaky salute, his arm and leg not quite in co-ordination. From the state of his bloodshot eyes, he was clearly suffering from a hangover. He climbed into the car and yawned, exposing the remains of three yellow teeth which wobbled when he spoke. 'Sleep now, sah. Very good. Haathi later.' He then passed out.

Aditya was not wrong about Indrajit. He drove with a cunning recklessness, the tropical landscape passing in a blur outside the window. We had only one accident when he swerved to avoid a bullock cart, clipping the back side-window against one of the animal's enormous horns. The glass exploded like a hand grenade with some of the fragments embedding themselves in Aditya's face. 'Lucky it wasn't my eyes,' he shrugged stoically, picking the glass out of his cheek.

It was late at night by the time we reached Daspalla. The town was deserted. There was no sign of the elephants. I felt as if I had been kicked in the stomach. 'Jesus!' I shouted, 'I just can't believe this. We've lost them. They could be anywhere ...'

'No sir,' Mr Tripathy announced calmly, pointing to large mounds like loaves of bread that decorated the road. 'Now we follow shit.'

We pushed on deeper into the night, our eyes glued to the black surface of the road, illuminated in the taxi's headlights, searching for the tell-tale signs. At intervals the trail would run dry and Mr Tripathy and Indrajit would make enquiries. Villagers, rudely awoken by the urgent shouting, would appear in their doorways, cocooned in blankets, looking bewildered and frightened. Reports regarding sightings of the elephants became equally bewildering – anywhere between two hours and six days. We reached a toll gate, where we received more accurate information. The elephants, we were told by the sleepy toll keeper, had definitely passed through. Did he perhaps know how long ago, we asked. No. Unfortunately his watch was not in working order. But he assured us it was not yesterday.

We were closer. The droppings were fresher and, as if on cue, Bhim woke up. 'Haathi close,' he said quietly, rubbing his bloodshot eyes, as he poked his nose out of the window. 'Can smell.'

We rounded the next bend. Three massive shapes loomed out of the night, their shadows dancing over the glow of a small roadside fire, around which lay bundles of vermilion and saffron rags.

'We'll pretend you're a tourist who has never seen an elephant,' Aditya whispered to me. 'Just stare in astonishment.'

As I got out of the car the rags suddenly billowed upwards and I found myself transfixed by three pairs of hot eyes that flashed like cash registers, curtained by matted tresses of long black oily hair. I forgot the necessity of our charade. As if drawn by a magnet, I was already moving towards the elephants.

Then I saw her. My mouth went dry. I felt giddy, breathless. In that moment the ancient wall crumbled and I walked through. With one hind leg crossed over the other, she was leaning nonchalantly against a tree, the charms of her perfectly rounded posterior in full view, like a prostitute on a street corner. I knew then that I had to have her. Suddenly, nothing else mattered and I realised with some surprise that I had fallen in love with a female Asian elephant.

As luck would have it, I had become enamoured with a perfect elephant, an elephant, even Bhim said, that made his heart flutter. She was young, between twenty-five and thirty years old and although in poor condition, due to mishandling and starvation, would in fourteen days in his care, turn into a lovely riding elephant. She had all the attributes – a healthy pink tongue unblemished by black spots, brown kindly eyes with no traces of white, the right amount of toenails, eighteen, five each on the front feet, four on the back, strong and sturdy joints and a perfect arc to her back. The other two elephants, he warned, were dangerous, and would quite likely kill somebody soon if they hadn't done so already. Take her, he advised me, it would be impossible to find better.

Anywhere between 10,000 rupees and 2 lakhs, I was told in Delhi when researching the price of elephants. A tusker is usually more expensive due to its ivory and prestige, yet a female is sometimes more desirable due to its temperament.

The odds were already stacked heavily in favour of the saddhus. To make matters worse a crowd had mysteriously assembled and was excitedly denouncing the saddhus as robbers and urging the 'rich firinghee' to buy all three elephants. My diary entry for the negotiations reads as follows: 'Their first price was 2 lakh. Our first price: 60,000 rupees. Their second price: 1 lakh 50,000 rupees. Our second price: 80,000 rupees. Their third price: 1 lakh. Our third price: 85,000 rupees. Their final price: 1 lakh. Problem. Stalemate. Holy men will not budge. Crowd now very excited. Go away and have urgent discussions over cup of tea. Tea delicious. Tripathy, Indrajit and Bhim advise stick to our price otherwise loss of face. Aditya says loss of elephant more likely. Return and offer 1 lakh. Holy men now refuse. Why? Holy men never go back on word and have hurt feelings. Aditya tells them will bring cash tomorrow. Holy men go back on word and forget about feelings but now want more. How much? 1,000 rupees. Why? In India, even numbers inauspicious, odd numbers auspicious. Bloody crooks. Agree. Crowd very disappointed.' (£1 sterling is approximately 26 rupees, give or take a little depending on fluctuations in the rate of exchange. 1 lakh equals 100,000 rupees, or £4,000.)

The mendicants, or beggars, told us that they would bring the elephant back to Daspalla. There they were more likely to find a suitable place to load her on to the truck that we would be bringing the next day. Before leaving I went to see her. I watched her flapping her huge ears, the ends of which were splotched with the palest of pink dots, as if somebody had flicked a paintbrush. I felt ashamed that I had bargained for her at all. I wanted to reach out and touch her, but found I couldn't, terrified that she might reject me. In the car on the way back I realised I didn't even know her name.

Mr Tripathy had forgotten about his suitcase full of elephants and now seemed as obsessed with acquiring an original elephant as we were. The next morning he and Indrajit went to organise a truck, while Aditya and I set off to find the zoo director to ask him whether we could keep the elephant there until we departed on our journey, and also if he would allow Bhim to act as mahout. We had reached the decision last night after three bottles of rum. Tripathy and Indrajit had vehemently opposed the idea, saying that he was too old, too weak and too drunk. Whether it was the alcohol or emotion I will never know, but the way that Bhim had accepted his position removed my doubts. 'Sah,' he said proudly, drawing himself up to his full five feet and executing another shaky salute, 'Raja-sahib, Daddy, Mummy, my family now. Bhim look after.'

The director was somewhat surprised and sceptical at the speed of our success. He readily agreed to let the elephant reside at the zoo, but wanted it outside the main park due to the quarantine regulations. The place he was suggesting was next to Bhim's house, which suited us perfectly. But, he warned us, although he had no doubts about Bhim's capabilities with elephants, he did have a drink problem. However, if we were prepared to take the risk, he would not stand in our way.

We found our transport was waiting for us at the hotel. The truck was a machine of magnificent chaos. It was difficult to ascertain on first inspection which was the front and which the back. It was the hippies' ultimate chariot, a relic of the Sixties and flower power, bedecked with garlands of flowers, effigies of gods, good luck charms and strings of fairy-lights that twinkled on and off prettily on application of the brakes. On the back was written, 'USE HORN PLEASE, OK' and underneath, 'TATA' which I thought was a message of farewell, but was in fact the make of the vehicle.

We set off to Daspalla stopping for a 'sharpener' in a bottle shop on the way. The proprietor, an ex-serviceman, excited by our visit, took out two bottles of beer and three glasses from a cupboard. The name of the beer was printed over a picture of Mohammed Ali standing over a fallen victim with his arms outstretched – KNOCK OUT, HIGH PUNCH, STRONG BEER, BREWED IN BANGALORE.

'On the houses, gentlemen,' he said, raising his glass. 'To England, India, elephants. God bless and the best of British luck.'

'That makes me proud to be an Indian,' Aditya said as we walked back to the truck. 'You have just witnessed something quite unique. In all my travels across this country, that is the first time I have been offered a free drink. It bodes well for our journey, my friend.'

'Luckily he didn't know you are a Maratha,' I remarked, 'otherwise his hospitality might have been of a different nature in view of the depredations committed by your ancestors in Orissa two hundred years ago.'

'Ah, the sword of the Marathas. Those were the days,' he said dreamily. 'You know, Mark, it was probably right here, on this very spot that my ancestors won yet another brilliant victory.'

'Actually it was at a place called Barmul Gorge which is somewhere near here. It was your last stand in Orissa. The English army, led by Marquis Wellesley, wiped you out.'

The mendicants were already sleeping by the time we found them in a deserted schoolhouse on the outskirts of Daspalla. I couldn't see the elephants but I could hear them feeding; sharp cracks of breaking branches punctured the still night air like pistol shots. Aditya squatted down beside one of the sleeping forms and I overheard a short, muffled conversation. The mendicant pulled his blanket further over his head, rolled over and went back to sleep. Odd behaviour I thought for a man who is about to receive nearly £4,000. Aditya stood up, his face registering a mixture of anger and disbelief.

'They won't sell. They've changed their minds.'

'You're joking.'

'I am not bloody well joking,' he hissed. 'You know what this bastard told me when I pointed out that he had gone back on his word and put us to a great deal of expense. He said it is our right to give people trouble. We do it all the time.'

Indrajit and Tripathy had now joined us. When Aditya explained the situation we had to restrain them forcibly from attacking the mendicants, who were now fully awake clutching an assortment of crude axes and spears, which I realised with horror they had probably used on the elephants.

'We are wasting our time,' Aditya said. 'There's only one solution. We will go to the police.'

The police station was empty apart from a bat circling a ceiling fan. From the back of the building we heard the sound of snoring. Indrajit disappeared. A few minutes later he returned followed by a disgruntled man with tousled hair, hastily tucking a khaki shirt into a crumpled lunghi. He waved us to a couple of chairs and slid behind a desk. He looked at me, as if he had just awakened from one nightmare and was now about to enter another.

Aditya explained the situation. The policeman blinked owlishly and painstakingly scratched out a report.

'In my opinion,' he announced finally, pushing back his chair and yawning, 'there is not seeming to be a crime committed.'

'There bloody well has been,' I shouted, losing the last vestige of self-control. 'They've got my elephant!' I threw down a visiting-card I had been given by a senior bureaucrat in the Orissa government.

To my astonishment, the policeman's eyes widened noticeably. In a matter of moments the entire garrison of the Daspalla Police Force were lined up in front of the desk and ordered to fetch the beggars. The posse returned with the man to whom Aditya had spoken. It would have given us some satisfaction if he had been driven at the point of a bayonet, or at least in handcuffs, but he seemed to be on excellent terms with his captors. He entered the station, helped himself to a cigarette from a packet lying on the desk, lit it from a match proffered by one of the policemen, and squatted down unconcernedly in a corner. A crowd had assembled outside the station. The majority were on our side, but a faction became demonstrative when a local quack told them I was buying the elephant in order to kill it. I would then, with the aid of a huge syringe, extract some magic potion which I would sell as an aphrodisiac. The police chief, sensing a riot, dispersed the crowd.

Up until now the mendicant had only revealed his name as Rajpath but when one of the police advanced upon him with a bamboo cane, he broke down in a well-rehearsed fit of histrionics, and whimpered that the elephant did not belong to him but to his boss who lived in a village near Benares in the state of Uttar Pradesh.

'Why in hell didn't he tell us that in the first place?' I asked Aditya incredulously.

For the next two hours a strange negotiation took place, during which the police acted as go-betweens. At one moment they would be deep in conversation with Aditya, Tripathy and Indrajit, the next with Rajpath through the bars of the station cell, behind which he now reclined. Meanwhile I waited outside and spent a pleasant night discussing the merits of the English and Indian cricket teams with one of the junior policemen.

In the early hours of the morning a solution was found. Mysteriously, Rajpath could now sell the elephant. Empowered by the owner, its destiny lay entirely in Rajpath's hands. He would be prepared to sign an affidavit to the effect as well as the sale deeds which we had brought from Bhubaneshwar. Both these documents would be witnessed officially by the police, and Rajpath would then set out immediately for Benares to deliver the money to the owner.

The deal was seemingly foolproof, except, I pointed out, for one salient point. In view of his previous attitude how could we trust Rajpath to deliver the money?

It was decided that Aditya would accompany him to Benares and conclude the negotiations with the owner personally. I had to fly to Delhi to sort out some visa extension problems. In the meantime, Mr Tripathy and Indrajit would keep watch over the elephant and we would meet back in Bhubaneshwar in a few days.

Arriving in Delhi, I found an article had already appeared in a national newspaper about my intended journey. The last paragraph read: 'more than anything else Mr Shand is looking forward to travelling at an elephant's pace in today's era of jet travel because it would enable him to absorb the surrounding elephant.' I assumed the last word to be a misprint; it should perhaps have read 'elements'.

My work finished I called on my friend and in his drawing-room ruminated over a name for my elephant. On a table there was a collection of miniature ivory elephants. He picked one up and handed it to me. It was exquisite. The body intricately carved in a pattern of tiny stars.

'In Hindi,' he explained, 'the word for star is "tara", more importantly Tara is one of our goddesses. What do you think of that for a name?'

'Tara, Tara, Tara,' I rolled it over my tongue. I liked it. It was a beautiful name for a beautiful elephant. A goddess and a star. She deserved nothing less.

A jubilant trio was waiting for me in the hotel room in Bhubaneshwar; Aditya handed me an impressive looking document studded with blue seals, a jumble of illegible signatures and a cluster of thumb prints. 'You are now the absolute owner of one female elephant named Toofan Champa.'

'Her name is Tara,' I interrupted.

'Then you are the absolute owner of one female elephant named Tara, aged about thirty years, height about seven and a half feet, with black forehead and black body, pigmentation spots on both ears, with eighteen toenails, six-inch tusks and healed wound marks on the centre of her back. By the way,' he added, 'Rajpath returned with me. An elephant, he tells me, takes time to get used to a new mahout. He'll work with Bhim.'

Over celebratory drinks he told me of his journey. At first he was worried that Rajpath might escape from the train, but the mendicant seemed so sad, and so subdued, that he spent the journey gazing mournfully out of the window until even Aditya began to feel sorry for him. When they arrived in Benares, Aditya employed the services of a lawyer, and they left by taxi to Lakeshar village, about two hours by road north-west of Benares.

The owner of the elephant, an elderly man, was obviously a figure of some standing. He lived in the largest house in the village and was not at all surprised to see them. Sitting by his side was one of the other mendicants who, it seemed, had gone on ahead to warn him. The rest of his family were also present. There were fifteen of them. At this moment, Aditya felt concerned. But everything went smoothly. The gentleman wanted to sell the elephant: there was no bargaining and the lawyer drew up the papers which were duly witnessed and signed. The money was then handed over, and each member of the family wanted to count it. This took time. Finally everyone was satisfied and the deal celebrated with cups of hot milk sweetened with sugar. As they were leaving the old man told Aditya that he would now buy another elephant. When he and his brother were young men and first married, their wives were unable to produce a male heir; a saddhu was consulted who advised them to keep 'Ganesh' near the house. They immediately bought an elephant, and some time later his brother produced a son.

'If he has to keep an elephant near his house at all times,' I remarked, 'what's it doing traipsing across Orissa?'

'He can't afford to keep it all year round,' Aditya explained. 'An elephant costs about 300 rupees a week to feed, which in India is a great deal of money. From November to March, our marriage season in India, he rents the elephant out. On such occasions, it is auspicious to have "Ganesh" present. During the rest of the year it will just sit eating money, so he makes a deal with mendicants like Rajpath. During the off season, he lends it to them and they make a lucrative living by begging. He also gets a cut of their takings.'

I was astounded. 'What a sensible arrangement.'

'It's actually quite a large business, particularly in the Benares area. Some of these landlords own up to thirty or forty elephants, or more. In many ways this is a good thing. Sadly, the use of elephants is dying out. Can you imagine India without elephants?'

Everyone in the hotel appeared to be involved in Tara's destiny. When I arrived, the receptionist told me my elephant had refused to get on the truck.

Aditya laughed. 'It was quite an event. These two' – he nodded towards Tripathy and Indrajit – 'were most upset. They wanted her to be waiting for you at the zoo. Indrajit even tried to ride her himself, as if she were some huge taxi. And poor Mr Tripathy nearly got flattened when she shot into reverse. The trouble was caused by the crowd. You can imagine the scenario – the shouting and jeering. She was a nervous wreck.'

'Where are they now?'

'On the road. Let's go and meet your new girlfriend.'

After driving about twenty miles we found them, taking shelter from the sun under the spread of a large banyan tree. It was, I realised, the first time I had seen her in the light of day. As often happens in life and love, she now presented a somewhat different picture. Even to my inexperienced eye, she appeared to be half starved. She lacked that roundness of girth that I had always associated with elephants. Her rib cage was clearly visible and her skin hung in folds like an ill-fitting suit. She looked at that moment exactly what she was – a beggar. It was only then, as I surveyed this immense bag of bones, that the enormity of the situation struck me. She was mine. I was the owner of an elephant, and the idea seemed so ludicrous that I began to laugh. Quickly I controlled myself for I thought – and this was even more absurd – that she might think I was laughing at her, and I had no desire to hurt her feelings.

I was also at a loss as to how to effect an introduction. She wasn't exactly an average pet, like a cat or a dog, or even a hamster, which one can pick up and cuddle or stroke and expect a contented purr or a wet lick or, in the case of the hamster, a sharp nip. However, she soon solved that problem. As I approached her nervously she stretched out her trunk and with the utmost delicacy began to explore the front of my shirt. She's making friends with me, I thought happily, enchanted by this apparent display of affection. It then stopped abruptly in the area of one of my trouser pockets into which she quickly inserted the tip of her trunk and deftly removed my lunch – an apple – and, with a squeak of delight, popped it into her mouth. It seemed the key to Tara's heart was going to be through her stomach. I dispatched Indrajit to buy her some food.

After two kilos of rice, which she consumed by poking her trunk into the sacks and sucking the contents out like a vacuum cleaner, four bundles of bananas and twenty-three coconuts, she seemed a little more replete and broke wind loudly as if to say thank you. As I watched her crunch up the last of the coconuts, her eyes, fringed by lashes long enough to suggest that they were false, closed contentedly.

3

Bandobast

IN HINDI THE word 'bandobast' means 'arrangement', and it was to bandobast that the next two weeks were devoted. On the 15th September the great festival of Ganesh was to be celebrated. We could not hope for a more appropriate and auspicious day on which to begin our journey.

Rajpath had spent five days with Bhim and Tara at the zoo handing over the reins of command. It was remarkable how quickly she adapted to her new master. Although the language of mahouts is universal – all originally derived from the ancient Sanskrit – local intonations are different. Rajpath's was strong and sharp. Bhim's was more sing-song and gentle. This encouraged me, for I had imagined an English accent causing terrible confusion. She was really a very clever elephant, though Rajpath told me before he left that she had one weakness: deep water. Always, he advised, shackle the front legs before her bathtime. Hardly a weakness, I thought. All elephants love water, even I knew that, and I forgot about it.

Her daily intake began with a morning snack consisting of thirty kilos of rice, wrapped in paddy, sprinkled with a few roots of turmeric (for digestion) and fed to her in bundles, like giant birds' nests, by Bhim. She then disappeared behind a mountain of fresh fodder, namely bamboo, the branches of Bud and Peepul trees of which she ate only the bark, and if she was lucky, some pieces of sugar cane. Having slowly worked her way through this she would reappear in the late afternoon when her larder would be restocked for the night. In addition she picked up tit-bits from the busloads of visitors to the zoo, and from my daily visits, when I would bring the icing on the cake – gur. Gur is unrefined molasses, and to elephants it is like foie-gras to a gastronome. They love it. The moment I arrived Tara would drop anything that she was eating, shoot out her trunk, flap her ears and stamp her feet like an impatient child. I became the candyman, and I admit the greater part of her affection at the beginning was due to this treat.

One difficulty remained. How were we to satisfy the appetite of such an enormous beast once the journey had begun? I had no idea where to find a chaarkatiya or food-gatherer.

'Not problem, Raja-sahib,' Bhim announced. 'My friend Gokul help us.' He introduced me to a shy young man with a mischievous face whom Aditya interrogated closely. Gokul's squeaky voice gained confidence with each statement, punctuated by laughter from Aditya. At last Aditya turned to me.

'Well?'

'He's our man. He's eminently qualified for the job. He has been a singer, an acrobat, a dancer, and most recently a tree feller. He now has a new ambition. He wants to be a mahout. Just like you.'

The legendary G. P. Sanderson, who was in charge of elephant catching operations in Mysore and Bengal in the late nineteenth century, reckoned a ton to be a good load for an elephant on continuous march. In his classic work, *Thirteen Years Among the Wild Beasts of India*, he also recommended that 'in hilly country seven hundredweights is as much as he should carry.' Now Sanderson was describing a male elephant and probably a large one at that. Tara was a female and in reality quite small, though admittedly at the moment she was doing her best to change her image. Her pack gear alone was substantial. It consisted of a soft quilted pad, about one inch thick, that extended from her withers to her rump and halfway down her sides. On top of this came the gudda or saddle, made of stout sacking stuffed tight with straw, six feet long, four and a half feet broad, eighteen inches deep, and weighing about one hundred and fifty pounds. It had a longitudinal opening which to some extent relieved the pressure on the spine, one of the most vulnerable parts of the elephant. 'Sore back,' Sanderson continues, 'often disables elephants for months, sometimes for years and may even result fatally.' On top of the gudda came the howdah, which can be an elaborate and ornate affair, but in our case simply resembled a heavy, four-legged rectangular table turned upside down with a cushion to sit on and rails at each end to prevent us falling off. The whole contraption was strapped on by means of one length of thick rope which went round her head and girth and up under her tail. To prevent chafing, it passed through a crupper, which was made not of leather but of metal, in the shape of a piece of bent pipe. 'Smoothness, not softness,' Sanderson insists, 'is the prime requisite in a crupper.'

Our personal gear, all the paraphernalia of a long expedition, tents, sleeping bags, cameras, cooking equipment, food, lamps, axes, kerosene, water, torches, and so on – hung from both sides of the howdah, so that the weight was distributed evenly and would rest on the upper part of her ribs, and not on her spine. This was all exclusive of her food, chains and shackles and, most importantly, the four of us. It became obvious, as I had been advised in Delhi, that we would need back up. With a vehicle to carry the bulk of our load, we could travel relatively unencumbered across the country, and then be supplied every few days at predetermined points of rendezvous. It sounded simple enough in theory, but whether it would work in practice remained to be seen.

Finding 'back up' was considerably easier than finding an elephant, and a jeep and trailer were kindly lent to us by friends for the duration of our journey. With the jeep came a driver, and without the driver we could not have the jeep, but there was, as Aditya and I agreed, something about Khusto that spelled trouble, though at that moment neither one of us could put our fingers on it. For a start, communication with him was a problem due to large well-chewed wads of 'paan' that were permanently wedged into his mouth, giving him the appearance of a squirrel with mumps. He was also more of a modist than a mechanic. The only spare part that he deemed necessary to take with him for this long and arduous journey was an extra rearview mirror, and he spent much of his time teasing his bouffant hair with the bright red comb he kept wedged in the back pocket of a tight pair of khaki trousers. Indrajit, on whose sagacity and faithfulness we had now come to rely heavily, also voiced his doubts about Khusto. To our great relief he insisted that he himself would come along as co-driver.

Although I knew he would decline, I asked Mr Tripathy to accompany us also. There were tears in his eyes. He clasped my hands, and I was as deeply affected as he was. 'I am too old for such things, sir. With my reward, I have decided to start a new business.'

I was intrigued. 'What kind of business?'

'I will become a miner,' he announced with marvellous inconsequence. 'I will find gold and diamonds. With my riches I will buy elephants.'

'But that was your last business.' I was now confused.

His wise old eyes filled with laughter. 'No, sir, o-r-i-g-i-n-a-l elephants. When you return to Orissa I will be selling them to you.'

4

Paint, Pujas and Pandits

WE HAD ASCERTAINED that the Sonepur Mela lasted two weeks, and that the peak day – Kartik Purnima (the day of the full moon) – fell on the 23rd November. Elephants could not be bought or sold before that auspicious date. To be on the safe side, we planned to arrive at the Mela around the 17th November, which would allow us sixty-four days to complete the journey. With the aid of some very out-of-date maps, we established a route. By my calculations (which were by no means accurate) the journey would be some seven hundred and fifty miles long, roughly the distance between John O'Groats and Land's End, or from New York to Chicago, or Sydney to Adelaide.

'Four miles an hour is a good pace for an elephant, but long-legged ones will swing along at five,' Sanderson wrote. Tara had the most beautiful long legs. Even if we were to be on the move for only four hours a day, starting early to avoid the heat, it seemed to me that we had plenty of time.

I could scarcely believe it. We were ready to begin our journey on the most auspicious day of the year. Some friends had arranged a special puja for our good fortune. Early on the morning of the 14th September, the day before we were due to depart, Aditya and I went to the zoo to watch Tara being made ready for the puja by some students from the art school in Bhubaneshwar.

Decoration of elephants is usually carried out by mahouts – specialists in the art, using chalk and coloured paste – who are familiar with the dangers, the vagaries and the fidgetiness of this large animal. They can work with assurance, secured by their knowledge. Understandably, the students were nervous. An elephant is a different proposition to the stillness of a canvas. They were also working in watercolours, and moved warily round her, applying dabs of colour with their paintbrushes. Tara now nervous as well, and perhaps annoyed by the tickling sensation of bristles on her skin, shook her head violently and flayed out with her trunk and tail, sending students, pots and paintbrushes flying.

Bhim and another mahout immediately took charge, forcing her to sit. They grabbed her trunk and her tail and held them tightly. Apart from her huge flapping ears Tara now remained steady enough for the students to work. With wonderful imagination, a trait seemingly inbred amongst artisans of Orissa, Tara was transformed into a bride. The insides of her ears were decorated with painted earrings of yellow diamonds and rubies, her forehead became a fringe of lacy pearls, her trunk a fretwork of flowers, lotuses, frangipani blossoms and blood red hibiscus, and around her legs appeared anklets of silver and gold. She emerged resplendent, a princess fit for the mightiest of kings.

When the truck arrived to transport Tara to Konarak, it was backed up against the side of a wide stone terrace about four feet high which fronted the zoo's museum, a long low building, from the roof of which bougainvillaea spilled. It was a venue, I thought, more picturesque than practical. The interior of the truck was littered enticingly with every kind of elephant delicacy – succulent stalks of sugar cane, thick sheaves of bamboo leaves and three or four large bundles of bananas. Bhim astride a closely hobbled, radiant Tara clanked up the steps on to the terrace. They approached the truck and then stopped. From where she stood she explored the back of the truck with her trunk. She crept all the way around it, testing and checking everything. She then leant forward, managing to reach the nearest of the delicacies which she popped into her mouth. Bhim urged her forward. She remained stationary. Two or three other zoo mahouts, armed with sticks, crept up behind her and began to beat the back of her legs, while another climbed into the truck and tried to interest her in the food. With a squeal of rage, she shot into reverse, scattering the mahouts and a group of enthusiastic onlookers in her path. She then halted and, regaining her composure, methodically consumed the contents of a flower bed which lined the other end of the terrace. Inevitably, a large crowd had congregated. They had not expected this added attraction on their day out at the zoo.

After three hours the experts (and there were a great many of them by then) decided that this was the wrong approach. I began to doubt their expertise and wondered if they had ever attempted such a manoeuvre before. The arrival of one of the other zoo elephants, a big docile female, who was in theory going to show Tara the way, proved it. She too refused to enter the truck. An impasse had been reached. There was only one solution. Tara, accompanied by Bhim and Gokul, would have to walk to Konarak, a distance of some thirty miles.

As I squeezed into the jeep, my backside wedged uncomfortably on a sack containing tins of corned beef and my head squashed at right angles against one of the metal roof struts, I agreed wholeheartedly with Louis Rousselet, who said of his travels in central India and in the presidencies of Bombay and Bengal that 'It is neither a slight responsibility nor a trifling matter to have to keep and maintain an elephant for a month or two.' I couldn't believe the amount of paraphernalia that had collected. Did an elephant journey really need all this equipment and all these people? But it seems I had got off lightly, for he goes on to tell us that 'a mahout usually takes his wife and children with him on the journey'.

It had been agreed that Tara and Bhim would meet us that evening at the government inspection bungalow, close to the great Temple of Konarak. By midnight there was no sign of them. A search party was sent out and returned without success. By 7.30 the following morning there was still no sign of Tara. The pandit who was to perform the puja deemed the early morning as the propitious moment for devotions. I had washed, had not taken food and was therefore clean.

For two hours I sat cross-legged in a sandy hollow outside the inspection bungalow which overlooked the Bay of Bengal. Facing me was a small, pink clay idol of Ganesh. Being a foreigner, I could not help feeling self-conscious and somewhat of a fool. Sand flies shot up my shorts and stung me on the backside. I was desperately worried about Tara. As the pandit muttered the last incantation in a cloud of incense, and I showered the little pink effigy with yet another handful of nuts, flowers and coins, news reached us that Tara had been located fifteen miles from Konarak. The Indians have a proverb, 'Listen to the elephant, rain is coming.' At that moment it started to rain.

In the driving rain, we piled into the jeep, pandit and all, to meet them. The old mahout was mortified that he had failed to reach Konarak punctually, but Tara had suddenly become lame in her front right leg and this had delayed them. The accommodating pandit performed a second puja, beside a little pond at the side of the road. This turned out to be a merry affair. As Tara's decoration had been washed off by the rain, Bhim anointed her forehead in a bright red powder, with the sign of the god Shiva, the Destroyer. The pandit blessed us all by dotting our foreheads with 'tikkas' and Tara was garlanded with marigolds and frangipani, which she happily consumed. At one point he blessed her by circling her head with sticks of incense. Thinking it was more food, she shot her trunk through the clouds of scented smoke. The poor pandit, already wary of this large, benevolent elephant, took a step back and fell into the pond.

It was now auspicious and appropriate for me to ride her, if only for a few yards. With Bhim tugging from on top of Tara and with the help of Aditya, Indrajit and Khusto, and a crowd of amazed local villagers pushing from below, I was hoisted on to her. In my panic I managed to climb aboard the wrong way round and found myself facing Bhim. I carefully turned round, and we set off to great cheers. It was the first time I had ever been on an elephant. I looked down the long drop, and as Tara gained momentum I knew I was going to fall off. Perhaps because I was sitting in the wrong position, her shoulder blades pumped up and down against my backside like pistons, and I felt myself going. Then I felt cold steel against my lower back and Bhim restored my dignity by hooking the curved point of the 'ankush' into my underpants.

In a way I had already started my journey. I felt elated, blessed and unbelievably smug. Leaning down, I kissed her on her large soft ear and whispered that I loved her. My confidence grew as we lumbered down that road. I turned and doffed my panama hat in what I thought was a most cavalier fashion, yelling at Aditya who was walking beside me, 'How do I look, my friend?'

'Ridiculous,' he said.

If the standard of our camp that night was any portent of the next two months, it looked like we would be in trouble. It was my fault, for the choice of the site in sandy ground amongst a forest of casuarina trees overlooking the sea was mine. I selected this scenic spot for two reasons. The first was that it was very close to Konarak, where the next morning we would officially start the great trek. The second was that I had developed a romantic idea of this journey. It was to be a journey of imagination, from the sea to the source, from the blue waters of the Bay of Bengal to the mighty Ganga at the ancient seat of the Emperor Ashoka's empire, Pataliputra. If only instead I had remembered my boy scout training. Tent pegs do not hold in sandy ground. I should have listened to Bhim, for chaining Tara to a slim, shallow-rooted casuarina tree was about as effective as tying her with a piece of string to a daisy.

It turned into a night of bedlam, not helped by copious amounts of rum which I had liberally distributed to celebrate our first camp. Khusto passed out. Bhim and Gokul could hardly stand. It was left to Aditya and me to try and control Tara. Three times she escaped, and in the process flattened an area the size of a football field. Dotted intermittently along the edge of the road were signs saying in big red letters: GOVERNMENT OF ORISSA FORESTRY DEPARTMENT. KEEP OUT. NEW PLANTATION. Eventually, under the threat of a ban on alcohol for one week, Bhim miraculously sobered up. With another of those shaky salutes, and after several attempts to climb aboard Tara, he announced that he was in full control and that he and Gokul would chain her to a sturdy tree about a mile down the road.

Aditya and I curled up inside a collapsed tent and fell asleep. One hour later we were woken by the sound of rattling chains and wild singing. Peering blearily out of the tent, I was amazed to see approaching us at top speed through the gloom, Bhim riding Tara, followed by a staggering Gokul. Mummy (Tara) had been a bad girl, Bhim informed us, and made a fool out of him. He had given her a good talking to and now Mummy knew who was the boss. Also Mummy had told him that she was lonely at the tree and wanted to spend the night near Daddy (Aditya) and Raja-sahib (me). So, with an incoherent mahout, a drunken chaarkatiya and a comatose driver, we spent our first night with Tara chained to the rear bumper of the jeep.

5

The Black Pagoda

AGAINST A FLURRY of protests I enforced a mandatory early-morning dip in the sea for everybody, to clear away the effects of last night's excesses. Only Tara was excluded after she had expressed great suspicion and then terror at the sound of beating waves and had run up the beach trumpeting, causing a group of amazed fishermen to drop their nets and dive for safety behind their boats.

As we entered Konarak the first rays of a glorious sunrise were illuminating the Black Pagoda, a temple of such solitary grandeur yet of such sensuality that my first impression was one of shock. I had been fortunate once, many years ago, to have visited an empty Taj Mahal on a bright moonlit night and had thought that nothing I would ever see could surpass it for its beauty. But the Taj Mahal is a mausoleum, a tomb, silent in its splendour while Konarak is alive, a constant motion of stone – celestial nymphs with swelling breasts and rounded hips, the rhythms of the lovers and the ecstasy on the faces of the erotic statues. Its energy is manifest in scenes of royal hunts and military expeditions, with infantry, cavalry and elephants marching in full regalia, speaking of the dream of an ambitious and mighty monarch.

Conceived as a celestial chariot of the Sun God, pulled by seven exquisitely carved horses and supported by twenty-four monolithic wheels, each of which represents the division of time, the temple was constructed by King Narasimha Deva the First of the Ganga dynasty of Orissa in the mid-thirteenth century AD. Twelve thousand men toiled ceaselessly for twelve years to complete this masterpiece, and it was named the Black Pagoda by the captains of coastal ships who used it as a landmark. Konarak is the peak of Orissan architecture about which it was said that the artisans 'built like Titans and finished like jewellers'. On the north side stand two lifelike elephants, their flesh rendered with wonderful realism. Between these stone elephants, dwarfed by their size, Tara made her ceremonial 'pranam' by lifting her trunk in salute. The head priest of Konarak came out to bless her.

In the shortening shadows of the Black Pagoda we set off triumphantly on our journey, applauded by a laughing crowd, many of them poking fun at the ridiculous figure striding out ahead, wearing a hat that had become a bonnet under its weight of garlands.

The countryside was lush, sensual and green (similar to Indonesia). Paddy fields dotted with clumps of bamboo and palm trees stretched for miles. Flashes of brilliant colour suddenly emerged as men in bright lunghis of emerald green, azure and saffron that had faded to salmon-pink stood up, gazed for a moment and then waved and shouted in greeting, their dark muscular bodies black against the green. Kites wheeled on thermals overhead and piebald and blue kingfishers hovered stationary above the fields. Then, wings pulled into their sides, they dived like arrows into the water and reappeared with frogs, fishes and small snakes in their beaks.

'What are those?' I said to Aditya, pointing to slim, glossy black birds with long, deeply forked tails that perched in lines on the telegraph wires, looking like a selection of chic little black hats displayed in a milliner's window.

'Drongos,' he said excitedly. Aditya was a keen amateur ornithologist and seemed relieved that my conversation was not going to revolve exclusively around Tara. 'They are clever birds,' he continued. 'They ride on the backs of grazing cattle and capture the insects that are disturbed by the animals' feet. With any luck, we'll see a racket-tailed drongo. They are much larger and have two long spatula tipped feathers like streamers in the tail. I have always longed to own one. They are superb mimics.'

Passersby stopped in amazement. Some just stared, open mouthed. Others turned their bicycles round to follow us and I overheard snatches of conversation with Bhim. 'Haathi-wallah, Konarak.' Then they smiled shyly clasping their hands together in greeting. But it was the children who went wild. At every village out they came, screaming and laughing and shouting. 'Haathi, haathi, haathi, haathi,' they cried and chased after us. One or two of the braver ones moved up in front of Tara and fed her bamboo and sugar cane.

At other villages we stopped and took tea, the best tea I had ever tasted, sweetened with sugar and cardamom. Tara was surrounded and paper bags of 'ludoos' (sweet yellow round cakes) were produced. She would delight the crowd by consuming the entire paper bag. Then she helped herself liberally to the piles of sweets and cakes laid out in trays in front of the shop. Sometimes her greed annoyed the owners and Bhim would smack her trunk smartly, reproving her, whereupon she would squeeze her small brown eyes shut like a naughty little girl. 'Mummy learn proper manners,' he told me seriously. 'She too greedy. She have bad habits. She Raja-sahib haathi now. She behave like one.'

Worryingly, Tara's foot did not seem to be getting better. She was walking with a pronounced limp, and it was Bhim who discovered the cause of this lameness – an infection caused by a wicked metal leg shackle with small spikes which pointed inwards that had been used on her by Rajpath. One of the spikes had caused a deep-rooted ulcer, but, Bhim told me, with hot-water compresses mixed with salt applied nightly she would soon be better. Until then, nobody was to ride her except him. The howdah, due to its weight, was abandoned. His knowledge of elephant ailments reassured me, but I fussed about like an expectant father.

It was a glorious day as I watched her plodding along in front of me, her tail swishing and her trunk shooting out from side to side, plucking at branches from overhead trees, flapping her great ears and munching with contentment. I felt wonderfully happy and patted her on her big, fat bottom.

'She really *is* lovely, isn't she, Aditya?'

'Yes, Mark.'

'No, I mean she is *the* most beautiful elephant in the world, isn't she?'

'Yes, Mark.' I could see I was going to drive him mad.

Considering it was our first day on the road, and that Tara was lame, we stopped and made camp by a wide river on the outskirts of a village called Nimpalla after covering a distance of only twelve miles. There are two basic requisites for a camp-site when travelling with an elephant: one is water, for bathing and drinking, and the other is a stout, thickly leaved tree to which one can safely chain the elephant, to provide shelter from the sun and perhaps obtain fodder. We were lucky to find both. Beside the river, a row of ancient Peepul trees stood like sturdy oaks. In a few minutes Gokul, with the agility of a monkey, and armed with an axe, had disappeared into the upper foliage and soon Tara's dinner came crashing to the ground.

For my benefit camps were, if possible, to be set up away from villages in the future. I had not yet become adjusted to the huge crowds I knew our entourage would attract. I realised I had no right to complain. I was travelling in their country, probably camping on their land. An elephant with a foreigner was understandably fair game, but I was still too much of a tourist to tolerate such human curiosity. As countless pairs of eyes scrutinised my every move while I struggled with Aditya to put up our ridiculously complicated tent, I was not in the most charitable frame of mind.

'Go away,' I roared, waving my hands like a demented marionette. A hundred pairs of eyes blinked once, my tormentors settled themselves more comfortably on their haunches and waited patiently for the show to go on.

'They won't go,' Aditya remarked quietly. 'Just ignore them.'

'Well can't you frighten them or something?'

'Perhaps,' he suggested, 'if you removed those white socks and covered up those ridiculous blue underpants they might think that you're a human being instead of a creature from outer space.'

'I'm going to take a bath with Tara,' I added grumpily, noticing Bhim leading her towards the river.

'That, my friend, will probably cause a riot.'

Watching an elephant take a bath is a delight in itself, but bathing with, or washing an elephant is something close to experiencing paradise. When I reached the river she was lying at full length with a contented expression on her face. Bhim and Gokul were busily scraping her with stones and the normally grey skin on her protruding backside was already turning black and shiny. Occasionally the tip of her trunk emerged like the periscope of a submarine, spraying them playfully with water before disappearing again and blowing a series of reverberating bubbles. I grabbed a suitable stone and, forgetting my self-consciousness, joined in the fun.

After half an hour my arms were aching, my fingers were bleeding, but I felt absurdly proud. Bhim, sensing my eagerness, gave me the honour of cleaning her trunk, her ears and around her eyes, something which usually only the mahout, who is most familiar to the elephant, will undertake, due to the extreme sensitivity of these areas. However, he made sure that the ankush was hooked around the top of one of her ears at all times.

'If Mummy feels that,' he explained, 'she give Raja-sahib no trouble.'

She didn't, except at one moment when she took a liking to my underpants (I'm glad somebody did) and dragged them half down. This caused hilarity among the crowd, now squatting on the side of the river bank. The whole process was then repeated on the elephant's other side. By means of a sharp command from Bhim, she lumbered to her knees and rolled over, creating a small tidal wave. Taking to my new job as a mahout's assistant too zealously, I found out the hard way that Tara did not like to be scrubbed on the soles of her feet. She was extremely ticklish, and being winded by the kick of an elephant was not an experience I would care to repeat. I still had a lot to learn, I realised, or rather she had a lot to teach me.

After feeding Tara we sprawled around a blazing fire, bloated from an evening meal of corned beef, lentils and rice, spiced with a few chillis. This was to be our staple diet, unless we could find the odd chicken or goat. None of us, it seems, were great chefs. Perhaps Indrajit might fill the position. Mugs were filled with carefully measured tots of rum and we drank each other's health, banging the tin mugs together and solemnly uttering the words, 'Jai Mata' (victory to the Goddess).

His inhibitions softened by the liquor, Bhim began to reminisce in a mumbling voice. 'Haathi, nicer than people. Only hurt if you trick. Never eat until haathi eat. If feed well always faithful. But not not steal haathi food. Haathi always know. Haathi wait. Then haathi attack. Many mahouts bad, steal haathi food. Bad mahout, dead mahout.'

I asked him why he had become involved with elephants. 'In blood,' he replied.

Many years ago his father was the chief mahout to the Maharaja of Mayurbhanj, so he had grown up with the elephants. But there was one incident that changed his life, and from that moment on he knew that his destiny was to work with the haathi. He was involved in a tiger shoot in the forest of Mayurbhanj organised by the Maharaja for some visiting dignitaries. His father and the other mahouts were riding the main elephants while he and another younger mahout, who were riding the supply elephants, became separated somehow from the main party. They ended up camping alone at night in the jungle. Bhim woke up to the sound of a tiger close by and then listened in terror as the tiger killed and dragged away the other mahout. His own elephant with instinctive protection had grabbed him by its trunk, pulled him between its legs and stood guard all night, trumpeting fiercely as the tiger stalked around. In the morning Bhim had ridden back to safety.

'Haathi, like Mummy. Guard child.'

Later as I lay in the tent I thought about what Bhim had told me. Even above Aditya's stentorian snoring I could hear Tara happily feeding – the crackling and crunching of branches followed by a contented munching. There was something reassuring about an elephant close by. It was like being guarded by a huge jovial nanny, and I fell asleep dreaming of tigers and temples.

A torrential rainstorm in the night was just a foretaste of the kind of weather that was going to dog us for the next two weeks. All the tents were blown down and the ground was ankle-deep in water. When I went to retrieve my air mattress from the mass of sodden canvas, it floated happily towards the river. In the half-light we struck camp quickly, cursing as we tripped over our tent pegs and guy ropes, serenaded by a deafening chorus of belching frogs which seemed to be laughing at our discomfort.

As another day's march began, Aditya and I walked gingerly. Blisters, or 'water bottles' as he more aptly described them, had begun to appear on our feet. Both of us were lame, and Bhim and Gokul had fever, shivering under umbrellas.

'Water bottle coming up under left big toe,' Aditya barked as he splashed along.

'Two water bottles under heel on right foot,' I replied wincing. 'God, they're painful! Do slow down, I can't bear it any longer.'

'Don't be so feeble. Crush them, forget the pain. Imagine what my ancestors had to endure.'

'Your ancestors,' I pointed out crossly, 'were generals and commanders. I bet they never walked anywhere; rode in great comfort on horses, I should imagine.' I turned to look at Bhim enviously, wondering whether I was ever going to ride Tara.

Our misery turned to laughter at the chaos Tara caused as we passed. Goatherds frantically tried to control their animals as they scattered bleating and panicking into the paddy fields. Bullock cart drivers on their way to the market, their ramshackle contraptions piled precariously with their wares, stood up and shouted, 'Hut, Hut,' mercilessly whipping their cattle like charioteers, urging them to pass us quickly. Sometimes they dismounted and covered the animals' eyes. It was to no avail. The bullocks, big enough in themselves, and sensing that something much bigger was threatening them, charged away uncontrollably foaming at the mouth, scattering their loads on the road. Three young men riding a small moped passed, whipping us in a fine spray. All three turned simultaneously, as if to double check that what they had seen was not a dream. The moped, out of control, snaked off the road and crashed into a muddy ditch. They were not put out in the slightest, laughing uproariously as we helped them out of their messy predicament.

Near the village of Hirapur we came across an exquisite and seemingly forgotten temple, surrounded by verdant paddy fields. We approached it by skirting a small lake in the centre of which stood a tiny, overgrown shrine, like a little gazebo in an English country garden. The temple was quite empty and of a curious design – a perfect stone circle about nine feet in height, standing open to the sky. Access was made by a narrow, low entrance way, which was no more than an interruption of the surrounding wall. Inside sixty-four perfect goddesses, carved in black chlorite, each about a foot high, sat in little niches facing an open pavilion in the centre. It held a beautifully seductive atmosphere and I imagined music, incense, flesh, colour, laughter, accompanying orgiastic love. The wall was built at just the right height so that people could not peep in. Later I found out that it was the Chausath Yogini Temple, one of only four in the whole of India, built in the ninth century AD. The goddesses or Yoginis were attendants on the goddess Durga, an image of whom at one time sat on the open pavilion in the centre. It was a place of worship exclusive to Orissa's kings.

On the main road we passed a tourist bus which screeched to a halt and reversed up alongside us. Excited cries of 'Slon, slon' poured out from the opening windows as I realised it was full of Russians. 'Slon' is Russian for elephant, and curiously the only word I know in that language. Tara, never one to miss an opportunity for food, worked the bus like a professional. Her long trunk dipped into every window emerging with oranges, bananas and apples, and finally a bottle of vodka which, before I could grab, she inserted into her mouth and sucked dry. Bhim reprimanded her fiercely by rapping the blunt end of the ankush on top of her bony head. This had about as much effect as hitting a hippopotamus with a lollipop, but I could see from the mournful expression on his face as he looked at the empty bottle, where his anger really lay. Luckily another was produced and we toasted each other uproariously.

'Do dra' (to the bottom literally, or bottoms up) came from the Russian contingent. 'Jai Mata,' from the Indians, a strange rumbling belch from Tara, and from the lone Englishman, 'Up yours.' With the aid of an elephant I had done my bit for 'glasnost' and 'perestroika'.

For a while the hot snap of the vodka warmed our bones and we swung along at a grand pace, forgetting about the rain. Bhim, looking like a cheerful, drowned water rat, sang a strange hooting melody that was muffled by the hood of the raincoat I had lent him. Tara now considered anything moving – whether a truck, a bus, a car or a cyclist – as meals on wheels and wandered, waving her trunk, into the path of these oncoming vehicles. Gokul hung on to Tara's tail giggling squeakily, performing an odd little jig. Aditya and I discussed blisters.

I struggled to keep up with him as he demonstrated what he called 'the loping gait' of a Maratha foot soldier.

Through the driving rain we could just make out the blurred outline of the Dhauli hills. On top of a prominent hillock, blinding white against a black sky, stood the Vishwa Shanti Stupa, the domed Peace Pagoda the Buddhists built in this century with Japanese collaboration, to commemorate the conversion to Buddhism of the great Indian Emperor Ashoka.

We took a short cut across some open fields to the River Daya, a river which was said 'to have run red with blood' during the horrifying slaughter of the battle of Kalinga, a massacre so enormous that Ashoka flung away his blood-stained sword and embraced the path of peace. It was on these very fields that the great battle had been fought. Under the black rainclouds, it was a bleak and eerie place. The wind moaned soulfully, pushing into us and making us shiver, less from cold than from something else, perhaps from the spirits of the one hundred thousand souls that had been slaughtered here. Tara sensed it too. She moved forward reluctantly, her trunk in the air, sensing, probing. Finally she came to a halt. Bhim tried to urge her and she let out a loud reverberating roar which I could only imagine was of terror. With her ears extended fully forward, she backed hurriedly away, then turned and fled.

'Mummy no like here,' Bhim yelled over his shoulder, struggling to gain control.

'Let's get out of here,' I muttered to Aditya.

'God knows how many elephants perished on this spot,' Aditya replied, shivering. 'This is an elephants' graveyard. After two and a half thousand years how is it possible Tara still senses that?'

Somehow I believed it possible, just as I believed the legend about the Emperor's conversion to Buddhism.

On these fields he had stood with a bloodied sword, gloating over the carnage around him. The skies opened and the Buddha appeared in a shaft of pure white light, holding in his arms a dead child. 'Give life back to this child,' the Buddha had pleaded. 'How can I perform such a miracle?' Ashoka had asked. 'You have taken so many lives,' the Buddha had replied. 'Cannot a man as noble and great as you give back just one life?'

We headed for the road that led to the Stupa where Khusto and the jeep were to meet us. There was no sign of Khusto. We waited an hour in the gathering dusk. Tara was fidgety and nervous, and her foot horribly swollen. We had to find shelter for the night and decided to head for the monastery, where the monks would certainly welcome us. We reached a wide, covered veranda with a large, shady tree conveniently near by.

'Perfect,' I said, jingling a brass bell attached to an iron grille. A faint smell of incense emitted from inside. There was silence. I rang again.

'Who is there?' called a nervous voice as a young Indian pressed his face up against the other side of the grille.

'Could I speak to the monks?' I asked politely.

'They are Japanese,' he replied.

'Well, that's very nice,' I said, 'but can I speak to them?'

'Gone away, in Calcutta.'

'Perhaps you could help us then. We need shelter for the night. We are all very cold, very wet and my elephant is sick.'

'You cannot stay here,' he stated firmly.

'Are you a Buddhist?' I asked.

'Yes.'

'Buddha Shuranam Gachami' (may the peace of the Buddha be with you), I greeted him.

'You cannot stay here,' he insisted.

'But we are weary travellers. We are not asking for much, just a roof over our heads and a tree to tether the elephant.'

'You are a foreigner.'

'Yes, but so what,' I shouted, starting to get angry. 'Buddhism is universal.'

'You cannot stay here. Please. It is a bad place. There are no lights and murders take place.'

Aditya shrugged. We limped off into the rain and several hours later found a deserted schoolhouse in the dark. After applying a hot poultice to Tara's leg, fashioned out of sanitary towels which had mysteriously appeared from Bhim's pocket, we collapsed in exhaustion, oblivious of our damp misery.

Early the next morning, as we were entering Bhubaneshwar, Khusto caught up with us. Through a paan-filled mouth, which did not conceal the smell of rum, he mumbled that he had had a puncture and got lost. Aditya and I decided that Indrajit could deal with Khusto. Tara's leg was our main concern and we pushed on to Nandankanan, which was on our route northwards, to consult the zoo vet. Bhim did not seem at all happy about our decision. Pouring scorn on the modern methods of medicine, he stated that it was he who always cured the sick elephants at the zoo. I was adamant; I could not bear to see her in such pain any longer.

6

In the Tracks of the King of Bliss

ON OUR WAY into Bhubaneshwar, we passed many young people beating drums, singing and carrying papier-mâché images – some gigantic, some tiny and, oddly, all pink in colour, for immersion in the river. It was Ganesh Chaturti, the last of the days dedicated to Ganesh, and their songs called upon the elephant-headed god to come back early next year. But the melancholic farewells were already alternating with excited hymns anticipating the god's return and it seemed to me that their continuity was like India itself, where the end of any event is always pre-empted by the birth of the next. The crowds turned, and it was as if they had found a new festival. To see an elephant on the day of Ganesh Chaturti was auspicious. A brass band, featuring trombone and trumpet players and a child dwarfed by a huge drum, joined us and we marched triumphantly into Bhubaneshwar like a circus parade.

At one time over seven thousand temples dominated the skyline of Bhubaneshwar, appropriate for a city that is called the 'Abode of the Gods'. It had started to rain as we approached the temple of Lord Lingaraj (the Lord of the Universe), the largest and most impressive of the temples in Bhubaneshwar, its vaulting spire soaring to a height of one hundred and sixty feet. The priests, seeing a foreigner, uncoiled themselves like pythons from wet stone entrances and slid menacingly towards me to extract money. But the sight of an elephant, or rather the sight of a 'firinghee' with an elephant, caused a clash of conscience; they didn't know whether to give to the elephant or to take from me. Being businessmen, they did neither.

At a busy roundabout a smiling policeman wearing a smart white solar topee hat and a cape saluted, blew furiously on his whistle and stopped the traffic to let us pass.

'Why be walking, sir?' shouted a rickshaw driver. 'I will be taking you anywhere for half price.'

'Patna? In Bihar?' I shouted back.

'Not being a problem, sir. Please be seated.'

'But it is at least seven hundred miles away.'

'Then I would surely die. Good morning,' and he pedalled away, his thin legs pumping furiously.

Indrajit and Khusto drove up in the jeep. We were now back to full strength. We instructed the two drivers to go ahead to Nandankanan to inform the vet of Tara's predicament. To rest her leg, we stopped at the Hati Gumpha cave (elephant cave) in the Udayagiri hills. Two stone elephants stand guard at the entrance. Inside, engraved on huge stone slabs, is the record of the reign of King Kharavela, the greatest monarch of Orissa, ruler of the mighty Kalinga Empire. Known as the 'King of Bliss, His Majesty the Mighty Conqueror, Sri Kharavela, the Possessor of Invincible Armies', it was he who pursued the Greek king, Demetrius, out of India. He came to the throne when he was fifteen years old and, in the twelfth year of his reign, led his vast army of elephants, cavalry and chariots towards north-west India, striking 'terror into the people of Magadha while making his horses and elephants drink from the Ganges'.

I liked the sound of this gentleman; perhaps it was just the name or perhaps it was that I, mounted on an elephant, was now firmly in the tracks of the King of Bliss. Like his royal elephant, Tara would drink from the waters of the Ganges.

As if to seal this bond, Tara's trunk suddenly snaked out and circled around the stone trunk of a guardian elephant. In elephant language this is the ultimate gesture of friendship.

At Nandankanan the vet made a perfunctory examination of Tara's leg and prescribed a week's course of strong antibiotics.

'How do I give an elephant pills?' I asked. 'In her food?'

'No, no, no,' he replied. 'This is a most serious infection. The course must be administered intramuscularly.'

'You mean injections?' I was terrified. 'I've got to give her injections! Oh, my God! I hate needles at the best of times. How on earth do I give an elephant a jab?'

'It is easy. Come,' he said. 'We will give her the first one now.'

I wished I had the confidence shown by J. H. Williams in his book *Elephant Bill*:

> One cut out all the fuss and just walked up boldly to the animal, gave it a good smack with the left hand and exclaimed, 'Hello, old chap.' With the right one thrust the needle through the hide and squirted in the vaccine. Then one gave it another smack and turned away, exclaiming, 'Come on,' to the next elephant. Elephants will bear a great deal of pain patiently and appear to understand that it is being inflicted for their own good, but they will only put up with it when the operator is full of confidence himself and feels he is making a good job of it, for an elephant can sense the absence of self confidence quicker than any other animal in the world.

'Can't you give her the first one?' I implored the vet, as I held a needle the size of a rocket-launcher in my shaking hand.

'No,' he replied firmly, 'you must learn immediately. Remember, plunge it in right up to the hilt. Once firmly in place, you can attach the plunger.'

'Which cheek?' I asked, nervously, standing behind Tara's enormous bottom. At that moment she turned her head and gave me a curious look.

'Either one. Whichever you feel most comfortable with,' he said airily.

After marking a spot in my mind I shut my eyes and plunged in the needle like a dart. With a squeal of rage she shot to her feet and trundled away with a broken hypodermic needle wobbling precariously out of her backside.

'That was very incorrect,' the vet remarked needlessly. 'It has to be a firm strong blow. Place the needle in straight. Now, we will try again.'

Tara was retrieved and made to sit. She gave me a look of pure venom. I repeated the process, this time with success, and even managed to pump the sticky fluid in efficiently.

'Repeat every evening for the next six days. You will soon find that she will become used to it. In fact, she will be grateful.'

Of this I was not convinced, especially when Bhim, who had been watching with distaste, came up and whispered in my ear. 'Raja-sahib,' he said slyly, 'Mummy in pain, Mummy know who give pain. Mummy cross with Raja-sahib. Better Daddy give injection. Raja-sahib hide. When injection over, give Mummy gur. Mummy then like Raja-sahib,' he smiled, winking at me.

As we were about to leave, after adding to our equipment a large box of hypodermic needles, syringes and glass phials, the vet pointed to two raised and hardened circles of skin on each side of her backside. 'You know what those are?' he said. 'Those are the marks made by the Lohatias, the men who in the olden days, when hunting wild elephants with lassoes, would hang on to the crupper ropes and spur their elephants on with a short club faced with iron spikes when extra acceleration was needed. This type of elephant capture was called Mela Shikar and the type of elephant used was known as a Koonki. They had to be very fast elephants.'

Looking at her now, as she stuffed her face with paddy, I wondered if she could catch a bus, let alone a wild elephant.

'Mela Shikar is now of course banned,' he continued, 'but it took place in north-east India, mainly in Assam. So you now have an idea where she might come from.'

Miraculously, Tara's leg already appeared to be improving. She could bend it more and we moved at a good pace over a wide, sandy, dry river basin in the shadow of an unfinished bridge. In the distance we could see the outline of Cuttack, the old capital of Orissa which, due to its unfortunate geographical position, wedged on a spit of land between two huge rivers, had been unable to expand. The capital was transferred to Bhubaneshwar in 1948. It was over one of these rivers that we now crossed.

Trucks and buses thundered perilously close. I had not adjusted to the fact that I was travelling with an elephant rather than a dog that might slip its lead, and I became foolishly anxious that Tara might disappear under the wheels of an oncoming vehicle. To my left, over a railway bridge, the Madras–Calcutta express train chugged imperiously. We were moving faster.

Cuttack was buzzing with an air of excitement, for the Russian circus was in town. Minibuses darted in and out of the traffic, their sides emblazoned with posters of svelte young ladies dressed in scanty sequinned outfits, balancing with arms outstretched on top of charging horses. Lions and tigers snarled from advertising hoardings and bicyclists with tannoys attached to the handlebars of their rusting machines excitedly described the entertainments of the Big Top. Pale-faced Russian artistes mingled with the crowd, and the circus strongman had managed to squeeze into a rickshaw's tiny seat. On his knee sat a dwarf. Tara and I greeted them all cheerfully but were met with a suspicious silence.

In the main square, fenced off, stood a marble statue of a splendid turbanned man with a beautifully refined face. Around his neck hung a garland of marigolds. He was the Maharaja of Paralakhemedi, a popular figure, responsible for making Orissa a state in its own right in 1936, separate from Bihar.

I was taken to meet the owner of *Samaj*, the oldest newspaper in Orissa. A venerable old man with exquisite manners presented Aditya and me with a wooden deity, and around our shoulders wrapped colourful appliqué-work blankets. He clasped my hand. 'Traditions are dying fast. What you are doing is an inspiration to the youth of Orissa.' Then he asked if I needed money. I was astonished by this genuine gesture of kindness.

On the outskirts of Cuttack we passed the ruins of the Barabati Fort. It was built in the thirteenth century and once consisted of nine courts, the first of which housed the elephants, the camels and the horses. All that remained was a crumbling stone entrance and a wide moat.

'This place has seen some action,' I remarked to Aditya. 'The Moghuls didn't behave too well, but it was your lot that really went to town.'

The invasions of Orissa had begun in AD 1205 with the purpose of securing the superior breed of elephants for which Orissa was famous. The most remarkable foray of all was made in 1360 by the Delhi Emperor Firoz Shah, who cut through the jungles of Orissa, crossed the Mahanadi river and occupied this fort, from which the King had fled. Here Firoz Shah spent some time hunting elephants, and when the terrified King sent envoys to negotiate for peace he replied, ironically, that he had only come to hunt and was amazed that the King had taken flight. The embarrassed Oriya King sent him twenty elephants and promised to do so annually as a tribute. Only then did the Emperor return to Delhi. Invaded and occupied by Mohammedans for five hundred years, the state of Orissa was plunged into further despair by the arrival of the Marathas.

'During the famine of 1770,' I reminded Aditya, 'when people were dying in their hundreds of thousands, you went completely berserk and, it is recorded, "raged like wild beasts across the country".'

'Tell me more,' Aditya said enthusiastically.

'It's not a nice story, but I must say you were efficient, in your extortionist greed.'

'Well there you are,' he replied. 'Nothing better than an efficient army.'

'Fortunately for Orissa your efficiency barely lasted a century. The British stormed the fort and the Maratha yoke was finally broken.'

'Bloody British,' he remarked with a laugh. 'Always poking their noses in where they're not wanted.'

Over the next few days we headed slowly northwards, gradually entering into rural Orissa, camping in government rest-houses and schools to avoid the discomfort of wet nights under canvas. The monsoons were still in full flow. Tara's foot had healed almost totally due to the injections that Aditya now performed expertly each evening. Bhim's sly plan didn't seem to be working as she paid rather more attention to Aditya than me. I was convinced that the vet was right; Tara was grateful to Aditya for healing her pain and they had become firm friends.

In preparation for my imminent training as a rookie mahout, Bhim had given Aditya a list of basic elephant commands which Aditya had written down for me phonetically. Mercifully there were only seventeen of them, not eighty-four as I had been told, and unless I learnt Hindi they just about covered everything. In the evenings, Aditya and I would wring out our wet, bloody socks and attempt to patch up the raw holes with Elastoplast, while I practised my commands.

Agit (Ah-git) – Forward/go

Peechay (Pee.Chay, like the name) – Back

Chai ghoom (like chime, like goon) – Right

Chi (like cheese) – Left

Chhee (like cheese again, but longer) – Dirty

Dhuth (like Dutch without the 'ch') – Stop, the most important command, which I never quite managed to master

Maar Thode (Ma, toad) – Break

A Dhur (A like Eh, Dur like Durbar) – Get this/get that

Oopar Dhur (Oo, pa, dur) – Reach up/grab

Mylay (My, lay) – Get up

Baitho (Buy, toe) – Down/get down on your knees

Theeray (Tea, ray) – Lie down/roll over on side

Theylay Chhup (Tea, lay, chap) – Drink

Bey (Bay) – Bitch

Lay lay (same) – Eat/take food/open your mouth. This one was pointless. Tara needed no encouragement

Utha (Oo, ta) – Lift

Bowl Bowl (same) – Speak/say thank you

This is easy, I thought to myself smugly, and was soon word perfect.

'I've learnt them,' I told Aditya. 'Test me.' I had hardly reached the 'Pee' of 'Peechay' before he exploded.

'For goodness sake, Mark. This is an elephant, not a dog. You sound exactly like that tweedy lady on British television who stomps around in green wellington boots saying "Sit. Walkies. Good doggy."'

'Barbara Woodhouse,' I interrupted crossly, 'was jolly successful.'

'Well, I can tell you my friend, this is a different ball game. Rather than speaking like some la-di-da debutante, put some life into it – "Dhuth,"' he roared.

Tara dug her front legs in and stopped dead. A mahout with lesser experience than Bhim would have fallen off. As it was, he lurched forward and buried his head in Tara's neck, almost swallowing the cigarette he had clamped between his teeth.

'Yes, I see what you mean,' I said humbly. 'I think I need a bit more practice.'

We stopped that night beside a lake surrounded by mist-veiled hills. For a change it was eerily silent; there were no people and only the soft 'clock clock' of wooden bells attached to the necks of the grazing cattle and the 'pit-a-pat' of something being thrown on top of our tents disturbed us. Tara, chained to a tree behind us, enthusiastically scooped up trunkfuls of earth and flung it over her shoulder, giving herself a mud bath. She soon resembled a giant molehill, but the coating of mud was an effective deterrent against the insects that were annoying her.

It was an evening of an old mahout's tales. Whether fact or fiction it did not seem to matter, and as the rum took effect Bhim, with his eyes closed, began to talk, not for our benefit particularly, or to anyone – just an old man's reminiscences because the time was right. He spoke contemptuously about the new methods of caring for elephants and of the people who claimed to understand them, but did not; of how it had been he who had been sent to capture a tusker rampaging in the jungles, causing havoc and destruction among the villages and to the people's crops, after all modern methods of capture had failed. The tusker had not been a wild elephant but a domesticated animal that had gone wild after being deserted by its mahout, probably a mendicant like Rajpath. Bhim had been sent for and had performed an old puja taught to him by his father, cutting the ear of another elephant, taking a little blood and offering it to a deity of Ganesh. Then he had been able to approach the tusker and within five days, soothing and comforting the distressed animal, had ridden him back to the zoo. He spoke of crossing the Simlipals, now a huge wildlife sanctuary, as a child, on top of a bus. The bus had passed under a rocky escarpment and he had felt hot breath and seen a flash of yellow hair as a tiger launched itself on to the bus and carried away the man sitting next to him. And he spoke of how the Maharaja of Mayurbhanj had presented the British Collector, who was returning to England, with a baby elephant; how the little calf had been hoisted by a 'big machine' on to the ship; how in return the Collector had presented the Maharaja with a thousand and one balloons of all different colours, shaped like animals, and of his amazement and delight seeing them float into the air around the ship as it slowly slid from its berth.

Later that night I was awoken by a soft tap on my shoulder and a rum-laced whisper in my ear.

'Come, quietly, Raja-sahib, you look Mummy sleeping.'

I crept outside and there, like a grey boulder, Tara lay quietly on her side, her trunk curled around her neck emitting a wonderfully soothing sound like bubbles escaping from a diver's mouthpiece.

'Mummy snoring,' he whispered. 'Mummy happy.'

7

Touch-me-not

OVERNIGHT, AS IF somebody had simply pushed a button, the monsoons left us, hurrying their black clouds further south. There was a distinct change in the air. It was crisp, alive; the early morning a few degrees colder and then warming as the sun rose. Autumn in India had arrived bringing with it long, hot, golden days of harvest, celebration and festivals.

As instructed by Bhim, we were to be on the look-out for the mimosa plant, otherwise known as 'touch-me-not'. If you caressed its small fern like leaves they closed quickly, like a shutting book. The plant was an essential ingredient in the puja that was soon to be performed, where I would take on Bhim as my guru. Bhim called it the 'full control ceremony'. Once Tara had eaten the blessed offering of mimosa and gur, he explained, she would be as obedient as a lamb and I would become the complete master. I was sceptical about this – not that I doubted Bhim, but because I doubted my abilities in controlling Tara, who was becoming friskier as each day passed. All the same I eagerly scanned the countryside for this plant. I was going to need all the help I could get. I was also encouraged by watching Gokul. He had apparently undergone a similar ceremony before we had started at Nandankanan and now was riding Tara with all the ability of a seasoned mahout, urging her along with shrill, squeaky cries.

We were well into rural Orissa, where fresh droppings were abundant, signalling that we had entered elephant country. At the top of the giant bamboo groves ringing the paddy fields were tree houses, constructed like large storks' nests, access to which was gained by long rickety ladders. These were anti-elephant machans in which the villagers would sit at night and, by means of fireworks, crackers, shouting and flaming torches, attempt to deter rampaging beasts from demolishing their crops. In one village, where we stopped for tea, a young man, the local teacher, approached me.

'It is indeed,' he said, 'a wonderful thing that you are coming today. A gift from the gods.'

'Namaste,' I replied, delighted by this welcome but slightly bewildered.

'You, of course, will stop and help us?' he enquired eagerly.

'Well, yes,' now completely bewildered. 'If I can.'

'It is the tusker, sir. It has decimated our crops. It has already killed eleven of our people. You,' he said pointing to Tara, 'will catch it with your elephant.'

'Catch it with my elephant?' I answered amazed. Tara was happily rummaging around by the side of the tea-stall in search of food. The thought of the four of us with Tara engaged in some mad Mela Shikar chasing a highly dangerous elephant was absurd, and yet it was wonderful that he imagined it as being so simple. 'I'm sorry. You see we are just travelling through your beautiful country and we are not equipped to undertake such a task. Can't the government do anything about it?'

'The government,' he replied crestfallen, 'will do nothing. The tusker has only killed eleven people, sir. It must kill twenty-four before they are even considering taking actions.'

This was but one of many similar situations that I would encounter on my travels concerning the growing imbalance in India between the rural man and the natural life of the elephant living in harmony. Both are blameless and both are victims of greed; greed caused by the desire for timber, and the consequent massive deforestation. Elephants are creatures of habit. They have, for centuries, followed the same migratory routes in search of food. They arrive and find none: their larder has been cut down, and in desperation they turn to raiding crops on which the villagers' livelihood depends. The villagers are helpless and, even if they could afford to buy modern firearms, would usually be loath to use them. The elephant is a revered beast. Even when, which is seldom, a licence is granted to shoot an elephant that has been established as a rogue, more often than not the kill is not carried out. They revert to modern methods of trying to drug the animal, which in reality is an expensive and impractical situation. In a local newspaper I had read about a problem tusker that had killed and was causing havoc in another area of Orissa:

> Licences were issued to kill it. When the hunters took position closer to the pachyderm to shoot him, they found that tears flowed from his eyes and he

> was supplicant. They dropped their plans and the tusker returned to the forests. The experts are of the opinion that the best way to tackle the situation is to capture the pachyderm. For every untoward incident created by the animal, they contend, there has been enough provocation by the timber merchants and the others who depend on the forest produce. The Minister for Forests who was informed of the case, vehemently opposed all proposals to kill the elephant. He asserted that he would instruct the forest staff to have him tranquillised and deported to the zoo where necessary arrangements with Rs 1 lakh would be made to get him trained under an expert mahout from Assam.

Sadly, this situation is worsening. The Indian elephant is simply running out of living space. Recently a herd of thirty were creating havoc as close as twenty miles to Calcutta. It is fervently to be hoped that desperate measures like culling will not be introduced, and it is up to man to redress the balance. The tiger, which until recently was almost extinct, is beginning to make a dramatic recovery thanks to the resources and expertise made available to 'Project Tiger'. The elephant must now be given the same attention.

At Mandahat, we came to another mighty river, the Brahamani. Some people had told us authoritatively that it was six feet deep and could be crossed, while others shook their heads, knowledgeably stating that it had burst its banks. The latter were right: no one could ford it. We took a short cut along a road which would lead us to another bridge at Kabatobandah, where we hoped to meet up with the jeep. The road soon turned into a track, and then into nothing, as we found ourselves amongst fields choked with baysharam, a kind of bush with long wavy stems sprouting lilac bell-shaped flowers, also known as 'shameless' for its gregarious, prolific and deep-rooted growth. It is considered a virulent weed which causes the Indian farmer enormous difficulties. The baysharam gave way to bamboo groves that had been decimated by wild elephants. In turn the bamboo led into sal forests still being decimated by human beings, in which the sound of a falling axe was always audible.

Considering their size, it is remarkable how elephants can move so soundlessly. Tara's footsteps, at their loudest, resembled the shuffle of an old man wearing carpet slippers. Because of this quietness, we encountered everything with an element of surprise, whether animal, human, bird or insect. Aditya was particularly happy. When we saw the flash of a golden oriole, a beautiful yellow bird with a jet black streak through its eye dipping away with a raucous *Cheeugh*, or the long ribbon-like tail of a paradise flycatcher, he would jot down his sightings excitedly in a small book. At one point Tara disturbed a carpet of big yellow butterflies that exploded into the air. A single butterfly, more courageous than its companions, attached itself firmly to the end of her trunk and after several vain attempts to dislodge it, by swinging it from side to side, she finally blew it off with a large sneeze.

The sal forests began to thin out and we moved carefully along the ridges dividing well-tended paddy fields. In corners of these fields were small tribal shrines situated under the spread of large shady trees. Dedicated to the goddess Devi, they consisted of groups of exquisite terracotta figures of horses, camels, elephants and bears which were offered as gifts to the deity, to ensure a healthy harvest to the indigenous Mundas. In the distance we heard the sound of drums. Spurring Tara on, we reached a small collection of thatched huts with pink walls surrounding a muddy courtyard where a Munda party was in full swing. A chain of men and women, dark muscular people with full lips and handsome high-cheekboned faces, were pounding their feet drunkenly in ankle-deep mud, performing a kind of ritual hokey-cokey.

At the sight of Tara looming over their compound, they threw their arms into the air, moaning loudly. The drum tempo increased, they whirled in ever-decreasing circles and finally collapsed laughing in an exhausted heap. A young woman wearing a brilliant azure sari, moulded to the contours of her body, untangled herself from the group and undulated over to Tara. She knelt gracefully and touched Tara's feet in obeisance. Each of her companions followed suit, and then offered us leaf cups containing a milky fluid which they had filled from large terracotta gourds. This was 'handia', a local rice beer. At first it tasted slightly bitter and fizzy, but after numerous replenishments, one was filled with a sense of contentment.

The drums started again. We were dragged to our feet and whirled round the compound. Now as drunk as our hosts, we proudly showed our paces. Aditya performed a sort of martial strut. I attempted to show them break dancing, which resulted in my head becoming firmly stuck in the mud, my feet waving in the air. Gokul, the professional, delighted the audience by doing somersaults, handstands and back flips. Even Tara, after draining one of the gourds, flapped her ears and shook her head while Bhim squatted with the elders and concentrated on the more serious aspect of things – drinking. When we took our leave the women presented us each with a frangipani flower, garlanded Tara, and blessed us for a safe journey.

We reached a small river where a flash flood had washed away the bridge. A man sat forlornly on the bank drying out a bundle of soggy letters. He told us that while attempting to cross, he had been knocked over by the current and his bicycle was now caught in a bundle of branches in the middle of the whirling water. Bhim and Tara waded into the river. Directed by his sharp commands of 'Uhta, uhta,' Tara lowered her trunk and plucked the bicycle from the branches as if it was a feather, depositing it gently in front of the grateful postman.

Out of curiosity, I penned a letter to myself in London and gave it to him. When I returned home three months later it was waiting for me. The letter was slightly worse for wear, with an added message written on the back of the envelope. 'For Haathi-wallah from K. Rath, postman, thanking him sincerely.'

Guided by a full moon that washed the landscape in a pale light, we finally crossed the Brahamani over a long concrete bridge. It was late by the time we found the camp and by the look on Indrajit's face we knew there had been trouble between the two drivers.

'Khusto!' he spat fiercely. 'No good, he take rum. He always drunk. No helping either. I put tents, I cook, he does nothing. So I hit him. Either he go or I go.'

Aditya and I looked at each other in despair. We did not need a domestic squabble and we couldn't afford to lose Indrajit. He was invaluable. We checked the rum supply. Indrajit was right. Out of a new case of twelve bottles of rum one was missing. We found Khusto sitting in the jeep nursing a face that was even more swollen than usual. He mumbled something incomprehensible and turned his back to us insolently.

'Leave this to me, Mark,' Aditya said angrily.

For the next ten minutes there was an angry exchange of words punctuated by metallic slaps as Aditya banged his fist on the side of the jeep. It stopped abruptly. Khusto's voice had changed. He was now pleading. Eventually he shuffled into the firelight and muttered an apology to Indrajit and offered his hand. Indrajit took it hesitatingly and then with an angry smile touched him on the shoulder. The crisis it seemed was over for a time.

'What did you tell him?' I asked Aditya.

'Simple, my friend. He has stolen, so therefore he is a thief. I threatened to take him to the police station. That did it. I have told him that from now on Indrajit is the boss.'

'Do you think it will work?' I said.

'We'll see. Anyway, I don't think Khusto's bad, just foolish. He told me that all his problems stem from being born with too small a tongue.'

'What's that got to do with it?' I asked incredulously.

'I have no idea,' he laughed. 'Anyway we shall be without them for a few days. We are entering the forests of Daitari tomorrow and Bhim has announced that Tara is fit enough to carry the howdah.'

'What about my puja?' I insisted anxiously. 'Why can't we find this bloody mimosa plant?'

'Slowly, Mark, remember this is India.'

'Slowly indeed.' At this rate I was going to walk to Sonepur, I thought, as I finished my mug of coffee.

We were sitting round the fire which had been made in the crumbling porch of a deserted house near our camp. Bhim suddenly jumped to his feet and pointed into the dark confines of the house. 'Nag, nag!' he cried excitedly. Everybody immediately disappeared and I was left sitting bewildered.

'What the hell's going ...'

'Get out of there, Mark!' Aditya shouted.

'Will somebody tell me what's going on?'

'Nag, nag!'

'What in the hell is nag?'

'A snake, you idiot! Cobra!' Aditya yelled from the jeep, from which he, Bhim, Gokul and Indrajit reappeared armed with axes.

'Jeeesus! A snake! Oh my God!' I shot out of the porch and fled towards Tara who in the circumstances seemed to be the safest bet, noting on my way that Khusto had climbed on top of the jeep. The boys advanced quickly into the house and a tremendous mêlée started. Shouts and screams followed by the sound of metal ringing on stone. I returned as nonchalantly as possible.

'Well?'

'Nag escape,' Bhim stated crossly. 'Big, maybe seven feet.'

'Seven feet!' I cried. 'Well, where is it now?'

'Maybe tent,' he leered happily. A thorough inspection of our sleeping quarters was made, but none of us slept well that night.

Early next morning before setting off, Aditya and I took a detour to visit Bhuban, famous as Asia's most populated village. Our mission was more than one of tourism: we were to buy 'bombs', anti-elephant devices that Bhim said we might well need over the next few days. The houses of Bhuban are so close together that their thatched roofs join over the narrow alleys, cutting out the light, and only single-line pedestrian traffic is possible. None the less, in the maze of shops selling brass and metal objects for which Bhuban has a reputation, we located the bomb-seller.

The bombs were hard and round, about the size of golf balls, and were wrapped in brightly coloured paper. When thrown against something hard they exploded like army thunderflashes. These ethnic grenades scared the hell out of me, and it was hoped that they would have the same effect on a wild animal.

By the time we returned to camp Tara was fully loaded. Unhappy about this sudden extra weight, she kept whipping her trunk back trying to undo Bhim's knots. From the front she looked like an old bag lady. Pots, pans, kerosene stoves and old sacks filled with tinned food hung from one side. Over the other flank dangled tents, sleeping bags, pillows, axes and cameras. All this paraphernalia had been placed in two white nylon hammocks that I had brought from England, so that from the back she resembled some grotesque model, wearing gigantic shoulder pads. As a deterrent against the hot sun, the top of her head had been oiled and it gleamed like a patent leather shoe. When Gokul, eager to see her reaction, exploded a bomb beneath her feet, she displayed the same patience as a nanny with a small naughty child, simply turning her head and giving him a look as if to say, 'Silly child,' and continued trying to undo the knots. It was not surprising that she didn't react. Rajpath must have taken her through so many town festivals that she was now indifferent to ordeal by firecracker.

There are four ways to climb on to an elephant. The first, and the one that we were about to adopt, is the easiest for the passenger and the most uncomfortable for the elephant. With a command of 'Baitho!' the elephant kneels and one clambers up on to the howdah by way of stepping on to the top of the front part of either leg, grabbing on to the ear, and hauling oneself up. In the old days a ladder would be produced or one would mount from a special block. The second way is harder. Upon the command of 'Utha! utha!' the elephant lifts either of its front legs and, grabbing the ear, one steps on to the leg and is raised up like an elevator. The third is over the backside. The elephant lowers one of its back legs, and one simply catches on to her tail or the crupper rope. The fourth, the expert's way, and the way that I hoped one day to achieve, is by the trunk. It looks so casual, elegant and simple. The trunk is lowered to the ground; placing a foot about in the centre, one holds both ears and is hoisted up and over.

Having awkwardly, but successfully climbed aboard, I settled into the howdah and noticed Aditya about to mount with his boots on.

'Take off your boots,' I said.

'What?' he exclaimed crossly. 'Why?'

'I don't know why. But from now on, no boots when riding Tara.' For some inexplicable reason I felt her to be as sacred as the deck of a yacht and I was delighted when I saw Bhim nod his approval. Grumbling, Aditya untied his boots, threw them up to me and climbed aboard. Tara immediately rose to her feet and we were lifted gently upwards. Elephant-back at last, I thought happily. We really have started the journey.

8
An Angry Tusker

> I do not know why it is, but the instant I am on an elephant I do not feel afraid for myself or anybody else. When the tall grass shakes and the elephants begin to scream, I ask whether it is a tiger or a rhinoceros in exactly the same tone I should ask the servants whether it is a partridge or a pheasant.
>
> Fanny Eden, Indian Journals 1837–1838,
> *Tigers, Durbars and Kings*

FROM THE VERY moment that Tara took her first step forward, I was filled with a complete sense of security, cocooned, wrapped in cotton-wool. I knew that while this wonderful benign animal lumbered below me, nothing could go wrong. From twelve feet up the view was spectacular. The landscape took on a different perspective and one could see both far and near – the blazing yellow of a distant mustard field or the early morning goings on over a mud wall of a village. But it was the feeling of invincibility that struck me most. My imagination ran riot, and I became the 'King of Bliss' surrounded by a thousand elephants, revelling in the horror and fear of my foes.

The experts told me that it would be uncomfortable, tedious and even painful to travel in a howdah. How wrong they were. I found the soft swaying motion relaxing, almost too relaxing. On occasion, I fell asleep, and just caught myself before I slid off. To prevent this, I fashioned a sling from a length of rope and found I could lie back with my feet hanging over her backside. Then, after plugging in my Walkman, I could recline like a Maharaja, listening to the strains of Italian opera while a huge, never changing empty sky passed by overhead.

Occasionally, like a tiny silver arrow, an aeroplane would flash far above. I felt sorry for the passengers squeezed into their pressurized chamber, hurrying from one destination to the next, unable to see the beauty that I was so fortunate to be enjoying. Gradually I was slowing down, slowing down to the pace of a country in which if one moves fast, one misses everything – and like a patient tutor Tara was influencing me, showing me the way.

We were now climbing steadily and passing through Orissa's mining belt – a dull, wide, angry landscape, dotted with huge rocky escarpments gouged out and scarred by blasting and bulldozers. In the distance I could see the forested ranges of Daitari shimmering blue in the heat haze. It was hot. As elephants do not sweat, Tara cooled herself down by looping her trunk into her mouth, extracting a mixture of spit and water and blowing it in a fine spray over her flanks and under her belly. Elephants, like camels, can store water. They have a kind of shut-off valve system that they can open and close as they wish. As the sun became fiercer, she piled a bonnet of straw and leaves on top of her head. Her great ears, the smooth skin behind their wide spread knotted with thick veins, flapped rhythmically, acting as ventilation under which Bhim would occasionally stretch out his legs and manipulate her with his toes to urge her on. Each toe had a life of its own, pushing, probing and playing like the fingers of a concert pianist. Then he would sit back on the front of the howdah and work her head with the heels of his feet, pushing forward and down. No commands were necessary. It was all being done by touch. Bhim told me to watch his movements carefully and learn. A true master remains silent. Considering my appalling Hindi accent, this would certainly make life easier.

Another example of Bhim's expertise came when Gokul, who would be walking alongside us, would change into the driving seat. Tara's pace would then alter considerably and she would slow right down, however much Gokul shrieked commands at her. She knew instinctively that she was now in control and exploited the situation mercilessly.

We made camp under a lone Peepul tree on top of a small hillock by the side of the road. The heat had sapped our strength and we slept for most of the afternoon. In the evening I went to feed Tara her gur. She greeted me with an affectionate rumble, wrapped her trunk around me drawing me closer, searching my body for her treat. The vet at Nandankanan had also given me some deworming powder for her, a little of which I had hidden in a thick ball of gur.

'Lay, lay! Tara,' I commanded.

She opened her mouth wide, exposing tiny six-inch tusks on either side and I caught a glimpse of her gigantic molars. I placed the ball on her fat pink tongue which was as soft as a blancmange and watched the obvious pleasure appear on her face. It changed quickly to one of 'You can't fool me' as she delicately removed the ball, placed it on the ground, broke it open with her trunk, blew the powder out, remoulded it and popped it back into her mouth. She did, however, like some medicines. As I kissed her goodnight, she reached into the top pocket of my shirt and pulled out a new packet of Setlers which she swallowed whole with relish.

Over the next few days we crossed heavily wooded highlands which in some places were as high as three and a half thousand feet, to Keonjhar, the capital of this large hilly district. The rocky ground, called laterite or iron sandstone, was of a sombre dark reddish colour. When I picked up a stone I was surprised by its lightness and the large round holes, like those of a sponge. All ancient temples, forts and palaces in Orissa are built with this stone, and, mixed with gravel, so are most of the roads. Our progress was slow as Tara picked her way carefully avoiding the sharp stones to prevent injuring her sensitive feet.

As we reached the summits which, from below, appeared as sharp peaks, we crossed extensive tablelands filled with green paddy in which women, wearing a colourful blaze of saris and large cane cone-shaped hats, were reaping the harvest. As the sun reached its zenith they shaded themselves under the trees, singing and combing each other's hair in the heat. We heard them giggling as we passed and they waved shyly.

'It reminds me of summer in England,' Aditya remarked.

'I didn't know you'd been there,' I said.

'Yes, in 1970. I worked in Kent, picking hops, although I didn't sit around like these girls. I worked from 5.30 in the morning until 7 o'clock at night. He was a bastard, that foreman, a real driver of slaves.'

'That's probably exactly what he thought you were,' I joked, 'fresh off a boat that had sneaked in somewhere on the coast at night.'

'I most certainly was not,' he replied indignantly. 'I hitchhiked all the way from India. But let me tell you, I felt like one the way that I was treated. I don't have many good memories of England at that time.'

'Well,' I murmured philosophically, 'here we are now, riding across India together on an elephant. What could be more apt?'

At that moment Tara shot out her trunk and grabbed a pile of paddy that was laid out to dry on the roadside. Bhim picked up the ankush and jabbed the sharp spiked end into the top of her head. She squealed, violently shaking her head in pain. I watched with fascinated horror as a large drop of blood bubbled from her skin. With a roar of rage I tore the ankush from Bhim's hand, grabbed hold of one of the ropes and swung on to the ground.

'That's it!' I yelled. 'The journey's over. I will not have my elephant hurt. You can all find your own way back.'

I stamped off down the road. Ten minutes later Aditya caught up with me. I stared at the bloody tip of the ankush.

'Forget it, Aditya,' I said. 'You can't say anything ...'

'Now listen!' Aditya shouted. 'Who in hell do you think you are? Elephant Bill? What do you know about elephants? Bhim would not use the ankush unless it was absolutely necessary. Before you interrupt, let me tell you what he told me. Tara was stealing. And I have just had to pay that poor farmer compensation. It is not Tara's fault though. She was taught these tricks by Rajpath. Many mendicants literally hold people to ransom by getting their elephants to pick up the paddy, unless the farmers pay up. Bhim has to break Tara of the habit of stealing and the ankush is the only way to make her understand.'

I sat down and stared moodily at my bare feet.

'Come on, Mark. Elephants are big powerful creatures. If you start pampering them you are in trouble. They are intelligent, cunning and deceitful. Believe me, the old man knows what he's doing. If he fails to convert her now she will only get worse.'

'All right, I'm sorry,' I said, slightly mollified. 'I guess I have a lot to learn, but one thing is for sure, you won't find me doing that. Shameless bribery with gur rather than sharp jabs with the ankush is going to be my method.'

'We'll see,' he replied. 'Just wait until you start riding her.'

We walked back to Tara who did not seem at all affected by her punishment. She was pulling up roots, smacking them against her legs to remove the earth, then stuffing them into her mouth. We climbed back on board and Bhim pointed at her head. 'See, Raja-sahib. I fix.' A small poultice of herbs was attached to the wound. 'No hurt now. Bhim sorry, but Raja-sahib must learn. Mummy learning also.'

Apart from the numerous anti-elephant machans dotted everywhere, the paddy fields that we now passed were surrounded by anti-elephant ditches seven feet deep, five feet wide at the top, tapering to about two feet at the bottom. Wild elephants are powerless to cross them except during the monsoons when the ditches silt up. Around the planted fields there were fences of twisted creepers in which wild mint grew in abundance, filling the air with its sharp aroma.

Then we entered the silent darkness of the forest and all was still again. Tara suddenly stopped, her huge ears spreading outwards. She extended her trunk upwards and moved it from side to side scanning and smelling the air.

'Haathi,' Bhim whispered. 'Close.'

Aditya reached for his camera bag. In the process he knocked it against a metal strut. With a sharp downward gesture of his hand Bhim indicated him to keep still and with another instructed Gokul to climb aboard. There was no noise, only the sound of dripping water. Then a sharp 'Tuk, tuk, tuk' split the silence and a coppersmith bird rang its alarm bell.

From the corner of my eye I caught a slight movement. A soft sound, almost inaudible, was the only indication that the foliage was being gently brushed aside. Like ghosts, three female elephants appeared and stood motionless on the road in front of us. I could feel Tara trembling beneath me. The wild elephants let out a deep rumble and extended their trunks towards Tara. They seemed much larger than her, more muscular, their bodies sculpted like sheet armour on a tank. Then as quickly and quietly as they had appeared, they disappeared.

I let out my breath and was about to reach for a cigarette when Bhim gave another of his urgent hand signals. We heard a movement, as if the grass were being crushed by some huge, unidentified force and suddenly a large male elephant with tusks almost three foot long confronted us. The tusks were not white, as I had expected, but yellow, and the tips dark from where he had been digging in the earth. Tara was trembling violently and Bhim was having trouble holding her steady. We were so close I could see the flies clustered around the tusker's mean little eyes. Without warning he rapped his trunk on the ground, emitting a terrifying sound that somebody once described as like 'shaking a large sheet of thin metal' caused by air being driven out of the trunk as it strikes the ground.

'Quick,' Bhim hissed. 'He angry. Throw bombs.'

Gokul, who always carried a permanent supply like a kid with fireworks, hurled one on to the ground. Nothing happened. It failed to explode. The tusker took one step forward, throwing his trunk contemptuously into the air, emitting a terrible shrill trumpet, as if warning us to keep our distance. It was so loud, so enveloping that one's senses reeled. I shook my head to clear it.

'For Christ's sake,' I whispered in desperation. 'Throw another.'

Leaving nothing to chance, Bhim picked up a bomb, laid it on the flat of the howdah and hit it with the ankush. There was a blinding flash, a puff of blue smoke, and when it had cleared the road was empty. We could hear the elephants crashing away through the trees, as delayed shock set in. But in that moment of silence, before terror turns to laughter, the primal energy of the absent beast still vibrated in the void. It seemed almost impossible to go forward. The silence of the jungle was no longer tranquil. It had become predatory.

'What would have happened if we hadn't got the bombs?' I asked, shaken.

'Maybe trouble,' Bhim laughed. 'Forget tell you. Mummy on heat.' He pointed to the temporal glands, two small holes from which a black viscous fluid was oozing, on either side of her face.

I remembered my amazement when I had seen an elephant's erect penis at the zoo. It was at least four foot long and as thick as a man's leg.

9

Firinghee Mahout

WE CAMPED BESIDE bubbling brooks and bathed in clear fresh water. The fodder was abundant and Tara ate well. Gokul trapped fish by making an ingenious dam-like contraption from his underpants and a hammock. Once a large black water snake became ensnared in it. We were all fitter and stronger. Aditya and I were beginning to lose our city bellies. Bhim had changed. Gone was the alcoholic ravaged face. His eyes were clear and he walked erect like a proud foot soldier. He explained it was nothing to do with the exercise but due to the good booze he was drinking. In Nandankanan, he told us, each day he drank two bottles of local hooch spiced with fertiliser to give it a kick. The pain in his stomach was sometimes so bad he was unable to walk.

We stopped that night at our most spectacular camp so far, next to an exquisite little colonial bungalow overlooking a vast, calm lake, where water swept noisily over a large concrete dam. Aditya and I went to bathe at the bottom of the dam. We sat with our backs against the cool stone as the water thundered over us, crashing past boulders into the valley below. As we walked back, something colourful caught my eye at the edge of the lake. It was a little offering of flowery garlands from which burnt incense sticks were poking out. Thick green sal trees swept up almost vertically from the lake and the ground was a carpet of crimson fallen flowers, like discarded silk handkerchiefs.

The occupant of the bungalow came out to meet us; an elderly man with a shock of wavy, white hair, wearing a smart khaki uniform on which the brass buttons gleamed. He was the dam-keeper and he had lived in this remote and beautiful place for the last twenty years.

'Don't you get lonely?' I asked him.

'I have my dogs, sir,' which were pressing up against my legs. He winked at me conspiratorially and glanced behind at a curtained window. 'Occasionally I am having company.' For a second the curtain drew back and a pretty face peeped out before hastily disappearing. 'But it is my garden that is keeping me busy. Please follow, sir. It would honour me to show you.'

It was indeed charming. Bougainvillaea spilled from the bungalow roof and night jasmine twisted round its small columns. A carefully tended vegetable patch lay on one side. On the other, surrounded by a ring of flame-of-the-forest trees, was an immaculate green lawn like a manicured croquet green on which stood an ancient Atco lawn-mower.

'I am apologising for the state of the lawn, sir,' he said regretfully. 'I now have to do it by hand. I am not able to get spare parts for my machine. The blades were worn down many years ago. I could probably be getting a Japanese one from the mining company, but they are no good. They do not understand lawns like the British do. If it would not be too much trouble,' he continued, 'could you be sending me a spare set of blades?'

'Of course,' I replied, 'if I can. It will probably take a long time as I won't be returning to England for some months.'

He smiled. 'What to do? I have all the time in the world.'

The trees thinned out alarmingly as we began to descend. Great trunks lay like slain corpses along our route, on which men worked feverishly chopping and sawing as if they were dismembering their victims. I supposed it would not be long before the beautiful forests that we had travelled through suffered the same fate. Under bridges, in order to avoid detection, villagers panned for gold, sifting the silt brought down by the rushing streams through concave boards. Aditya tried to photograph them but they hid their faces. Apparently their activities were illegal and if discovered were punishable by heavy fines.

At the village of Harichandanpur we met with Indrajit, Khusto and the jeep. The vehicle was surrounded by people, who grew to a huge crowd by the time we joined them. Sensing a reception like this, Indrajit had wisely made the camp about three miles out of the village. We tried to shake off the crowd, but by the time we reached the camp, hidden by a small rocky escarpment and surrounded by mango trees, we found ourselves hemmed in by about five hundred people. Eventually even Aditya got fed up with them and hurled a well-aimed anti-elephant bomb. The result was most satisfactory and they fled, but not too far, only as far as the rocky escarpment where they sat, patiently like hyenas.

Indrajit managed to find a couple of chickens and provided us with a very passable dinner. I congratulated him profusely, hoping that this flattery would induce further culinary prowess; our food up until then had been somewhat bland. Just before falling asleep I remembered the mimosa plant.

'What about my puja? When is it happening?' I enquired urgently of Aditya, who was cocooned like a mummy beside me.

'Tomorrow,' he said sleepily. 'It's all arranged.'

'But why tomorrow? What about the mimosa? I can't do it without the mimosa. Tara won't listen to me,' I banged on anxiously.

'Tomorrow, because …' He replied wearily, 'Bhim has decided it is an auspicious day. And as for the mimosa, well, do you really think it will make any difference?'

'Well, yes, I believe in those sort of things now. After all, India's full of them and you are always expounding the theories of the unknown and the supernatural, and the higher levels of cosmic consciousness.'

'Far out, man,' he replied and fell asleep.

We were woken in the middle of the night by a terrible commotion. Tins were being banged, people were shouting hysterically and the glow of fire lit up the interior of the tent. Aditya and I shot out to a scene from a Ku Klux Klan film as the villagers swept across the fields with lighted torches.

'What's going on?' we yelled.

'Bhalloo,' came Bhim's muffled and bored voice from the interior of his tent. 'Mummy not crying, so no trouble.'

Aditya laughed. 'It's a bear, Mark. It's been feeding on those ground-nut fields over there. The look-outs must have discovered it.'

The bear had succeeded in attracting the crowd away from us. Apart from one solitary silhouette, the escarpment above the camp was empty. I crawled back into the tent, contented.

'Rabbits and hares,' I said, poking my head out of the tent in the morning.

'What, where?' Aditya croaked, waking up quickly.

'No, no, it's only a silly English expression which you are supposed to say on the first day of every new month, and today is the first of October. But they must be the first words otherwise the charm doesn't work and is considered unlucky.'

'Just as well,' he yawned sleepily, falling back into his cocoon. 'Today is your puja. Today you ride Tara and you are going to need all the luck in the world.'

Against a lemon-tinged dawn sky we bathed Tara in a small, deep, circular rock pool that was choked with weeds and lilies. It was so perfect that it might have been made to order. Bhim and Gokul were worried about the possibility of snakes, so we threw buckets of water over her while she stood pulling at the weeds. When the crowds began to return, Tara was saddled quickly and we set off.

Indrajit and Khusto had already left on a secret shopping mission to Keonjhar. I guessed it might have something to do with my puja. I had seen Aditya slipping Indrajit a piece of paper. They were to meet us later on that day. I was consumed with curiosity and longed to interrogate Bhim about what part I was to play in this ceremony. I was still concerned about the absence of the mimosa plant. I wanted to know everything, but Bhim seemed very detached and pushed Tara along with clinical efficiency. Fields of ground-nuts – the poor man's almond – stretched out on each side of the road, broken by small hideouts – anti-bear machans. We had left the hunting grounds of the Haathi and were in the territory of the Bhalloo. Remembering the confusion he had caused last night, I saluted the bear again.

On a telegraph wire a handsome Oxford and Cambridge blue bird with a big head and a heavy black bill chuckled as we passed underneath.

'Roller or blue jay,' Aditya exclaimed excitedly, fumbling for his notebook. 'Your luck is in, it seems. The roller is considered very auspicious because of its colour. It represents the god Shiva, whose neck turned blue when he swallowed the poison of the world.'

'Far out, man,' I quipped nastily. I was still fuming about the lack of importance Aditya had attached to my mimosa plant.

Suddenly our progress was halted. Four policemen, astride bicycles, formed a road block. One of them was holding up his hands, as if stopping traffic.

'Good morning, Mr Sands,' he said.

'Good morning, officer,' I replied bewildered. 'Have you come to arrest me?'

'Good heavens no, sir, just to escort you.'

'Escort me. Why? Are we in danger?'

'No, no, Mr Sands. Just orders from headquarters.'

'What headquarters? Whose orders?'

'Bhubaneshwar, sir. I am not knowing who, but if you are comfortable we will begin.'

I never did unravel this mystery. It was a genuine escort and a very jolly one at that. Two policemen wobbled precariously in front while the two behind swerved to avoid the contents of Tara's breakfast which thudded down in front of them at irregular intervals. Buses and trucks and bullock carts were all pushed aside as the officer blew furiously on his whistle. One felt terribly important. The police station which they insisted I should inspect was spotless and neat, with gardens surrounding the pretty white bungalow built by the British in 1927. Inside it was cool, the cells were empty; there was no crime here they told me. Hanging next to a rack of well-oiled Lee Enfield .303 rifles and a bunch of handcuffs was a curious looking object like a grappling iron attached to a long rope.

'What is that for?' I enquired.

'For drunks, sir,' the officer replied. 'Many people are drinking now because of the harvest. Sometimes they drink too much and topple down wells. We fetch them out with that.'

At mid-day we passed a long granite ridge. Bhim pointed saying, simply, 'Puja.'

At a small stream the old man and I immersed ourselves in the muddy water to cleanse ourselves before the ceremony. Then we ascended to the ridge's bleak summit. It was an eerie, lonely place shrouded in metallic clouds. The wind tugged at our clothes and the clouds moved together becoming a monstrous black umbrella.

'It's going to rain,' Aditya said suddenly, breaking the silence. 'You know this is really extraordinary, it is considered ...'

'Yes, I know,' I interrupted flippantly, 'if it rains it is considered auspicious.'

'For once, Mark,' he said unsmiling, 'just try to be serious. For some inexplicable reason the gods are favouring you. Now pay attention, for Tara's sake, and I will tell you what to do.'

The jeep pulled up on the road far below and Indrajit and Khusto struggled up the hill, carrying an assortment of packages. Indrajit unpacked the boxes. On a big metal platter he placed bananas, two coconuts, bundles of incense and small arrangements of coloured flowers. I was told to undress and my waist was wrapped in a starched white dhoti, the traditional dress of the Indian when at worship. Around my neck was placed a saffron gumcha, a cloth about the size of a small sarong, and my forehead smeared with vermilion. Bhim was dressed identically. I faced him trying to keep a serious expression on my face. This was difficult as I could feel the cold tip of Tara's trunk exploring the back of my dhoti.

Picking up the offerings between my clasped hands I made my namaste to Bhim and placed it at his feet. I repeated this three times, each time bending to touch his feet. He placed his hands lightly on my head and recited a mantra. I completed my obeisance by a gift of money, 500 rupees, adding one rupee to make the total uneven and therefore auspicious. We both faced Tara. Her forehead shone crimson with the mark of Shiva. Bhim then uttered a mantra over Tara, circling her head with sticks of burning incense. We smashed the coconuts in turn and anointed her feet with the milk.

'Raja-sahib,' Bhim instructed, 'now make mantra to Tara. Then we ride.'

Caught unawares, I closed my eyes and recited in a loud pious voice a poem by Hilaire Belloc,

> When people call this beast to mind,
> They marvel more and more,
> At such a little tail behind
> So large a trunk before.

Luckily, the boys did not understand. They smiled approvingly at what they thought was an immensely powerful English mantra. On the other hand Aditya understood only too well and shook his head in despair.

Anxious that the next and most difficult stage of the ceremony went smoothly, I surreptitiously slipped Tara a large chunk of gur.

'Please, Tara,' I whispered in her ear, 'make this easy for me. Be nice. If you are', slipping another piece, 'there is plenty more where this came from. We'll have secret midnight feasts together. I won't tell Bhim. You know he doesn't like you eating too much as it upsets your stomach.'

She rumbled quietly and squeezed her eyes together as if winking at me in approval of our conspiracy. I might as well have been talking to the moon. When I placed my foot on her lifted front leg and grabbed her ear, she shook her head violently. I found myself being swung wildly – my dhoti unfurling – backwards and forwards like a rat being shaken by a terrier, and then with a spine-jarring thud, I landed on the ground.

'Traitor,' I muttered angrily, 'the deal's off,' and smacked her hard on her trunk. She looked only slightly remorseful but the next attempt was successful, only because I was aided by Gokul who pushed giggling from below, and by Bhim who pulled sternly from above until I was settled unceremoniously on her neck. Still, on reflection I didn't blame her. If I had been used to the nimble light tugs of Bhim, Gokul and Rajpath I would react similarly to the sudden dead weight of a hundred and eighty pounds hanging like a limpet from my ear. Determined, at least, to regain some measure of dignity, I dug my toes firmly behind the ears and said 'Agit.' Nothing happened. She remained stationary, turning her head to look at me with a puzzled expression.

'Come on, Barbara,' Aditya yelled. 'You can do better than that. It's not "Aaahgit," like "Amen," it's a short command and don't mumble. Yell.'

This time I yelled. To my surprise Tara lumbered forward and we set off down the hill.

'That's it,' he shouted encouragingly. 'Keep at her. She has got to learn that you are her master. Keep your back straight, have some pride. It is a great moment for you. You are the first "firinghee" mahout.'

As if my action had met with approval from the gods, it started to rain lightly, and then mysteriously stopped.

The eight miles to Keonjhar were sheer agony, chaotic and slow. I had now changed my riding position, sitting at the edge of the howdah to work her with my heels, digging them in continuously. Then, to guide her, I flicked my toes under her ears. After a mile I felt as if I had completed the Tour de France. My legs ached mercilessly and my toes were a bleeding mess. Oblivious, Tara wandered from side to side like a hungry locomotive, stopping at bamboo groves to feed at her leisure. However much I pleaded, kicked or cajoled, she did exactly what she wanted. It was like trying to steer a bulldozer for the first time. Bhim, perched behind me, did his best, rectifying my mistakes like a patient driving instructor.

'You just need practice,' Aditya remarked nonchalantly from where he lay sprawled on the howdah. 'You can't expect to be an expert overnight. Bhim has told me it will take at least a week before she will be used to you. During that time,' he said happily, 'you will be unable to wash, sit down or sleep. And do you realise,' he continued, even more happily, 'that as you are now Bhim's pupil you will have to do everything for him?'

'What do you mean?' I grunted, wiping the sweat from my face.

'Well, for instance, you must prepare his food, wash his clothes. All sorts of things.'

'Christ,' I said bitterly. 'I've come all this way to ride an elephant only to be turned into a bloody valet. The sooner I find that mimosa the better.'

The sight of this uncontrollable elephant on which sat a cursing, wild-eyed Englishman dressed like a saddhu, caused a variety of reactions in passersby. Women quickly ushered their terrified children to the safety of their houses. Some men shook their heads in total disbelief, while others doubled over in laughter. At one village, a group of men sitting drinking tea on a 'charpoy' laughed so much that it tipped over backwards, and six pairs of thin, brown legs waved like tentacles from underneath. Bhim spent a voluble afternoon alternately satisfying their curiosity, controlling Tara and pacifying me. Eventually he got fed up. In answer to the standard question of 'Where are you going?' he would snap 'England.'

At a small roadside house an old man with a long grey beard shuffled out from inside and stopped us. He sank to his knees, prostrating himself in front of Tara while she gently rubbed her trunk through his hair. A beautiful girl in a blood-red sari with a frangipani blossom behind her ear followed suit. After washing Tara's feet with water, she presented all of us with garlands of jacaranda flowers. There was a sudden sharp cry of pain behind us. A little boy, the girl's son, ran screaming to his mother, holding a small brown hand to his face. Blood seeped through his fingers. He had been standing too close to Tara's tail, watching in fascination as she whipped it back and forth to brush off the flies. The thick, long, hard hairs at the tip had struck him in the cheek, splitting it like a melon. Aditya quickly pulled out the first-aid kit and after cleaning the deep wound, patched it with Elastoplast.

'I am sorry,' I said to the girl and the old man. 'I'm afraid it will leave a nasty scar.'

'Sorry, why be sorry?' he said quietly. 'Your elephant has done my grandchild a great honour. He has been blessed by Ganesh. He will always be lucky.'

10

Tara's Tantrum

BY THE TIME we reached the outskirts of Keonjhar it was dark and I was both hoarse from shouting commands and exhausted. Once an old British hill station, the town lay at some elevation and for the last ten miles I had forced Tara up steep inclines. After that the thought of spending the night under canvas was just too hideous to contemplate. I went to visit the Collector, a charming, easy-going man, who immediately arranged for us to sleep in the Circuit House, built by a former Maharaja of Keonjhar some eighty years ago, which was now usually reserved for visiting dignitaries and judges.

It was a splendid, solid example of English Colonial-cum-Indian palace architecture, spoilt only by a coat of vile mauve paint. We had the place to ourselves. After chaining Tara to a mango tree in the large, walled garden, we spread ourselves out in a suite of four rooms on the first floor leading on to a spacious veranda. It was surrounded by a pretty wrought-iron balcony, furnished with old-fashioned teak and wicker planters' chairs with extending leg-rests, marble-topped ebony tables and, best of all, a large refrigerator which we quickly stocked with beer. As we sat looking out over the twinkling lights of Keonjhar, a white-coated attendant filled our glasses and looked disdainfully at Indrajit's line of dripping clothes festooned around the balcony like mourning flags. Obviously he had been used to more respectable guests.

After the luxury of hot baths and a decent dinner, Aditya and I lay out in the long chairs in the darkness.

'We might spend a few days here,' he remarked, settling himself more comfortably and taking a long pull of beer. 'We're well on schedule and it would do us all good to take a rest,' he added, noticing me trying to sit sideways in the chair.

'No, I'm fine,' I winced. 'I think we should push on.'

'As you wish. But I was really thinking of Tara. Bhim has told me she is a little under the weather.'

'What?' I said, falling into his carefully laid trap. 'In that case, we must rest.'

Like Tara with her gur, Aditya had successfully discovered my Achilles' heel. Unable to walk, I crawled over to the side of the balcony. I could just make her out, dusting herself happily while leaning up against the tree, with one back leg crossed over the other.

'Goodnight, my love,' I shouted. She turned, lifting her trunk, emitting a half trumpet, half squeak, like a suppressed sneeze. I smiled happily. I was getting there.

In the morning Aditya and I set out in a rickshaw to visit the old palace of Keonjhar which we had been told was just a crumbling empty shell. The rickshaw driver's leg muscles bulged with the effort and his breath came in short, sharp bursts as we climbed steadily out of town. Then we picked up speed, freewheeling down hills lined with shops where men made metal pots, banging them into shape with small hammers. Out of the clouds appeared a fine crenellated wall overgrown with creepers, and furnished with tactically sighted look-out turrets embellished with arrow slits. Leaving the rickshaw we passed through an ancient gateway, its great wooden doors hanging askew from rotten hinges. We could make out the ruined palace overgrown with jungle and stained green with mildew, but still showing traces of former elegance. We wandered down a weed-covered pathway, choked with wild roses and shaded by towering palm trees.

At the main entrance, guarded by a pair of heavy bronze cannons moulded in the shape of tigers, we were met by a group of scruffy young urchins who announced that they were the keepers of the palace and would be pleased to show us around. They led us into the Durbar Hall which had been capped at one time by a fine frescoed rotunda and was now open to the sky. The floor was covered in bird shit. Graffiti was scrawled on the walls: 'The world is a servant to money' and 'Life is nothing but pain'. In the ballroom, they told us, a vast crystal chandelier used to hang from the ceiling, where a family of swallows now had their nest. As we felt our way along dark dripping corridors, bats erupted around us and screeched away, brushing our faces with their velvet wings. In the Deity room a black outline was all that was left of a solid gold statue, stolen twenty years ago, and in a corner, flaking with rust, was the Royal Nagara – a huge metal war drum. Noting my interest, one of the little boys explained with the air of a professional guide that there were once two war drums covered in human skin. In warning against invading armies, they would reverberate of their own accord.

'What happened to the other one?' I asked.

'Gone walking, sir. To lake.'

Under a large mango tree, which we were told was a thousand years old, stone slabs covered a dried up spring. Legend said that anybody entering the water disappeared. Keonjhar took its name from this. It means 'spring' in Oriya.

Our young guides ushered us into a large, pretty courtyard surrounded by small pavilions. In the centre stood a marble fountain designed as the open petals of a lotus flower. The floors of the pavilions had once been mosaic and were still studded with a few remaining pieces of lapis lazuli. An ornate, gilded, empty frame was propped up against a wall, a reminder of an opulence long gone. This was the entertainment chamber where once the Maharaja had received his visitors, plying them with opium-based sherbets and sweetmeats as they relaxed on silk bolsters, while dancing girls had whirled in front of them. To make his foreign guests feel at home, the ruler had commissioned carved scenes, which still ran along one wall – a two-masted ship in full sail; a lady in European costume with a small boy in knickerbockers hanging on to her full skirts; a train puffing over a bridge. One of the boys asked as we were leaving if we wished to meet Her Highness the Rajmata.

'The Rajmata!' Aditya exclaimed incredulously. 'She still lives here?'

We waited in a small, dripping courtyard surrounded by tubs of long cactus-like plants called 'mother-in-law's tongues' and from whose shape and sharpness they have taken their name. Where once we would have been forbidden to enter we now stood – in the old zenana.

The boys reappeared carrying in their arms an old lady dressed in a simple cotton sari and scuffed rubber sandals. After laying out a strip of torn Aubusson carpet, they placed her carefully in a rickety wicker chair. Behind her, in the gloom, her attendants fluttered about like ghostly moths, their faces veiled. The boys informed us that the Rajmata was unable to speak, but she could hear and see.

Aditya stepped forward and touched her feet in obeisance. For a moment the sad eyes cleared and she smiled gently, as if remembering better times; times when the palace had bustled with activity, times of glittering banquets, the rustle of silken saris, of colour, and, above all, of respect. Now she was reduced to this, a proud old woman left with nothing. A wave of great sadness swept over me.

The boys' devotion to the old lady was touching. No one looked after her now, they told us angrily as we were leaving. Her relations had abandoned her. She had been robbed at gunpoint three times. Everything had been taken. They had begged her not to keep her valuables under her bed, but like many old women she did not trust banks.

'You know these western states were once famous for human sacrifice,' Aditya told me on the way back in the rickshaw. 'Traditionally, the Rajas of this state had the right during their coronations to have a man brought in front of them, whereupon they would cut off his head, and give rent-free land to his family as compensation. After the British arrived and banned capital punishment, the Commissioner, on hearing of this custom, quickly travelled to Keonjhar to put a stop to it. As you can imagine, everybody was highly upset, but the Commissioner, a practical fellow, managed to appease the ruling Raja and solve the problem. The chosen man was duly brought forward. The Raja swung at him with his sword without actually making contact and the victim collapsed on the ground feigning death. He was then ordered to disappear from the kingdom and to be very careful never to be seen by the Raja. He was in fact declared dead and the family duly compensated.'

'Typical British ingenuity,' I crowed. 'At least we did achieve something.'

Early next morning, Aditya and I were woken by a frantic Indrajit and Gokul. 'Tara escape!' they exclaimed, 'in big tank [reservoir]. Won't come out.'

'Where's Bhim?' I growled, sleepily.

'Sleeping. Drink too much rum last night, so we take her for bath.'

'Wake him up now and meet us at the tank.'

When we arrived there was no sign of Tara. The surface of the water was calm. Alarmingly, the tank was enormous. (I remembered the case of an elephant that went for a two-hundred-mile swim, island-hopping across the Bay of Bengal. It took twelve years to complete its journey and the distance between some of the islands was at least a mile.) Suddenly from the far side of the tank, the tip of Tara's trunk broke the surface, blowing a spray of water like a fountain into the air. With a trumpet of pleasure she flung herself forward like a porpoise and disappeared again, delighting the large crowd which had by now gathered around the tank.

Bhim arrived carrying a spear, the ankush, a selection of fruit and a large sack of gur. 'Not Mummy's fault,' he said angrily. 'Gokul forget chain legs. Rajpath warn.'

Gokul squeaked with indignation stating that he was unaware of Tara's penchant and if Bhim had not drunk so much this never would have happened. Aditya calmed them down before a fight broke out, suggesting they should concentrate their energies on getting her out.

Standing in the shallows, Bhim started calling Tara, a banana in his outstretched hand. She immediately reacted, came surging across the tank to stop a few yards from the bank. In the meantime, as Gokul could not swim, Indrajit, armed with the spear, had managed to circle behind her. He waited, treading water frantically with the tip of the spear aimed at her backside. As she came a little closer and reached out her trunk, Bhim retreated, enticingly. She came closer still, almost into the shallows. With a quick lunge, she whipped the banana out of his hand, popped it into her mouth and reversed into the water. Turning to face Indrajit, who had been almost swamped by the wave, she blew a jet of water at him, performed a kind of elephant back-flip and surged away, trumpeting triumphantly. The audience applauded deliriously.

This ploy was repeated a number of times. All were unsuccessful. Finally Bhim turned to me. 'Raja-sahib call Mummy.'

Aditya had gone to call the police to see if they could disperse the crowd that were not helping matters. He returned with one policeman who upon seeing Tara cavorting in the water, tucked his bamboo cane under his arm and settled down to enjoy the fun.

I followed Bhim's instructions. 'Tara! Tara!' I yelled authoritatively, waving a lump of gur in my hand. 'A dhur! A dhur! Lay! Lay!' The people watching howled with laughter on hearing my accent. Some of them mimicked me accurately.

Again Tara came quickly across the lake. At the sight of the gur, she placed two large front feet on the muddy bank. I gave her a small piece and then as quickly as possible, grabbed hold of one of her ears to try swinging up on her back. She turned quickly. For a moment I was pulled through the water like a beginner trying to water ski, letting go as I swallowed a mouthful of dirty water. I started to swim back, gasping and choking. I felt something long and sinuous encircle me, and like a lifesaver rescuing a drowning man, Tara pushed me forward, depositing me in a wet bundle in the shallows. She trumpeted again and looked at me mischievously before returning to her watery playground. 'Mummy no come now,' Bhim stated. 'We leave her. Mummy come out when cold.'

That evening, almost twelve hours later, I was sitting on the veranda of the Circuit House when Gokul shouted excitedly, 'Tara coming!' Looking down, I saw her trotting happily into the garden. At last, I thought, thank God for that. Unfortunately our troubles were not over. Each time Bhim and Gokul tried to shackle her, she backed away, after ripping the chains from Bhim's hands and throwing them into the air.

We tried the old food trick. One of us fed her while the other tried to snap the two front chains together. It failed. After shutting the garden gate, we drove her into a small area surrounded by two walls. We advanced on her purposefully, shouting 'Baitho, baitho!' jabbing the spear into her back legs. She charged at one of the walls, almost demolishing it. Slightly stunned, Tara stood quietly for a moment. Seizing his chance Bhim quickly scrambled on to her and took control with the ankush. Gokul then chained her. She looked unusually remorseful, squeezing her eyes shut when I rapped the end of her trunk with a small stick.

Tara's tantrum was over, but I couldn't be angry for long. After all, it was Sunday and Gandhi's birthday. It was a holiday and she deserved some fun.

II

Death in the Jungle

WE HEADED NORTH-WEST into the state of Mayurbhanj, traversing a high plateau towards the great tiger sanctuary of the Simlipals. To our left, a few miles from the Bihar border where it looped down to its most southerly point, lay the ancient city of Kiching, in the tenth and eleventh centuries AD the capital of the Bhanja kings.

Having waited so long to ride Tara, I now dreaded it, the pain was so great. To ease the stiffness in my joints, I walked. We passed a procession of men carrying a small bundle wrapped in straw and strung from a long pole. A police chief idled slowly in a jeep behind. We stopped to talk with him. The bundle contained the body of a young tribal girl who had been found early that morning raped and mutilated by the roadside. Tara became increasingly fidgety as if the sight and the smell of this morbid situation was utterly distasteful to her.

Curious, I asked Bhim whether he had ever known an elephant to have eaten flesh. He shook his head vehemently, then narrowed his eyes as if searching for something that had happened a long time ago. Reluctantly, he recalled an incident. It had happened during a state occasion. A Maharaja was being carried in a silver howdah, on the back of a ceremonial elephant, ridden by its mahout. Suddenly the elephant snaked its trunk back, grabbing the mahout's leg and pulling him to the ground. As in the old days, when in certain states in India executions were carried out, the elephant stomped on the mahout's head, splitting it like a ripe melon. Gathering the gory contents in his trunk, it had blown out a bloody spray, spattering the Maharaja. Shocked and outraged, the Maharaja immediately ordered the elephant to be destroyed. The other mahouts, however, begged him to reconsider. This mahout, they told him, had for many years treated the elephant with the utmost cruelty. The Maharaja, passionately fond of this favourite elephant, believed their stories and spared it. The elephant never misbehaved again.

'There was one situation in which an elephant did actually eat a human being,' I told him. 'It happened in a zoo in Switzerland many years ago.' Bhim looked at me with disbelief. 'This elephant called Chang was punished for misbehaving and confined to his stable. Chang had a great admirer, a young girl who was so upset that she broke into the zoo overnight to feed and console him. She did not return home. In the morning the elephant keepers found traces of blood on the floor and, lying amongst the fodder, a human hand and a toe. On further investigation Chang's droppings revealed her undigested clothes, hat and handbag. The keeper persuaded the authorities to spare the elephant's life but some years later Chang grabbed his keeper and battered him to death against the bars. Chang was then destroyed.'

'Pah!' Bhim uttered contemptuously, spitting out a thin red stream of betel juice, and, leaning forward, covered Tara's great ears. 'No listen Raja-sahib, Mummy. He telling bad things.'

About eight miles from Joshipur, the point of entry into the Simlipals, I got on Tara and we joined a busy trunk road which straddles the continent from Calcutta to Bombay. The harder I was on her, the better she behaved and Bhim told me that I was beginning to make progress. My main problem, however, was avoiding the trucks that thundered by perilously close. I spent a tiring day digging my big toe under her right ear and shouting 'Chi, chi,' to turn her on to the verge. Once there, progress was even slower. It was lined with trees. At every one she helped herself to the overhanging branches, ripping them off and plucking the leaves, then stripping the bark before moving on to the next. Determined to put a stop to this greed, I banged the blunt end of the ankush repeatedly on her head. She simply shook her head and took no notice, occasionally showing her mild displeasure by blasting me in a fine spray of spittle.

She was none the less beginning to earn her keep. A number of the trucks that passed us would stop. The co-driver would stretch out a hand and place a coin in the tip of her trunk which she would then curl upwards and deposit the money on her head. Blessed by Ganesh for a safe journey the drivers would clasp their hands together, make their namastes and move on. Sometimes her trunk would shoot through the open window, almost demanding payment. When we reached Singada, our pockets jingled with coins. We now had established a way of financing our journey. Rajpath had taught her well.

A large weekly market was taking place at Singada. I threaded Tara through the mass of humanity and animals, causing a stampede. Bullocks and goats knocked over food stalls and Tara liberally helped herself to the spoils. Soon our jingling pockets were empty as we forked out compensation. Squatting in small groups, tribal women radiant in brilliant red and blue saris were selling 'handia', the local hooch, handing it out in coconut shells. Anklets jingling, others weaved through the crowds replenishing supplies, their smooth, strong, braceleted arms supporting large terracotta gourds on their heads. Everyone appeared to be drunk, throwing around their hard-earned money liberally, enticed by the miracles that were on offer.

Two travelling Rajput medicine doctors, wearing bright red turbans over strong thin aquiline faces, excitedly advertised the virtues of their wares which lay coated with flies in small trays in front of them. Most popular were the aphrodisiacs – dried intestines of snakes, toads' feet and a particularly strong brew of cobra tongues and boars' semen. At another stall a large crowd gathered round a man surrounded by baskets containing many different kinds of snakes. The crowd gasped as he rolled up his sleeves. Taking a snake's head, he forced its mouth open and plunged the fangs into his arm. Writhing in mock agony, he tied a bright red thread just above where the snake had struck, and then slowly straightened his arm. Miraculously he was cured. The threads, he extolled to the crowd, were blessed and stopped the effects of the poison instantly. He was a good salesman and business was brisk.

Short of Joshipur we stopped at a roadside tea-house. A dazzling array of trucks was parked outside. A small wiry man with slanting eyes, his face a deep ruddy colour, engaged me in conversation. He was Nepalese and a co-driver on one of the trucks.

'Take me with you to England,' he pleaded. 'I will be your bodyguard. I am excellent at fighting.' He pulled up his shirt exposing a livid lumpy scar that ran from his navel to his right nipple. 'I killed the man who gave me this,' he said proudly. 'These people,' he continued contemptuously, gesturing at some tough-looking characters who were sitting drinking tea, 'are weak. Nobody can match a Gurkha.'

'I don't need a bodyguard,' I replied. 'You see I have an elephant.'

'Ah, in that case you are in good company. It is not my lucky day.'

As we entered Joshipur, a motorcyclist wearing a uniform, goggles and a leather aviator's cap, slowed down, gave us a curious look and then drove on. He then stopped, turned round and passed us again. He repeated this manoeuvre several times, as if unsure of something. Finally he shouted, 'Are you Haathi from Konarak?'

'No!' Aditya yelled back. 'We are the Haathi from Calcutta. The Haathi from Konarak be arriving later.'

'More Haathis arriving?' he said puzzled.

'Yes,' Aditya said airily. 'Tomorrow one from Delhi and then another from Bombay.'

'Oh, goodness me, this is most confusing,' and the man raced off.

'Bloody officials,' Aditya laughed, 'that's fixed him.'

Joshipur is where one actually enters the park, but it is from Baripada, the capital of the state of Mayurbhanj, some forty miles away, that the permissions are granted. Through the window in the office I noticed a powerful radio.

'Would it be possible to send a message to Baripada?' I asked politely of a young bespectacled forest officer.

'It is not working,' he snapped nervously. 'Park closed. No one allowed in.'

'But your brochure', I argued, 'informs one that the park opens on the 1st October. It is now the 5th.' There was no answer. Two mystified Australians, who had come all the way from Delhi, were still waiting after four days to see the game park.

'We are wasting our time, Mark,' Aditya said. 'Indrajit should drive us to Baripada and we will find the man in charge. Maybe we can contact the Maharaja for whom you have a letter. He might be able to help. In the meantime, Bhim, Gokul and Khusto can stay with Tara.'

When we reached Baripada we discovered that the Maharaja was 'out of station' and the forest officer had disappeared, 'gone to the market', we were told. Through local information we found out the reason. There was a man-eating tiger abroad and it had just killed somebody in the south of the park. No one was allowed in. Desperate that we should cross this great game park, whose beauty had been extolled to me from the beginning of my journey through Orissa, I telephoned the authorities in Bhubaneshwar. I pleaded and pushed. The park was enormous, I argued. Over three thousand square kilometres. It was unlikely that I would bump into the tiger. Finally, we were granted full permission to go anywhere in the park, but only by jeep, not with the elephant. Reluctantly I agreed. It was better than nothing but I felt sad that I wouldn't be able to share this wilderness with Tara.

We waited three hours for the forest officer, a tall man with a limp handshake, who seemed anxious to be rid of us, issuing a letter immediately and nervously avoiding any reference to the man-eater. On the way back to Joshipur we stopped to stretch our legs at a roadside tribal shrine. Effigies of cows and horses and two black granite elephants stood garlanded by night jasmine. An old pandit came out of the shrine and blessed us. In the darkness Aditya and I looked at one another.

'Are you thinking what I'm thinking?' he said.

'Yes,' I replied.

We opened the letter and studied it under the jeep's headlights. It was addressed to the officer in charge at Joshipur.

> I talked with CWLW at ten p.m. today and he confirmed our earlier decision re the pet elephant will not be allowed inside Simlipal. They may keep the elephant at Joshipur. Accompany these persons in park jeep to Chahala and Barehipani but avoid Jenabil because of the man-eating problem. But do not tell them this. The roads are not OK. Tell that.

'But the people who collect honey from those sheer rock faces are deeper in the park. We'll miss seeing them,' I said. We had been told about them in Bhubaneshwar. Their methods of collecting honey were spectacular and unique to the Simlipals.

Indrajit came over and Aditya translated the contents of the letter. He was silent for a moment. 'Perhaps we lose park jeep in jungle,' he shrugged. 'If lost must go where we can.'

The next morning Indrajit, Aditya and myself left the camp. Earlier I had asked Bhim if he would like to come, but he wanted to stay with Tara. 'Mummy unhappy both Raja-sahib and Bhim go away three days,' he said. 'One day okay.'

The park jeep escorted us into the Simlipals. It was like entering another world; a world that had been untouched for centuries. The tracks were overgrown, lined by tall sal trees. The air was fresh after the monsoons. In sunny clearings peacocks stood motionless, fanning out their glorious feathers, and high above them mynah birds chattered noisily. At intervals we would catch the flash of gold and white and a spotted deer would turn to look at us before picking its feet daintily through the undergrowth. Everywhere was the evidence of elephants, old and fresh droppings littered the road. In the 1986 census four hundred and fifty elephants had been counted and as many as ninety tigers.

Through a bower of orchid-lined trees, we arrived at Chahala, an old shooting lodge of the Maharaja of Mayurbhanj, now converted into a tourist camp. It was gothic in design with vaulted ceilings and large open fireplaces. It had been painted a hideous violet and green. Surrounding it was a deep anti-elephant trench and beyond, strategically placed salt-licks for game. At five o'clock the next morning, as the mist still hung heavy in the air, we watched bison and barking deer approach the salt-licks, followed by a small herd of elephants, including two babies who held their mothers' tails with tiny trunks. From the distance came the deep cough of a tiger. The animals moved away quickly, the little elephants squealing in alarm.

From a raised log cabin at Barehipani, the source of the Buldha-balanga River, we gazed across a wide gorge and watched a thirteen-hundred-foot waterfall thunder beneath us. In Hindi 'barehi' means thread and 'pani' water. In the dry season, only a thread of water falls like a single silver arrow. The old forest ranger complained bitterly about the elephants. Every week, he told us, they destroyed his garden. Most years the log cabin had to be rebuilt because wild elephants rubbed their sides against the thick wooden poles. I thought sadly of Tara. How she would have loved this paradise where elephants roamed free, untouched and undisturbed.

As there was no news of the man-eater, our guides thought it safe to take us to Nawana, the village of the honey collectors. We descended from the hills crossing wide grassy meadows, alive with wild flowers. On the outskirts of the village, we parked the jeeps and entered a small mud-walled courtyard. It was empty except for a young man with one leg. The villagers, he told us, were far away on the other side of the park taking honey from the tree bees. It was only during the winter that they collected from the rock bees. I was bitterly disappointed.

'How is the honey collected?' Aditya asked him in Hindi.

'It is a dangerous business, sir. We lower ourselves on thick vines down the rock faces in which the bees make their nests in small caves. When we find a nest we light a torch and throw it in. The bees come swarming out and we collect the honey.'

'Don't you get stung?'

'Sometimes, sir. But we smear our bodies with herbs and always chant our mantras before work. On a good day we can collect twenty-five kilos of honey.'

'What happened to your leg?' Aditya asked, I thought rather impolitely.

He smiled ruefully and rubbed the stump. 'It is our wives, sir. They tie the vines on to trees at the top of the rock face. There they stand guard. Unfortunately,' he added, 'my wife liked another man. It was a long fall. I was lucky.'

I told the park rangers that I wanted to talk with the villagers when they returned from collecting honey. They agreed to let us stay at Nawana. They would return in a few hours to collect us.

'You want to go Jenabil? Now chance,' Indrajit said excitedly after they had left. 'Maybe seeing tiger?' Aditya and I looked at each other nervously.

'Well, why not?' I said to Aditya after some deliberation. 'We've missed the rock bees and we've come all this way. Let's go.'

The track was overgrown and from the absence of tyre marks nothing had passed this way for months. A tree blocked our way. Struggling to lift it we disturbed a herd of wild elephants feeding nearby, camouflaged by the solid green wall of the jungle. The ground shook as they crashed away, trumpeting wildly. At Jenabil the tourist lodge was empty. In the small village Indrajit found a man who knew where the tiger had killed. At first he was reluctant to take us, but with the promise of a healthy reward, he agreed. I told Indrajit to ask him whether we might catch a glimpse of the tiger. The man looked astounded and launched into an urgent tirade.

'This is not a joke, sir,' he replied angrily. 'This is a big, male tiger. It was a man-eater that killed my friend, and it will kill again.' Our bravado deserted us instantly. We fell silent. The man continued. 'We are poor people, sir. We go into the forest to collect lac [resin produced by coccid insects from which incense is made] from the trees. Each day, before entering the forest, our pandit tells us which side of the road to go to avoid bagh. That day there were ten of us. The pandit told us to go to the right but my friend, Sri Ram Naik, decided he would go the other way. A few days earlier he had spotted a good healthy tree. He was a brave man and had, on several occasions, fended off bagh with his axe. It is an everyday occurrence. We and bagh must try and live together. He was big man, like you,' he pointed at me. 'He took his young son with him. His remains are still there. The police were too frightened to go in to collect them. We must be very careful, bagh is still around.'

We reached a place where an axe cut marked a tree standing by the road. 'This is the place,' he said quietly. 'We go in here. Take sticks and make plenty of noise for bagh can be sitting two feet away and you will not see him.'

Aditya and I realised we were embarking on something both dangerous and stupid. We had no guns, only elephant bombs, which Indrajit cheerfully distributed to each of us. He seemed oblivious of the danger.

We stepped cautiously into the jungle, up to our waists in thick undergrowth. Large bamboo clumps, caressed by the wind, rustled urgently, warning us to take heed. We followed the guide in single file, Aditya and I firmly in the middle. Indrajit took up the rear. At intervals the guide would stop and check his route. Finding another cut in a tree, he moved on. We yelled. We shouted. We beat the bushes, feeling naked and defenceless. We reached a clearing. The bushes were flat, the surrounding trees raked with claw marks. Pointing at the dried muddy ground, the guide indicated large round indentations, the size of soup-plates – the tiger's pug marks.

On a small outcrop of rock, a faded blood smear; then a rubber sandal, and another – they were an odd pair. Close by a torn and bloody lunghi lay rotting in the ground. Finally a skull, gleaming yellow in the pale sun.

'It was here, sirs, that it happened,' he told us. 'My friend was looking up at this tree. Bagh struck silently from the back. From the other side of the road we could hear his screams. We rushed over, but he was already dead. The bagh had him by the throat. We tried to recover the body but bagh was too big and too angry. He came at us, and we ran.' Our guide shivered as he looked up at the tree. '"O my Father I am dead." Those were his last words. His son told us.' He shivered again. 'We must hurry out of this place, sirs. It is not safe.'

I turned the skull over disturbing a colony of ants, feeding on a flap of skin. There was nothing else. The man had been completely devoured. No bones; just the skull left as a warning. I wanted to take it but Aditya stopped me.

'Leave it,' he advised me. 'It has become part of his jungle.'

We collected the remains of his things. Now a small pathetic bundle, once worn by a strong, brave man. They deserved better than to rot in the jungle; we would take what was left to the Ganges for immersion in the holy river.

Our guide took us to the dead man's house. It was empty. His family had already left, paid a compensation of 2,000 rupees. A few broken cooking pots littered the floor. Stuck to a mud wall were coloured crayon drawings done by his children; of a field, of a cow and of a man looking up at a tree, behind him stood a yellow-striped cat with a big pink tongue and long whiskers.

If the welcome I received from Tara was an indication of her affection, I was a happy man. She positively vibrated with excitement, coiling and uncoiling her trunk like a giant watch-spring, straining against her chains and uttering sneezes of contentment. For a change she did not immediately open her mouth. She simply touched my face with the wet tip of her trunk and stood perfectly still, her eyes closed, resting against me gently. A feeling of pure pleasure swept over me and then one of equal panic as in just over a month I would have to say goodbye and would probably never see her again.

Bhim wanted us to visit his family in Baripada. As we left, Tara seemed almost resentful, hurling a branch petulantly into the air. Bhim's mother and father lived in an old tiled house which stood defiantly, like an ancient spider, in an encroaching cobweb of modern buildings on the outskirts of the town. In a neat room dimly lit by oil lamps and a small cooking fire, a tall, elderly man sat erect in a rocking chair. When we entered, he came quickly to his feet belying his age, and saluted smartly. Unlike Bhim, his face was curiously unlined, almost boyish, and, apart from one rheumy eye that glittered milkily in the gloom, he seemed in the best of health. When my eyes adjusted to the darkness, I noticed his wife squatting in the corner, fussing over some pots. After offering us tea, she returned to her place, but I could feel her accusing look boring into me. She mumbled something and Bhim laughed in embarrassment.

'She worried Raja-sahib take only boy England. Never come home.'

Aditya took both her hands in his, and reassured her that this was not true. She seemed to relax a little but still continued to eye me with suspicion.

The old man was anxious to talk of the old days, and in a soft proud voice told us he had been the chief mahout of the late Maharaja and during his tenure had often been to the Sonepur Mela. There he had purchased elephants for 6,000 rupees each and had taken three months to ride them back. At one time there had been twenty elephants in the royal stables. They were so well trained that during tiger shoots they had moved so quietly not even a leaf was disturbed on the trees.

He touched the rocking chair proudly. It had been presented to him by the Maharaja when he retired. As Aditya and I were leaving, he took me aside. 'Elephants are like human beings, Sahib,' he whispered. 'They like companionship. Don't leave her for too long. Every evening before you sleep, talk to her. Tell her stories.'

To check again if the Maharaja had returned we drove to Belgania Palace. Formerly built to accommodate royal guests during the Durbar administration, it was now his home, as the original larger palace in the city had been turned into a college. Situated on a small hill with commanding views over Baripada, it was a big picturesque colonnaded building, like a grand Florentine villa, the colour of burnt sienna, approached by a sweeping drive lined with flame-of-the-forest trees and jacaranda. An ageing chowkidar received us. We settled ourselves comfortably to start with, in easy chairs on a broad loggia, and then more nervously as a large, scarred Dobermann came and joined us. 'Brook you bloody dog. Get down,' a voice boomed as Brook began to take particular interest in one of my legs. A large, balding, unshaven man, dressed in a stained kurta and a dhoti, appeared. He looked tired. Black rings circled his eyes.

'Forgive me for keeping you waiting,' he said, 'but I was just finishing my puja.' With a smile he held out his hand and enquired our names. 'Patankar,' he said suspiciously. 'That's a Maratha name, isn't it?'

'That's right, sir,' Aditya replied proudly. 'I come from Gwalior.'

'Hmm,' he mused. 'Interesting. An Englishman and a Maratha. A friend and a foe. Two hundred years ago we suffered badly under the Maratha yoke. In fact, we joined forces with the Marquis Wellesley to stop you entering Bengal from the south. One of my ancestors, Rani Sumitra Devi, the adoptive mother of the *de facto* ruler of Mayurbhanj, was honoured by the British Government in recognition of her meritorious services. You must', he said pointedly to Aditya, with an amused twinkle in his eyes, 'have had a very nostalgic journey through Orissa. Anyway, we are all friends now. Let us have tea. I will call my wife.'

It was the kind of tea that one longs for on journeys such as this; cucumber sandwiches, cream cakes and endless Benson and Hedges cigarettes (my usual brand which I had not smoked for two months). They were supplied kindly by his wife, a member of the Nepalese royal family, a beautifully coiffeured lady, smelling wonderfully of Worth perfume, wearing a pale, powder-blue sari and dashing diamanté-studded glasses. To begin with she was a little shy but when our conversation turned to shopping she became very animated, eagerly praising the merits of Harrods and other famous stores.

'Where did you find your elephant?' the Maharaja asked.

'In a dreadful place called Daspalla,' I replied.

He laughed. 'Daspalla was famous for two things. The best elephants and the most stupid people.'

I told him of our journey through the Simlipals, which had once belonged to his family. On hearing of our exploits at Jenabil, his attitude was one of horror, telling us that our behaviour had been both foolish and irresponsible. However, he was grateful for the information and for what we had done.

'Sri Ram Naik always collected the resin from which I make my own incense. I knew him well. He was a splendid man.' As we were leaving, the Maharaja presented me with a plastic bag. I opened it. Inside were pieces of crystallised bark. 'This is resin,' he explained. 'Sri Ram Naik's last delivery.'

On the outskirts of Joshipur, we met up with two female elephants, the larger resembling an old and dusty tramp, dwarfing her little companion who hung on to her tail with her trunk. Both elephants were in poor condition – gaunt, almost skeletal. They stood listlessly, not bothering to brush away the flies that crawled over their eyes, from which dripped a white mucus. They greeted Tara placing their trunks into her mouth. Standing beside them she shone – a beautiful Maharani attended by two dowdy maidservants.

'Haathi no good,' Bhim said disdainfully. 'Both no see.'

We stopped to talk with their mahouts, mendicants who were working their way south through Orissa. By November, they would return to Benares, where the elephants' owner lived, a rich pandit who kept a stable of forty elephants. The elder man sported a curling, white moustache, his greedy eyes never leaving Tara. He offered to sell us the smaller elephant for 60,000 rupees. As if to show her off, he yanked down viciously on the ankush which hung from a rusty pin, piercing one of her ears. In resignation, she simply shook her head slowly. He then offered half this price for Tara. His contemptuous proposal was met with howls of derision from us, and we moved on laughing, ridiculing his impudence.

Then it hit me. My laughter died. A feeling of cold dread swept over me. I had been offered a price: however absurd, it was still a price and for the first time I became aware of Tara's destiny. In that brief moment, the entire context of what I was doing changed. It was no longer the romantic ride on an elephant across India that I had dreamed up so flippantly – a whim to satisfy my ambitions. It was reality, however camouflaged by the colour and the beauty – it was there, hard and completely unchangeable. Tara was my responsibility, her future life lay in my hands and every step she took brought me nearer to that moment. I tried to force it into the back of my mind. But it was now there, hanging like a relentless black shadow.

12

Double Dipper

IN A MATTER of a mile, the difference between Orissa and Bihar became visible. It was like suddenly parting the leaves on the edge of a rain forest and stepping into a scorched desert. Gone was the colour, the lushness, the laughter, the languid sensuality that manifested itself in Orissa, to be replaced by a harsh, suspicious and angry terrain. It showed in the quality of the tea, the sudden absence of fresh paan, the drabness of the lunghis, the condition of the villages and, above all, in the people. Our attitude changed accordingly. Bhim and Gokul became nervous and unsure of themselves.

Soon after we entered Bihar an incident occurred that exemplified this new feeling. An aggressive, stocky man with a bald head that gleamed like a billiard ball in the sun approached us driving a large loaded cart pulled by two bullocks. In an attempt to prevent the inevitable chaos, I steered Tara off the road and faced her away from the bullocks to allow them to pass as I had done in Orissa. He shouted at me angrily to get my elephant out of the way. I had already done this, but to avoid an unpleasant scene I moved a little further, at least two hundred yards off the road. He drove his bullocks forward, whipping them with a bamboo pole, and he had just come abreast of us when they panicked. Snorting with fear the bullocks raced along the road for a few yards, flew over a ten-foot drop to land in a muddy paddy field the other side, snapped their harness and made off quickly. Unimpressed as I was with his character I could not help but feel admiration for his driving skill. From a position with bullocks, cart and driver in mid-air, he landed the contraption like a seasoned jet pilot.

Unfortunately he did not reciprocate with admiration for Tara and me. He came stomping up the bank, gathering a few villagers on the way. 'This is my village and my road,' he spluttered furiously. 'Your elephant is a menace.'

'Excuse me, sir,' I interjected politely, 'this may be your village, but a road is built for the purposes of travel. Anybody can travel on it, including an elephant which, I would like to point out, is not a menace. If you recall, I moved off the road to let you pass.'

'Unless you give me compensation of five rupees I will impound your elephant,' he shouted. If he had been more civil and not insulted Tara, I would have paid gladly.

'How do you think you are going to impound my elephant?' I demanded angrily, flicking her behind the ear. She rolled her head and moved towards him. His eyes filled with alarm as this large beast loomed in front of him. He did not reply and we moved on.

Fortunately this feeling did not seem to be constant. At Majhgaon, a predominantly Muslim village, we were entertained royally by the elders, splendid old men in dhotis with long white beards. Delighted to see Tara, they crowded around her placing coins in her trunk, and even crushed paper money. Under the impression that the bank notes might contain something to eat, Tara investigated carefully, before dropping them despondently. Clearly, when she had been with Rajpath she had not received such riches.

One of the elders, the village tailor, took me into his shop over which a sign proudly proclaimed IMAM TAILORS, MAJHGAON. PERFECT FITTING LADIES AND GENTS. GOD MAKE A MAN, WE MAKE GENTLEMAN.

'If I may say so, sir,' he said, 'for an Englishman you are poorly dressed.' Measuring my waistline, he presented me with a pair of violet bell-bottom trousers and a matching shirt. 'Now,' he said, eyeing me critically, 'you look like a gentleman.'

Indrajit and Khusto managed to find a quiet campsite that night. To celebrate the halfway point of our journey we drank a great deal of rum. Unsteady and feeling inexplicably maudlin, I made my way over to where Tara was chained. I sat down in front of her and a feeling of great sadness swept over me. It was then that I knew I could not sell her. The two blind elephants and the sight of Tara when she had been with Rajpath, convinced me. I had to find her a good home. She would never be a beggar again. I drank more of the rum, wondering unrealistically if I could take her back to England. Not to some concrete zoo but to a wonderful estate where she could retire and live happily.

Many years ago the Duke of Devonshire had faced a similar situation. He had met a lady who enquired what she could bring back for him from her travels in India. He had replied jokingly, 'Ah, nothing less than an elephant.' To his astonishment, some months later, an elephant duly arrived. It was kept in a large enclosure in the grounds of his house in Chiswick, developing an undying passion for the gardener, who put the animal to work. The elephant brushed the paths with a broom held in its trunk, picked up grass cuttings and watered the plants with the aid of a can. Its dexterity and extraordinary intelligence did not end there. The Duke's guests were entertained after dinner as the elephant pulled the cork from the port bottle and handed it to the butler. Unfortunately, like many elephants, it developed a taste for alcohol and died of consumption in 1829.

Even as I realised I was fantasising I felt a presence behind me. Aditya settled himself beside me and we gazed in silence at Tara.

'You know, Aditya,' I said eventually, 'I ...'

'I know what you are thinking, Mark,' he interrupted. 'I feel the same. She has become part of me as well.'

'What are we going to do?' I asked desperately.

'I don't know. But Sonepur will be full of elephant experts, and I give you my word we will find a solution there.' Unable to shake off the feeling of unease, I went to bed.

Suddenly, late in the night, the fly of the tent was ripped open and Bhim tumbled drunkenly inside. 'No time left,' he shouted urgently. 'Journey soon over. Raja-sahib learn ride Mummy like good mahout. I watch today. No good.' He climbed on to Aditya's back, hooked his legs around his waist and proceeded to give a demonstration of toe movements. 'Daddy now Mummy,' he cried. 'Watch good, Raja-sahib, Bhim show you.' For the next half hour Aditya's legs were kneaded and crushed and his kneecaps grazed from the pressure of Bhim's horny toenails. Eventually Bhim exhausted himself and passed out.

'At least he's keen,' I remarked to Aditya as we carried him back to his tent.

'We were lucky to find him, Mark,' he replied. 'He cares.'

We climbed back into the tent. I was just falling asleep when a long, sinuous shape slid past the back of the tent, pressing against my head, which was wedged against the canvas. I sat bolt upright and shook Aditya. There was no need. He had felt it as well. I crawled quickly towards the front of the tent but Aditya grabbed me.

'Stay inside,' he said calmly, and yelled at Indrajit to investigate. A wild commotion followed. Then Indrajit poked his head in holding something long and bloody.

'Nag,' he said happily. 'I get it' – and he held up a five-foot cobra.

It was now getting cold in the mornings. We started later and later, waiting for the sun to rise, before facing the icy cold water when bathing Tara. We travelled slowly northwards passing people preparing to celebrate Dussehra, the festival which commemorates the victory of the warrior goddess, Durga, the consort of Shiva, over the buffalo-demon, Mahiasura. Drunkenly, they lay in the shade of large trees where hooch stalls had been set up. The powerful smell of 'handia' or 'raci', as it is known in Bihar, hung in the hot air. With nose and trunk filled respectively with this irresistible temptation, both Bhim and Tara were finding it hard not to stop.

One evening we became part of a travelling circus. As we set up camp we were joined by a band of roving snake-charmers, delightful, gregarious rogues sartorially resplendent in bright yellow turbans decorated with feathers. Around their necks on beaded strings hung little leather pouches containing remedial herbs to cure snake bites. They carried their reptiles in circular, flat wicker boxes; six cobras, a krait and two lazy pythons.

Their presence attracted an even larger crowd than usual who watched spellbound as the cobras undulated hissing from the boxes and danced to the rhythm of little wooden drums. Bhim, not to be outdone by this slick showmanship, delighted the crowd further by coaxing a variety of sounds out of Tara both from her front and rear end.

Once out of the intoxication of the tribal belt, we crossed a landscape bleached white from the smoke of a large cement factory. Nearing the town of Chaibasa, we could almost have been in England, on a sharp, sunny, frosty morning. Each leaf and blade of grass was covered in a fine white powder that sparkled in the sunlight. To avoid this white wasteland we took a small back road. Spanning it was a tall wooden bridge under which a fast river flowed.

I urged Tara forward. After putting one foot cautiously down, she backed away. No inducement could make her cross it. Without me so much as uttering a command, she simply took over and wandered further up the river bank. After testing the depth she splashed over. On the other side we met a man who told us that the bridge was unsafe. It was now only used by pedestrians and cyclists. Three weeks ago a taxi driver had driven his vehicle halfway across and the timbers had suddenly splintered. Luckily he had managed to reverse to safety.

Similar incidents of an elephant's extreme cautiousness have been recorded. One was during the Sepoy rebellion in 1857. A general, riding an elephant, had been leading his army towards a bridge which spanned a deep ravine. Similarly, persuasion proved useless – the elephant refused to cross. The general, trusting his elephant's sagacity, had the structure examined, finding that the enemy had cut away the main supports.

The outskirts of Chaibasa reminded me of an English country village. In British days the town had been the centre of administration for south-eastern Bengal. We crossed green fields dotted with clumps of giant mango and taller Peepul trees. In the distance the spire of a church trembled in the heat haze; fine sturdy trees, shading broad boulevards, gave relief from the hot sun and made a passing snack for Tara. It must have been a pleasant place to be stationed. But according to the Bengal District *Gazetteers*, a Mr Rickards wrote in 1854, 'There is everything in Chaibasa to make a person want to leave it ... it has not a single attraction.' And a Dr Bell in 1868 added, 'those officers who have mastered the Ho language and have become intimate with the people like this station, but with the executive services of Bengal generally it is regarded much in the light of a penal settlement.'

At a small bank we stopped to change travellers' cheques. The manager could not understand why I wanted to travel through his state. 'When God created Bihar, Mr Shand,' he told me, 'He was in a very bad mood.'

The exquisite church, whose spire we had seen shimmering in the distance, was of the Lutheran order and still retained its original stained-glass windows. Built a hundred and eighty years ago, it had an aura of dignity and simplicity, quite unlike its Roman Catholic rival nearby, a modern atrocity glittering like a seaside fun palace, complete with an ornate grotto-like shrine in which the Virgin Mary was lit by red and blue lights. Inside, converted tribals polished an already gleaming marble floor in which the giant gem-studded cross was reflected.

As we left Chaibasa for Seraikella, where we had been invited to stay by the Raja, we stopped to watch a game of cricket played by some college boys. A fine pull through mid-wicket sent the ball skimming towards us. It stopped just in front of Tara. She eyed this foreign object with interest and then cautiously rolled it around with the tip of her trunk. Satisfied the ball was inedible she stamped on it, embedding it into the hard ground. A group of players had by now run over. They stood in front of her silently, undecided about what they should do. One of them, braver than the rest, stepped forward.

'Excuse me, sir,' he asked politely. 'Um, could we be having our ball back. It is the only one we have.'

'Of course, I am sorry,' I said confidently, commanding Tara to move back and dig out the ball. Nothing happened. She stood firmly in place, flapping her ears. I repeated the command. Again she ignored me. I dismounted, rapped her on the trunk and dug the ball out myself. 'Here you are,' I said, embarrassed and furious at her behaviour, tossing it back to them.

'Maybe your elephant is liking playing cricket,' one of them suggested with a laugh.

'Oh yes, she is really very clever.' Taking the ball back, I tossed it at Tara. She did nothing. There was a soft thud as it hit her in the centre of her trunk. I repeated the manoeuvre to no avail. Eventually, I threw the ball back to the players. 'She's just out of practice.'

'You old bag,' I whispered to her. 'You let me down. You may be a slow learner, but that was pathetic. After all you are an Indian elephant. You should bloody well know how to play cricket.'

My accusations were a little unfair. Although an elephant is slow to learn, with practice it will repeat almost anything faultlessly, just like the amazing elephant cricket team that the famous animal trainer John Grindl of Bertram Mills's Circus succeeded in coaching. In his book *Elephants* Richard Carrington records that a pair of elephants would take up their stations at opposite ends of the arena, one with a cap and pads and holding a bat in his trunk, while the other bowled. On either side four or five others were ranged as fielders. At the word of command the bowler threw the ball down the pitch and the batsman took a ferocious swipe at it with his trunk. More often than not the bat connected and the elephant would plod down the arena for a run. Meanwhile, one of the fielding elephants would stop the ball and throw it at the stumps. It took Grindl several months of patient effort to perfect his act. He began by standing in front of the batting elephant, grasping both bat and trunk in his own hands. Another man would then bowl the ball and Grindl would guide the elephant's trunk to hit it. After many hundreds of attempts, the elephant grasped the idea and hit the ball on its own. A similar technique was employed with the bowler and fielders. Thereafter there was no holding them, and they would play the game with enormous enthusiasm.

In the blistering heat the road to Seraikella stretched before us unendingly. My stiffness had now almost vanished. Hard yellow calluses decorated the ends of my toes, but the sides of my legs were blue from bruising, where Tara's great ears hammered ceaselessly against them.

I was beginning to feel comfortable with her and perhaps she with me. My self-consciousness was vanishing and I barked at her fiercely when she tried to steal paddy or slow down unnecessarily. Considering she was supposed to be a

Koonki elephant, she moved remarkably slowly and I had continually to work on her to achieve an even pace. Gradually the habits of a beggar elephant were dying and I felt she was acquiring a new pride.

En route we picked up our first hitch-hiker, a young tribal who displayed great excitement on seeing a large dead snake in the middle of the road.

'What on earth was that all about?' I asked Aditya.

'Our friend has expressed a wish that the snake would come alive and bite him.'

'What …!'

'He believes that it belongs to the lowest caste of snakes. It is, in fact, an untouchable. Therefore once our friend bears this mark, all other snakes will avoid him.'

We dropped off our logical companion on the outskirts of Seraikella. By the time we entered the town it was dark. Power-cuts added to the confusion as Tara picked her way with uncanny sureness, waving her trunk constantly as a blind man uses his stick. Elephants are short-sighted animals and rely on their remarkable proboscis to sense rather than see their way. At one moment we padded silently in a complete black-out, the next we found ourselves in the middle of a busy, brightly lit street. At the sudden sight of this huge animal, bicyclists fell off their machines and passersby shouted in alarm. A man on a brand new red Vespa suddenly swung out in front of us.

'Welcome to Seraikella. I am relation of the King of the princely state of Seraikella. Excuse me,' he added with an embarrassed laugh, 'that is not quite correct. I am relation of the ex-King of the ex-princely state of Seraikella. Please follow me.' Guided by this curious outrider, we made our way through a maze of twisting streets eventually arriving at a pair of large wooden gates, which were thrown open.

Waiting in the palace courtyard were the Raja, a plump, bespectacled man, and his younger brother, tall and elegant, who spoke perfect English. The Raja performed a small puja and anointed Tara's feet. Then he pointed to a huge, ancient frangipani tree, the roots of which were embedded in the wall, almost as if they had started life together. He told us we could chain Tara there. Bhim made a closer inspection of the tree and shook his head.

'Excuse me, sir,' I said to the Raja, 'my mahout does not think this tree is strong enough. I am afraid my elephant will destroy it.'

However much I appealed, the Raja insisted that it was the right place, telling me that the tree was five hundred years old, sturdy and particularly auspicious to the family, making it essential that Ganesh should rest there. As we followed the Raja and his brother, I heard the crack of the first branch being snapped off contemptuously.

Through a narrow porchway Aditya and I were led on to a spacious lawn where the Raja suggested we pitch our tents. He then disappeared to watch television and we settled down to talk with his brother.

I was interested to hear that Seraikella and Kharsawan, a neighbouring principality, were the only two states in all of British India that were never required to pay taxes to the British. In 1793 a friendship treaty had been signed between the ruling Raja and the East India Company in recognition of Seraikella's protection of the Company's salt industry, by preventing salt smugglers from entering the kingdom. Aditya was more pleased to hear that the treaty was also granted in connection with the help that the Raja's armies had supplied to the British against the ferocity of the Maratha invasion.

Then the Raja's brother spoke about the Chhow dance. Seraikella is famous for this dance, which is performed in honour of Lord Shiva. Now, the Chhow is almost completely organised and financed by the Raja's brother, himself a leading dancer, who has taken his troupe to London, Paris, Rome, Munich and New York. All the dancers are male. All wear masks. The choreography requires that the dancers should express the moods through the limbs alone, since if the mask is discarded, the face then becomes the major focus of attraction. The Raja's brother had arranged for us to see a performance – a dress-rehearsal only, he apologised – in the village of Govindpur.

We left the boys to put up the tents and drove with the Raja's brother to the village. In the mud courtyard of a farmer's simple home, the dancers were dressing for the performance. Lying incongruously among the terracotta milk urns and the cows, were big steel costume trunks covered in colourful stickers from grand hotels in Italy, England, Germany and other European countries. The dancers, all clad in costumes of exquisite finery, coloured their hands and the soles of their feet with vermilion, their faces now obscured by painted plaster masks. Surrounded by cattle stalls and lit by kerosene lamps, we were entertained to a superb display of the Chhow dance. Through the movement of the feet alone, as they leapt, turned and gyrated to the rhythms of the drums and other instruments, the dancers suggested not only the more traditional legends but also brought to life their own humble, daily occupations, such as fishing and hunting.

In the Peacock Dance, the young dancer managed to convey all the vanity of this colourful bird by moving only the upper part of his body to emphasise the extended fan of tail feathers. Another, dressed as a bee, seemed actually to hover, vibrating the sequinned wings attached to his back, as he darted around yet another dancer dressed as a flower. Sometimes, in this particular dance, the wings are made of stone, so one can imagine the stamina required.

What impressed me most was the avid concentration of the village audience, particularly amongst the small boys watching. I have found many times, when attending a dance in other remote areas, the audiences' concentration centred rather on the tourist, or the click of the camera. But here Aditya and I were totally ignored. The small boys' eyes were glued to the scene in front of them and, like young critics, they applauded a fine move or criticised a mistake.

On returning to our tents on the palace lawn, we discovered the boys in a state of considerable excitement. They were all vying for the attentions of the maidservant to the Raja's wife, a deliciously attractive young woman, who was heartlessly teasing them. All through the evening, I had received reports of how she had given Gokul and Khusto a 'dipper' and then Indrajit a 'double dipper'. Even Bhim, distracted for a change from booze and Tara, joined in, announcing firmly, to the derision of the others, that she obviously preferred older men as she had given him a 'triple dipper'. It all sounded somewhat pornographic until Aditya discovered that a 'dipper' was nothing more than a wink. The whole game was later put to an end by the Raja's wife, who banished the girl to her room.

Early the next morning I fetched Tara for her bath. Where once had stood a five-hundred-year-old frangipani tree and a wall, now lay a mass of splintered branches and crumbling stonework, occupied by an elephant with an innocent expression on her face. I unshackled her and headed for the river. Luckily, as it was the first time I had taken her alone to bathe, she was very quiet, almost lackadaisical, and behaved impeccably, but I was still very much on guard against her sudden pranks.

The River Kharkai was wonderfully clean and swirled its way across smooth, round boulders, having started its journey at the waterfall at Barehipani in the Simplipals. We waded into the cool, refreshing water. Tara sank slowly down on her knees, allowing me to dismount, and then rolled over happily on to her side. For an hour, I scrubbed her from the tip of her trunk to the end of her tail. Exhausted, I stretched out on her stomach and took the sun while she lay quietly, half submerged, beneath me. Around us a group of men went about their morning ablutions without concern, speaking softly to avoid disturbing us.

I rode her back to the palace, where I found a forlorn-looking Bhim standing nervously behind the Raja, who was surveying the damage. I apologised profusely.

Although I could see he was both astounded and quite upset, he assured me that it really did not matter. In another five hundred years, he told me, another tree would stand there. After all, he added, it would be something that he could tell his grandchildren.

He garlanded Tara with flowers from the fallen frangipani tree and we left. On our way out I noticed Indrajit looking anxiously at a high window in the turret of the palace. It opened slowly and a slim hand darted out dropping a single orange marigold. Indrajit picked it up and placed it carefully behind his ear. 'Double dipper,' he said happily. 'She like me the best.'

13

Full Control Ceremony

WE STARTED THE steep ascent of the South Bihar highlands, leading to the great ranges of the Chota Nagpur Plateau, which eventually wind downwards to the flatlands of the Indo-Gangetic plain and our final destination of Sonepur.

The gradient became progressively steeper, our path often blocked by boulders which had been swept down the hillsides during the monsoons. In places we were confronted by fallen trees, which Tara threw aside like twigs. In the early morning, the narrow tracks, lined with lantana bushes, became a tunnel of sparkling cobwebs filled with fat, black and yellow spiders which, being venomous, terrified me. Tara decided that a straight line was the best approach, and I spent hours wielding the ankush, brushing the spiders out of my face and then panicking as I felt something crawling down my bare back.

The sal forests were being systematically destroyed by the local villagers, for cash and for new fields. In deep valleys between the hills, the remaining topsoil and the trapped water yielded good rice crops and, on the peaks, where only a few trees remained, 'Jhoom', or slash and burn cultivation, was taking place.

We reached the summit of the South Bihar highlands and made camp, affording a fine view of the Chota Nagpur plateau, a watery blue massif in the distance. The tribals of this area, the Bhumias, are a wild and shy people, hunters who rightly claim that the forest belongs to them. Animists with long flowing hair, they wore head and arm bands made from snake vertebrae and knotted red loin-cloths. Most of them carried axes instead of bows and arrows, adopting an easier form of survival. They seemed out of place in this devastated landscape.

In the middle of the night Tara trumpeted loudly. I rushed over and found her straining at her chains, rapping her trunk on the ground and then signalling with it towards some bushes. I threw a bomb into the darkness. There was a scrabbling in the undergrowth and, in the beam of a torch, I saw the bushy back of a bear charging down the hill. I felt sorry for the creature, which must have been sauntering home, self-absorbed in the custom of bears, his belly full, to doze through the daylight hours in his lair. Confronted by this enormous and enraged elephant hissing and trumpeting loudly, he probably suffered terrible indigestion.

The next day, at a village called Biribanki we disturbed a colony of bats that blackened the sky and then returned to hang like clusters of black grapes from the trees. The villagers were disappointed to find that we were unable to shoot them as we were not carrying firearms. In this region bats are considered a great delicacy.

We reached a deep, impassable nullah or ravine. Indrajit coaxed the jeep carefully but when it could go no further he doubled back and arranged to meet us in a few days at Sarwada. We loaded Tara with provisions and set off, glad to be rid of the jeep and its mechanical problems. Now I could concentrate totally on Tara.

She was refusing point blank to listen to my commands and treating me with almost arrogant disdain. In a sulk I decided to walk for the rest of the day. We had entered the Bible belt and passed neat, white-washed churches in every village. Young girls with long hair gathered in pigtails and tied with pink ribbons, wearing blue skirts, white shirts, long socks and sandals, swept the courtyards with religious fervour. Two young boys fell into step beside me. Their names were Daniel and Imai, and they told me they were converts to the Anglican Church of North India. They were on their way, they said excitedly, to attend a five-day church seminar in the town of Muru.

'What religion are you belonging to?' Imai asked me politely.

'Well, I suppose Church of England, Protestant, but I don't take it very seriously. I go to church usually once a year at Christmas.'

'Once a year?' they gasped. 'But that is very bad.'

'I don't have the time, boys,' I continued poker-faced. 'You see, nine months of the year I live in England where I like to beat my wife, and when I go away I chain her up and come to visit my elephant. I never beat my elephant, though.' (Not much, I thought.) 'All men beat their wives in England. And drink. And do other things,' I said suggestively. 'Would you like to go to England?'

'Oh yes, sir,' Imai replied. 'Very much. I would like to see the beatings and drinkings and other things. In fact,' he continued wistfully, 'in our village we used to ...'

'Imai,' Daniel said sternly. 'That is enough. We will make a report of this at our meeting.' As we parted company, he turned and shook my hand. 'Sir,' he said sombrely, 'you may have a fit body, but you have a cracked mind.'

Completely out of context with the surrounding landscape, high upon a hill stood a magnificent red brick church with a high circular turreted spire. It was the Church of the Immaculate Heart of Mary, first constructed by Belgian missionaries in 1874. As the community grew and more money became available, the church was finished in splendid style in 1910.

The padre invited us in for tea, but banned Tara, who could easily have fitted underneath the large entrance. Instead she poked her trunk through the open window while I fed her a continuous stream of biscuits. It was light and airy in the nave, where the ceiling soared two hundred feet. The vestry walls were lined with clocks. There must have been fifteen or twenty of them, all showing different times – even a cuckoo clock which would chime wheezily and shoot out a rusty spring. As we were leaving, the padre pointed to the large collection of pouches attached to long wooden poles.

'Isn't it wonderful,' he announced in a condescending way. 'The people are so poor here that they are unable to give money. Instead they fill the pouches with rice.'

'Alleluia,' I said, and walked out.

We met up with the jeep near a village called Keora, where again people were celebrating the festival of Dussehra. Revellers lay unconscious at the side of the road, in ditches and the wisest in the comfort of small paddystacks. One man, more steady on his feet than most, hung on to Tara's tail, begging for a cigarette. Aditya gave him one which he promptly tucked behind his ear. He then stumbled forward in front of her and lay down and begged for another. Bhim shifted his feet fractionally behind Tara's ears and she reached down to grab the back of the man's trousers and dangled him in the air. By the perplexed look on his face, he seemed unsure of whether he actually was being held aloft by an elephant or simply having a drunken hallucination. He let out a scream of terror, whereupon she deposited him gently on the side of the road.

We pitched camp beside a wide, marshy lake filled with wild duck and surrounded by mango trees. Before eating, Bhim approached me holding something in his hand. It was the illusive mimosa plant.

Gently I took the plant from him, staring at it reverently. So this was what I had been anxiously searching for for hundreds of miles. I was a little disappointed.

I had expected something more exotic, instead of this lifeless green sprout that resembled a common weed. But, when I brushed its tiny fern-like leaves with my finger-tips, the plant became alive, the leaves closing rapidly – touch-me-not. Excitedly, I realised that in my hand I was holding power. The power that could tame an elephant. Bhim broke into my reverie: 'Raja-sahib. Now have mimosa. Now do "full control ceremony".'

The full control ceremony! This was my final puja. The puja that would turn me into a mahout! I ran down to the lake, bathed myself, combed my hair and put on my dhoti and gumcha proudly. When I returned to the camp Bhim presented me with a small ball of gur, wrapped in this precious plant.

'Well, I'm ready,' I said enthusiastically waiting for directions.

'This is your puja, Mark,' Aditya said. 'Between you and Tara. It's entirely up to you what you pray for, but after you have finished, feed her the offering.'

'OK,' I said. 'Just a moment.' I dashed into the tent and retrieved my copy of *The Elephant-Lore of the Hindus*. Turning to the chapters on 'Favourable marks' and 'Marks of characters' I knelt down in front of Tara and whispered, 'Oh, beloved Tara, who trumpets with a roar like clouds full of water. With sparrow-like honey colour eyes. Whose reddish trunk tip is as radiant as red lotuses. Whose back is long and curved like a bow. Whose temporal bosses are hairy, and large, like the swelling breasts of a lovely woman. With broad ears, jaw, navel and pudenda. With copper coloured lip and palate. You, that are beautiful, who has an odour like the white water lily, sandalwood, orange tree and lotus. Whose face beams and who has the cry of the koil [cuckoo]. You are blessed with the character of the god. O princess you are worthy of a king.'

'What did you recite this time?' Aditya asked. 'Humpty Dumpty?'

I ignored him and solemnly placed my offering of gur into Tara's mouth. She rolled it around inside for a moment narrowing her eyes at me, as if making a decision. Satisfied, she swallowed it, and reached out to touch my face with her trunk. Then she farted loudly. By the terms of the puja, the moment she swallowed that gur, she had accepted me as her master.

'Got you, you old bag,' I said triumphantly. 'Now you'll listen to me. Just you wait and see.'

I sat down for a while and watched her. I now felt I knew her inside out. Immediately she confronted me again with my own ignorance, proceeding to do something so clever, charming and human that it left me speechless with admiration.

She rummaged amongst her fodder and selected a suitable branch. Holding it in her trunk, she stripped the leaves away and began peeling the bark back. For a moment I thought she was simply going to feed. Instead after discarding the bark, she broke the branch into four separate lengths and laid them out in front of her. She selected one and sharpened it to a point against her chains. Satisfied with the shape, she began to clean methodically between her toenails like a manicurist, digging out the dirt, then wiping the tip of the stick in the grass. Her beautification complete, she blew spittle on her toenails and buffed them with the end of her trunk until they gleamed blackly. I later found out from Bhim that there are sweat glands between an elephant's toes. It is essential they are kept clean to prevent clogging.

Male elephants 'in musth' have been known to use the same process to clear the temporal glands, which can become blocked with discharge. On occasions, certain rogue elephants that have been shot have been found to have a broken piece of twig jammed tight, like a cork, into both glands. Some experts surmised that they had been driven mad by this and, unable to remove the blockage, had turned aggressive.

The next morning, my confidence unlimited, I decided to attempt the expert's way of mounting an elephant – by the trunk. With a certain panache, I grabbed both her ears, placed a foot solidly on her trunk and shouted authoritatively 'Utha! Utha!' I don't recall much about the next few seconds – just a slight sensation of air passing quickly under my lunghi. Then to my surprise I found myself sitting firmly on her neck.

'You see,' I said triumphantly to Aditya. 'That's due to the mimosa. I'm now the master.'

'Except that you are sitting on her back to front,' he replied acidly.

'That's just a small matter. I'll correct it in time. You see, I had my eyes shut. The most important thing,' I said smugly, 'is that I did it. You're going to try it next.'

Accompanied by Gokul, we plodded down to bathe in the lake. Wading into the shallows, Tara obligingly lifted her leg so that I could climb off.

'Chain her front legs, Gokul,' I said.

'Chains? No chains. Raja-sahib forget,' he squeaked. 'Wait, Gokul fetching.'

I stood beside her, holding on to one flapping ear. She looked out at the tempting flat surface of the lake and with almost an apologetic shake of her head, she whirled round and ran squealing into the water, surging across it like a stately liner, much to the annoyance of the ducks who took to the air in a flurry of beating wings.

'Come back you bloody nightmare,' I yelled. 'Come back at once. I feed you! I spoil you! I honour and praise you! and still you insist on making me look a fool. When I get you out of there things are going to change.'

Grabbing the ankush, I plunged into the water and swam out towards her. I circled behind her, jamming the ankush hard into her fat bottom. 'Move, you tub of lard,' I spluttered, treading water frantically. Whereupon she disappeared. Moments later I felt my backside being prodded. I whirled around and managed to clamber on her back, holding tightly by both ears. With a squeal of delight, as if I was now her new playmate, she dived, and I found myself being bounced along underwater as she tiptoed along the bottom of the lake. My ears began to pop. Remembering what Bhim had told me about an elephant holding its breath for the same length of time as a man, I somehow held on. Just as I thought my lungs would explode, we surged upwards, taking great gasps of air.

'You see, fatso. You cannot …' and before I could catch my breath, down she went again. This time I had to let go, spluttering to the surface. She popped up a few yards ahead and looked mischievously at me. 'All right, Tara, enough's enough. I'm going for help.'

I swam to the shore. She followed me closely. As I climbed out she looked sad that the game was over. Shaking with rage and cold I marched into the camp where Aditya and Indrajit were having breakfast.

'The all powerful mimosa,' Aditya crowed, and both of them collapsed in laughter.

'Where's Bhim?' I demanded. 'He's coming with me. And so are you.'

'He can't swim,' Aditya remarked, 'so what the …'

'I'm quite aware of that,' I replied icily. 'I'm going to use my lilo. He can lie on it with the spear and we can push.'

It would have been an odd sight anywhere, but on a remote lake in the middle of Bihar, it was a miracle. Drunken Dussehra celebrants shook themselves from roadside ditches and haystacks, rubbing their eyes in amazement, as if their hangovers could not possibly account for the sight. Passersby stopped and stared, and I heard the church bell tolling as if gathering people to see this unusual spectacle.

Bhim was decidedly sceptical about the lilo. He prodded it suspiciously, but I convinced him that it did float. Lying down gingerly, he held the spear firmly ahead of him, and we pushed out into the middle of the lake. Tara came whizzing over, fascinated by this new arrival. Poking the lilo, she flipped her trunk underneath it tipping Bhim into the water. The old mahout disappeared in a wash of bubbles. Aditya fished him out and, ignoring his protests, rolled him back on. With Bhim as the central attack, we closed on Tara, in a kind of 'V' formation, jabbing the spear continually into her legs and backside. At last we began to force her towards the shore.

'Boat sinking,' Bhim shouted anxiously. Indeed it was, and water began to lap over the sides.

'Hang on, Bhim,' I yelled. 'Just a few more yards.' Tara, perhaps realising that this was no longer a game, lumbered out of the water and raced at full speed towards the camp.

'Leave her to me,' I said firmly, following her. For the next two hours we played a kind of cat and mouse game. Unable to resist the large chunks of gur that I held enticingly in my hand, she would trot forward and slowly push out her trunk. I would remove the gur and with the other hand, in which I held a thick piece of rope, whack her as hard as I could. She would rush off squealing, bursting through the camp, scattering tents and pots and pans. In the end, her greed proved greater than her patience and, with a look that said 'the game's up', she stood meekly while I chained her front legs together. As I locked the final link, a bedraggled Bhim reached over my shoulder and punched her on the trunk.

'Now Bhim shoot Mummy!!' he raged. 'Like soldiers shoot great tusker, Ganges, dead, in water!'

We managed to calm him down, but it was only after he had finished the better part of a bottle of rum that he finally told the story.

The elephant, a big old tusker called Ganges, belonged to the Maharaja of Puri, the Gajpati – The Lord of Elephants. Ganges was a splendid, gentle animal, cherished by the family, being used only for the most important ceremonial occasions. The town of Puri is situated on the coast of Orissa, and early each morning the elephant's mahout, dressed in a red uniform, rode him to the beach where the fishermen would be unloading their night's catch. The mahout would make a selection for the palace kitchen and then Ganges would carry the fish back in his trunk. At the beginning, Ganges had clearly indicated his displeasure by refusing to perform this task. Being a herbivore, the stink and slime that cloyed his sensitive organ would have been most distasteful. However, being a disciplined elephant, and, no doubt goaded by vicious jabs from the ankush, he eventually carried out his duties punctiliously. One day, his dignity badly bruised, Ganges decided he had suffered enough. Throwing down his noxious burden, he charged at a tree, intending to smash his mahout in the overhanging branches. Somehow, the mahout survived the impact and hung in the tree until the elephant moved away. Ganges returned to his stable in the palace, where the Rajmata, the Maharaja's mother, as was her habit each morning was waiting to feed him. Alarmed by the absence of the mahout, she called for help. Obviously very disturbed, Ganges broke away before he could be chained, and rushed through the heavily populated streets of the town, where, amongst the crowds, he singled out and attacked passersby who were wearing red. Fortunately, only three people were killed and he finally came to rest in a nearby lake. By now, his mahout had returned, announcing that the elephant had gone mad. Acting on his recommendation, orders were issued to destroy the elephant immediately. As Ganges wallowed happily in the water enjoying his bath, a squad of soldiers lined the banks and emptied their magazines into him.

'Not tusker's fault,' Bhim said, his bloodshot eyes watering. 'Bad mahout,' and curled up next to Tara to finish his rum.

'How far is it to Ranchi?' I asked Aditya.

'About eighteen miles.'

'Right,' I said, climbing on to Tara. 'No stops. We're going straight through.'

Having perhaps sacrilegiously drawn a skull and crossbones with a white sunblock on her forehead, I dug my toes viciously behind her ears, rattled the ankush against the howdah and set off.

As elephants can sense fear in a human being, they can also sense anger. Perhaps it was this that vibrated through my body, transmitting itself to her, so that she finally realised I could no longer be exploited and began to respond accordingly. Gone were the days in which she would amble from side to side, travelling at her own convenience and pace. We fairly swung along. She misbehaved once, grabbing a handful of paddy from a passing cart. It was the last time she did it. Automatically, I stuck the point of the ankush sharply behind her ear. As she trumpeted in pain I winced, horrified by my actions. I felt instantly sick. Blood welled from where I had spiked her and I watched, mesmerised, as it spread over the side of her head.

'Good, Raja-sahib,' Bhim shouted from where he was walking behind. 'Now Mummy listen.'

Terrified that I had injured her seriously, I drew both my feet back into her neck, a trick that I had seen Bhim perform many times. Surprisingly she stopped dead in her tracks. Bhim inspected the wound.

'Not problem, not problem,' he consoled me. 'Not need medicine.'

But I was beyond consolation. After cleaning the wound with Dettol I stuck a large patchwork of Elastoplast over it, which she inspected suspiciously with her trunk before ripping it off, and throwing it on to the road. The blood had already dried, and I spent the rest of the day anxiously brushing away the flies.

We climbed steadily, up the southern fringe of the Chota Nagpur plateau. Cultivation surrounded us. There were no trees. This area had never recovered from the ruthless exploitation of the timber demands during the Second World War. We made camp under a large iron-girder bridge a short distance from Ranchi, the major city of this region.

The next day Aditya and I left by jeep to visit Ranchi, accompanied by a young crime reporter who had come out to meet us. He told us it was a relief to discuss elephants rather than murders. Bhim and Gokul in the meantime would make their way slowly around the vast town's outskirts towards Pisca, near where we had been invited to stay with the sister of a friend from Delhi.

In earlier times, the salubrious climate of Ranchi had induced many Europeans to settle, and going by the sumptuousness of the former Government House, they were determined to live well. About four hundred labourers and two hundred masons were employed in the construction of Government House. The woodwork was executed by Chinese carpenters. Portland cement was used as mortar. The floors and ballroom were lined in teak and the card-room in marble. The gardens, designed in an Italian style, were filled with imported plants. Once a town of great character, Ranchi was now almost completely industrialised, with the dubious honour of having the highest crime rate of any city in India.

We called on one of Ranchi's most venerable characters, a charming old Anglo-Indian lady called Marie Palit. A wildlife expert for thirty years, she had observed tigers from a tree-house she had built in the jungle. Now a sprightly eighty-five years of age, she told me she had started life in London, where she had studied to become a beautician and hairdresser in an establishment called 'Dolls', before marrying one of India's most eminent surgeons who had received the OBE. Her house was named 'Cobwebs'. When she had first moved to Ranchi some seventy years ago, the track leading to it was a tunnel of silken threads and she had been loath to disturb the occupants. Over tumblers of sherry she dreamily recalled a misty morning when the Duke of Gloucester, 'a charming man on a beautiful horse', had ridden over from nearby Government House to breakfast with her. A keen shikari in her day, she had shot everything except a hippopotamus and a man.

In the meantime, Bhim and Gokul were nearing Pisca. When we caught up with them, Tara was meandering from side to side, occasionally giving a small lurch as she tripped over one of her legs. Both Bhim and Gokul were asleep on top of the howdah – Gokul spread out on the back with a happy expression on his face – Bhim with his head on his chest, snoring loudly. As I got out of the jeep, Tara greeted me with a happy, lopsided grin and sneezed loudly. A blast of distinctly alcoholic breath hit me in the face. They were all drunk, having been to a roadside party. Bhim explained that the hot sun had made her thirsty, and it was impolite to let her drink alone.

Through some pretty, stone park gates, we could see a drive lined with jacaranda and wisteria bushes, at the end of which we could hear the sound of laughter and chinking of glasses. We had arrived at Tikratoli Farm. Our hostess was sadly in hospital, but her son was there to greet us.

On the lawns, surrounding a picturesque ornamental pond filled with rare species of water birds, a group of well-dressed men and women sat in easy chairs, chatting and draining the last of the pre-luncheon cocktails as if at some country weekend in England. We felt we were entering a dream as the scene was so alien to the vagabond life that we had led until now.

'Good afternoon,' I said as normally as possible, taking off my sweat-stained turban, as if I had arrived by car with my suitcases in the boot. I yanked hard on Tara's ear to stop her helping herself to the abundance of carefully planted shrubs.

'Welcome, Aditya and Mark,' he said expansively. 'Everything's arranged. Park your elephant over there,' he pointed to a suitable tree. 'Your boys' quarters are all prepared. Would you like to wash before lunch, or just get stuck into the drink?'

We spent an idyllic two days eating off china plates, using silver knives and forks, drinking out of pre-chilled beer mugs and bathing in big porcelain baths filled with piping hot water. Our travel-stained, filthy clothes were freshly laundered. We began to feel almost human again. Tara was utterly spoiled by the children of many friends who came to meet us, and the boys had an opportunity to have a rest and check out our paraphernalia. The jeep was stripped down and tuned. Tara's pack gear, which was coming apart at the seams after the endless days of travel, was repaired and patched up for the final part of our journey.

Our host arranged a press conference. Apart from one journalist who thought I was an 'exploiter' rather than an 'explorer' and another who was amazed I had not been at school with Rajiv Gandhi, it went off well. The State Bank of India presented me with a banner which read THE STATE BANK OF INDIA APPLAUDS THE SPIRIT OF ADVENTURE. I was delighted. My association with these institutions has never been amiable.

Lured by the comforts of Tikratoli Farm and the superb hospitality of our host, I was tempted to stay longer, but I could feel complacency setting in. It was time to move on. McCluskiegunge, Hazaribagh, the vastness of the Indo-Gangetic Plain, and the mighty Ganges lay ahead.

14

McCluskiegunge

Our Homeland At Last. A Wandering Homeless Community Will Now Have A Real Home. The Land Of Our Dreams Is Now A Reality. Our Proud Possession Where We Can Get Together And Build Our Very Own Farms And Vineyards, Our Towns And Suburbs And Grow To Be One Of The Peoples Of India.

THESE WERE THE stirring words of E. T. McCluskie, an Anglo-Indian engineer from Calcutta, in the *Colonisation Observer* of 1933, after he had leased ten thousand acres from the Maharaja of Chotanagpur to build the first independent community where Anglo-Indians could make a life and grow into a nation through unity and co-operation. In its heyday, just before the war, three hundred Anglo-Indian families had settled in the colony, living in style in splendid villas surrounded by extensive farmlands. They brought with them every modern amenity; a departmental store, a club, a dispensary, a nursing-home. There were schools and churches. Hockey, football and cricket were played. Lavish balls were thrown, where the ladies rustled in the latest fashions from London and Paris, while gentlemen in black ties drank their chotapegs of whisky on the manicured lawns and discussed 'home', some of them never having been there. When the war came many able-bodied men, especially of the younger generation, joined the armed forces, never to return. Others fled in fear of reprisals from the Indians when the country was on the threshold of independence.

All that remains today are a few of the original families, possibly twenty-five, still living in their mansions, full of pride and spirit, cherishing memories of better times.

P. D. Stracey, himself an Anglo-Indian, wrote a somewhat harsh, but accurate, account in *Elephant Gold* of what the Anglo-Indian represented:

> I was a typical product of British Indian stock and western upbringing, an Anglo-Indian or Eurasian, as a person of mixed descent is known in India and further east. My community had evolved as a distinct entity among the many races of India and came to occupy a particular little niche in which traditions and respectability of a smug British pattern kept us aloof from the country in which we lived and earned our bread. We had once been of great service to the conquerors of India in building up the various strata of administration at a time when it was impossible to find enough people for the jobs which call for toughness and enterprise, but suddenly we had fallen on evil days. Still, we were the second line of British power, always at call to suppress unrest and disorder and to prop up authority during the period of India's struggle for independence. We were 'little Britishers' largely unconscious of the anomaly of our position, completely unaware of the indifference with which we were treated by the Europeans on one side and the Indians on the other, although, no doubt, in the eyes of the world, a tragic product of British rule in India.

Before 1946, the colony was for Anglo-Indians only and the land could only be sold to them. Subsequently, this restriction was removed, with the result that settlers sold their land, usually for a very low rate, to entrepreneurs who, over the years, have developed their own small businesses into thriving factories. When the wind blows from the north-west, the fumes of the largest open-cast coal mine in Asia blows its filthy, choking, smoke over McCluskiegunge. The mine is spreading greedily, and if nothing is done to preserve this unique settlement it might well become part of this monstrous pit.

McCluskiegunge, or the 'Gunge' as residents call it, spreads over nine square miles of heavily wooded, undulating hills, through which the Calcutta–Delhi railway line runs. In the old days, McCluskiegunge was filled with retired railway personnel and was a main stop on this line. Now the station is but a watering halt for the coal trains heading north.

Perhaps the term Anglo-Indian represented what I was when I rode into McCluskiegunge, an Englishman on an Indian elephant. For two days I found myself going through a series of mixed emotions: nostalgia, sadness and anger but, above all, admiration for the spontaneity and honesty of these people, who went out of their way to make me feel at home.

I passed white gateposts bearing the names 'Greenacres', 'Park Grange', 'The Nest', 'Honeymoon Cottage', 'Mini-haha' and 'The Gables', which led up carefully tended driveways in which labradors and terriers bounded down to greet me with their vigorous barking.

'Come here, Flossie, sit.'

'Jungo, you bloody dog, get down.'

'Sorry you weren't here a few days ago, you'd have met Podge, he got bitten by a cobra. Still, old Eva's bitch has just had a litter.'

'Come in, come in. You must be hot. I've just made some fresh lemonade, or perhaps you would like something stronger. Not a bad vintage this year. You can have guava, mulberry or elderberry wine. I suggest you try guava. It's got a bit of a punch.'

Stepping into the cool of verandas, luxuriant with bougainvillaea, I was shown proudly around the houses. Some were decorated with English chocolate-box covers pinned to the walls and prints of horses and foals, puppies and Beefeaters. Others were more elaborate. Heavy sideboards were littered with silver frames, holding faded photographs of friends and relatives back home. In the room of one house sat a Steinway grand piano, its woodwork eaten by white ants. Over well-trimmed hedges residents wearing panama hats and clutching secateurs and watering cans or baskets of cut roses, gladioli and large wild daisies, discussed their gardens and worried about the condition of their orchids.

I took tea with Mrs King, an elegant Eurasian lady, clad in crisp coloured chiffon scarves. Over cucumber and cheese sandwiches she told me that she had suffered a heart attack yesterday morning. That same afternoon she had destroyed a snake's nest containing thirty-eight baby cobras, but was determined to be up and about today to greet me. She sweetly presented Tara with a garland of marigolds. Nearby, I visited Mrs Matthews, a widowed Indian lady, whose husband had served as a doctor in the British army before spending most of the war as a prisoner of the Japanese. She now receives a pension from the British government in recognition of his services. Mrs Thipthorpe posed for a photograph in a red wool dress and pearls, proudly clutching her deceased husband's Service and Coronation medals, while Stanley Potter, the Gunge's oldest resident, whose house was called 'Dunroamin', lent me his valuable collection of the *Colonisation Observer*, dating back to 1933.

At 'Bonner Bhavan', whose grand wrought-iron gates were designed as peacocks, I talked with Dolly Bonner, a bitter but intelligent and controversial old lady who told me that she had never fitted in, warning me against visiting certain other residents who were not 'the right sort'. She really believed that between the time of British departure and Independence, the Anglo-Indian, who she considered to have a superior education and a greater understanding of administration than most Indians, was better prepared to take over the reins of government in the new India.

I lunched with Jit Roy, once a keen shikari, who brought his own food in a tiffin carrier – roast pork and potatoes. He carried his toothpicks in a small leather wallet. Immaculately dressed, he wore flannel trousers, silk shirt, a paisley foulard, and highly polished brown brogues, topped off by a brown felt trilby. A fan of the BBC World Service, he had requested a song on 'The Pleasure's Yours', in memory of an old friend and resident of the Gunge who had died recently, and had heard it was to be played for him that very night. Later I drank with Brian Callaghan, a former boxer who had trained in the same gym with Henry Cooper. He had returned to the Gunge to look after his sick mother.

The next day, at a pretty white bungalow nestling in the hills, we met one of the area's richest residents, eighty-eight-year-old Ida Mukerjee, an Anglo-Burmese lady who with a thirty-year-old boyfriend seemed determined to enjoy life to the full. Passionately traditional she had ostracised her son for marrying a local Adivasi (tribal) girl, forcing him to eke out a living selling fruit at the station. Four years ago, their young son had disappeared on a coal train heading north. Perhaps he had chosen this way of life at the station, in the hope that one day his son would return.

Kitty Teixaira, once regarded as the most eligible and beautiful girl in McCluskiegunge, had been dealt an equally tragic destiny. Her mother, a domineering possessive woman, had deprived her of any education, forbidden her to mix in society, keeping her a virtual prisoner. On her mother's death Kitty had inherited a large decaying property and no money. She had since married 'a bad sort' and, like Ida Mukerjee's son, struggled to make a living by selling fruit at the station. We met her there surrounded by three dirty snotty-nosed kids, a strikingly handsome young woman, with a haunting sing-song voice, dressed in a ragged sari.

'Keep away from Clem Mendonca,' we were warned. 'He's mad.' But we paid no heed, determined to meet the Gunge's most eccentric resident. It was dark when we arrived at the blacked out and silent house. We banged on a heavy iron grille, recoiling instantly as two snarling shapes sprang against it.

'Who's there?!' a voice growled from inside.

Nervously we introduced ourselves, as a powerful torch beam blinded us. Bolts were drawn back and a head poked out cautiously, scanning left to right. 'You haven't been to see those bastard Camerons?'

I shook my head. Earlier I had been told of a terrible feud that raged between the Cameron brothers and Clem Mendonca.

'Come in,' he said. 'But I'm keeping the lights out. I'll face them in the open, but I'll be damned if I'll sit like a duck in a shooting alley.'

We seated ourselves at a small table. The soft glow of a kerosene lamp illuminated an arsenal of crossbows, rifles and shotguns. Leaning against the wall was a thirty-foot aluminium boat. 'Captain' Clem Mendonca had served forty-five years in the Merchant Navy. Dapper and compact, he bristled like an angry otter. 'Glad you're not a Geordie. I'd have thrown you out. Worst crews I sailed with!'

Suddenly he jumped to his feet, crept over to the window and scrutinised the blackness outside, a pearl-handled Smith & Wesson .38 revolver appearing mysteriously in his hand. 'That's Cameron,' he yelled, and I just managed to stop him shooting Indrajit, who was smoking a cigarette. He noticed me eyeing the boat.

'I'm off soon,' he announced. 'Can't stand this place. Got to get back to the sea. No Camerons there – just you and the elements.'

The arrival of Bhim announcing that Mummy was lonely cut short our visit with Mary Morris. In five minutes, however, managing to look chic in a pink fluffy dressing-gown, this spirited elderly lady had captivated us with her wit and charm. Fortunately our paths would cross again.

A unique monument to a forgotten era, McCluskiegunge hopefully will survive. Already some influential people with the right values are starting to buy property for their retirement. This would have pleased E. T. McCluskie. He sounded a splendid man, and I found a tribute to him on his death in a 1935 *Colonisation Observer.*

> He might have built a palace grand, superb,
> Which rivalled many a Raja's rich demesne
> And revelled in a gay luxurious ease
> Like lordly Nabob. But he chose, instead,
> The better way: his fadeless name to write
> On heart and mind of a down-trodden race,
> With pen of fervent zeal dipped in gold ink

Of memory pure, eternal as the soul.
Let others grovel in mire of hoarded pelf –
'To serve' his maxim. And his deeds transformed
Lapra, waste village, into city fair –
McCluskiegunge! Fit for a worthy race
To dwell in, whose inheritors, while time doth last
Shall rise and call him blessed.

To avoid the long dull road route to Hazaribagh, we cut across the open coal mines of Ramgarh. If there was such a place as hell, this was it. Spread like some virulent rash across the landscape, the pits were linked by a roller-coaster of conveyor belts. Grinding excavators fed waiting trucks, like greedy prehistoric birds. In minutes, we were covered in a fine coal dust and were up to our ankles in black slime, choking and wheezing as the filth hit the back of our throats. It was Tara who suffered the most. Her trunk, which she continually dipped on to the track to find a safe route, became clogged with black sticky waste, which she blew out as if cleaning an old-fashioned fountain-pen.

We passed the towns of Daccra, Rai, and Bacchra, ugly places with ugly names. Crossing a glistening inky river, we washed our faces, a pointless effort, as if we had used a bar of trick soap. Brick factories, monstrous effigies to progress, belched smoke from their tall chimneys. Bhim told me that sometimes elephants were used to drag the steel cars up from the pits; his words were a chilling reminder for me of Tara's destiny. Most of the labourers were converted Santal tribals and I wondered whether they realised, when they took the good path from their quiet traditional life, that they would end up here.

After crossing the main Calcutta–Delhi railway line, we stumbled through a series of deep nullahs, and then, climbing again, reached a narrow forested plateau. As if a door had suddenly been slammed shut, hell was behind us. Along a narrow path lined with wild mint, jasmine and bridal bouquet, and alive with bird-song, we met happy groups of Santal tribals. The men stopped and offered us fruit, but the women and children, terrified of Tara, slipped quickly into the hedges. After we had passed, we saw them kneel, making their pujas in her footprints.

That night we camped close to a field of wild mustard, flanked by a clear bubbling river and a railway bridge arching gracefully over a deep ravine. It was a moonless night and in the limited radius of the firelight the area seemed to shrink to the size of a cellar, with a ceiling of stars, a wall of trees on one side and a crescent of tents, each lit by the dim glow of a kerosene lamp, on the other.

In the gloom, almost invisible, Tara stood quietly like a statue, occasionally disclosing her position by a rhythmic flapping of her ears.

Winding down off this razor's edge, in the morning we crossed the Damodar River, a roaring impassable torrent in the monsoons, but now like a mill pond. Egrets waited patiently for a passing minnow on little islands of exposed sand. The avarice of the Moghul emperors was excited by reports that diamonds were to be found in these rivers that criss-crossed the Chota Nagpur plateau. In fact, there is a legend that the Koh-i-noor diamond was discovered in the River Koel.

The track now petered out completely. Guided by two drunken tribals, Tara forced her way through thick Lantana bushes, disturbing partridge and 'jungli murghi', the Indian jungle fowl, a bird similar to a chicken but with a long tail, that explodes from its cover like a rocket. Finding the path again, we descended on to the Hazaribagh plateau, a patchwork of greens and pale golds where paddy and surguja were cultivated. In the distance to our left rose a misty mass of violet hills.

The villages were clean, large and well constructed. Courtyards filled with marigolds and sunflowers led into darkened rooms with thick mud walls. Instead of windows, there were a few strategically placed openings allowing the air to flow unhampered, making them deliciously cool. The roofs of the houses were tiled. Women were decorating the outside walls by a method of hand painting, dipping their fingers into a mixture of straw, ash and water and combing their fingers in long wavy strokes across the walls, creating swirling evocative patterns of trees and lotus flowers. When the painting dried the women would apply lime and red earth to add colour. With its tall cypress-like trees this terracotta landscape reminded me of the rolling hills of Tuscany.

Nearing Hazaribagh we encountered a small encampment of Birhor tribals. Traditionally nomadic hunters and jungle dwellers, their existence relies on the game that they can catch. They are a shy, little-known people who are now forced to change their ways due to deforestation, lack of hunting grounds – and by the lure of better housing donated by the government anxious to obtain the tribal vote. They are squat, dark and flat-nosed, similar to the aboriginals, wearing their hair long and straggly. Known as the 'leaf people', they construct their dwellings, resembling large hollow bonfires, from tightly packed leaves. If a Birhor builds a new hut, and it leaks once in two years, he is thrown out of the tribe. Masters of fieldcraft, they practise a simple and highly effective way of trapping game. For large animals, such as boar and hares, they use nets propped up on sticks, into which the game is driven, effectively entangling themselves as the sticks collapse. For birds, a small wire snare, like a noose, is used, which is carefully camouflaged by piles of leaves.

This encampment was unique, providing a contrast between those who succumbed to civilisation, living in new government-built houses, and those who still lived in the traditional leaf dwellings. The leaf house was tidy, the mud floor clean, while the government house was in chaos, pots and pans littering the floor and the wooden window-frames used as firewood.

We were accompanied into Hazaribagh by the Birhor medicine man, a splendid character carrying a sack full of oddities – lizard tongues and claws for cramps, silkworm cocoons for constipation and various roots for impotence. I saw him later selling his wares outside churches and government offices. He did thriving business, and the thought of some fat official suffering from constipation swallowing a silkworm, or dabbing his private parts with a root to improve his sexual prowess, made me very happy.

While taking Tara to bathe next morning, Gokul disturbed a nest of hornets and was badly stung. Jumping off Tara, he ran back to camp screaming. He was in severe shock, his body a mass of burning lumps. Meanwhile, Bhim went to retrieve Tara. Unaffected by the hornets that buzzed angrily around her, she was feeding happily nearby. An hour later he returned.

'Didn't you get stung?' I asked him incredulously.

'Once,' he replied smiling, pointing to a large lump on his head. 'But die, drunk. Eat Bhim blood.'

Later we drove over to see Mary Morris, whom we had met briefly in McCluskiegunge. She was staying at a large convent, formerly her family house and now a hostel for local Adivasi girls. By torchlight, owing to a powercut, we celebrated her seventy-fourth birthday over rum and fruit cake. She had been born in Ranchi and had left for London to train as a hairdresser and beauty specialist at the Mayfair Salon in Hanover Square. Having received her diploma, she had worked at grand hotels throughout Asia and became the Maharani of Jaipur's personal hairdresser. For a period in the Fifties, she worked at Steiner's in Grosvenor Street, where, she proudly informed me, her clients had included Yvonne Arnaud, Vivien Leigh, Jennifer Jones, Valerie Hobson and the Queen of Jordan. She had served as a nurse in Chittagong (now Bangladesh) during the war and escorted patients on ambulance trains from Calcutta to Lucknow. She had been awarded the 1939–45 medal, the Burma Star and the War medal.

She showed us postcards of herself as a vivacious young lady always on the arm of a handsome man, either in civvies or uniform. One portrayed her standing in front of the Taj Mahal surrounded by a large crowd of men. She laughed, her blue eyes twinkling.

'One woman with a hundred men – all to myself on a moonlight night at the Taj. Not bad, eh? Those, of course, were in what I called my salad days. Now I am just an old woman.'

'Not old, Mary,' Aditya said, 'just seventy-four and still capable of putting life into two weary travellers.'

'Flattery, my dear boy, will get you everywhere.'

That evening, Bhim decided Tara needed to get drunk. For once, it was not just an excuse so that he could join in, but because she needed a full night's sleep. She was very tired and the alcohol would act like an anaesthetic, ensuring her a long rest.

Mahouts often doctor their elephants, as we were to discover at the Sonepur Mela. Bhim prepared a mess of oats and gur in a bucket. He poured in two bottles of rum, moulded three or four sloppy balls of the mixture and shoved them into Tara's mouth. When drunk, elephants are like human beings – their reactions varying according to their characters. The naturally good-natured appear even more so, the aggressive become downright dangerous. Everybody, except myself, was dispersed. Bhim explained that although Tara would not cause any trouble, it was better she was with the two people she knew best and trusted.

At first nothing happened, then I noticed slight defects in her co-ordination. Tara always stood with one back leg crossed over the other and attempting this now, she found she could not feel her back legs at all, moving them from side to side with a perplexed expression on her face. Her huge head fell aslant and she began to whip her trunk up and down as if it were some kind of toy. Slowly her eyes closed. She became still. One of her front legs slid slowly forward, then the other. For a moment, in a most undignified fashion, she seemed to crouch like a giant cat. Finally, with a contented rumble, she rolled over and passed out.

'Mummy have hangover tomorrow,' Bhim murmured, opening another bottle of rum. 'Better Bhim as well. Then Mummy and Bhim ill together.'

15

The Land of the Buddha

A FEW YEARS ago, the inhabitants of Hazaribagh were terrorised by a man-eating leopard, which had killed with alarming frequency. Some people surmised that the killings were carried out by a pack of wolves which had acquired a taste for human flesh by consuming the bodies of deceased prisoners left to rot outside the prison. That prison, once Asia's largest, lay to our left as we made our way towards Hazaribagh National Park.

Tara was suffering from a hangover and would not be coaxed into moving faster than a shuffling amble. Bhim stopped regularly at small canals to enable her to slake her raging thirst. I felt sorry for her. Unlike humans, she could not sweat out the alcohol. To add to her misery, she carried a full load. We were taking a short cut over rough terrain to the Grand Trunk Road where the jeep would meet us in a day or so. Barring mishaps, we would arrive on the 7th November at Bodh Gaya, where I had arranged to meet my friend, the photographer Don McCullin, who was to accompany us for the last part of the journey.

We passed slowly through a herd of cattle. Around their necks hung wooden bells, emitting a sound like heavy raindrops hitting water. We stopped to talk to the cowherd, an Oraon tribal, who showed us a selection of these bells. Each was exquisite and of a different design, and each unique in its sound, enabling him to distinguish in which direction individual cows had wandered. Aditya offered to buy one. The cowherd refused saying that he would offend the soul of the tree from which he had fashioned the bell, having asked for the tree's blessing before cutting it down. The tree is always chosen and felled on a Saturday and the bell then made on Sunday. During its creation, no clothes can be worn.

In Assam and Burma, elephants also wear bells so that at night, when the elephants are set free, their mahouts can keep a check on their whereabouts.

However, blessed with that ingenious proboscis, they fill the bells with mud and wander undetected, stealing into cultivated areas to enjoy night-time feasts.

In the afternoon I tried to push Tara along at a faster pace. She kept crossing the road from side to side, as if selecting a special path. At first I thought it was due to her hangover but, after scolding her a few times, I realised this was not the case. At intervals, her trunk would swing up and deposit a pile of small rocks on to the top of her head. Then I spotted the reason for the obstinacy, which she was deftly showing me. The path was littered with small, sharp stones, and her slow, cautious movements were simply to avoid injuring the sensitive soles of her feet. This little show of sagacity gave me more pleasure, perhaps, than anything I had experienced with her so far. She had taught me so much.

We camped beside a dirty nullah, amongst a grove of date palms near a village called Kotapisi. Due to lack of firewood, I commanded Tara to uproot a thick palm stump which proved more obstinate than I had expected. She bent it backwards and forwards using one of her front feet, then loosened it more by using her full weight, pushing with her 'bushum'. Working steadily, she eventually ripped the stump out of the ground with a great tug of her trunk.

In the middle of the night Tara escaped. Following a trail of flattened grass, from dragging the uprooted date palm that she had been chained to, we found her in the middle of a lush paddy field. It was as if a combine harvester had been at work. Half the field was neatly cropped. We did not blame her. It was becoming difficult to satisfy her appetite, and unless we paid exorbitant prices, the owners of trees were reluctant to let Gokul cut fodder. We sat up all night, taking turns to watch her, leaving early to avoid an ugly scene. A final descent through dense jungle, from which we could hear the roar of traffic, led us to the Grand Trunk Road which links Calcutta and Delhi.

Delighted by the smooth surface of the tarmac, Tara swung along at a grand pace, unaffected by the diesel fumes from passing trucks that choked us and made our eyes water. It was a great shock. Suddenly the stillness of the forest, the clear bubbling rivers, the dazzling bird life and the colour and joviality of the tribals became a distant memory.

We stopped at a tea-house for breakfast. As the trucks pulled in and out, a few drivers threw coins at Tara's feet, which she picked up and placed on her head. We needed the money badly. It was Sunday and the banks were closed. The jeep had not as yet turned up. We were going to have to work the road. Bhim was indignant. Mummy was not a beggar now, he exclaimed angrily. She was a princess, and he refused to have anything to do with our venality, not that we had collected much by the end of the day.

'Generous bunch, the Biharis,' I remarked to Aditya as I glared at another passing truck, like a hitch-hiker glaring at a motorist who has failed to give him a lift.

'It's not so much that,' Aditya explained, 'it's because they don't want to stop. There are so many ambushes on this particular stretch that even the truck drivers are frightened. You wait until tonight. You'll find it difficult to sleep when the trucks join into one long convoy to cut down the risk.'

It was dark by the time we met up with the jeep. Suitable camp-sites were now impossible to locate. We ended up in somebody's back garden, just off the highway. Aditya was right – the constant rumble of passing trucks, the hiss of air brakes and the crunch of badly changed gears continued all night. To pass the time, we placed bets on Tara's height. Using the old method, we had to guess how many times a piece of string would wind around her foot (which was approximately twenty-four inches) to equal her height, taken at the highest point of her back. Khusto and Indrajit said twenty, Gokul, twelve. Aditya and myself, convinced we were correct, knowing Tara stood at seven and a half feet, from the sale document, stated five. Bhim, with a quiet chuckle, guessed two, a decision met with howls of derision. Extraordinarily he was correct. Twice around Tara's foot made her eight foot, just a few inches off her actual height. Going by Khusto and Indrajit's judgement, she should have been sixty feet tall.

The next day we continued along the Grand Trunk Road, the flowing artery of India that for many years has been the conveyor of life and legend.

'Prostitutes,' Aditya exclaimed excitedly, pointing to a colourful encampment of painted ladies sitting by the roadside, their eyes thick with kohl, smoking hookahs and chattering like mynah birds. 'Probably on their way to the Sonepur Mela.'

Seeing Tara, they cooed, whistled and called to us suggestively to join them for breakfast. They stroked my arms and legs, playfully pulling at my hair and smelling me. They wrinkled up their noses in distaste and started giggling.

'It's your fair skin, Mark,' Aditya explained, laughing. 'They find … how do I put it' – trying to be polite – 'you well, different. As a firinghee, they're saying you must be rich. So they're discussing prices. But because you are riding an elephant they are prepared to give you a discount.'

Bhim stood beside Tara, with a lascivious expression on his face, whispering to her quietly. Quite suddenly, her trunk shot out, grabbed the hem of the nearest sari and pulled sharply upwards. The girl gave a shriek of alarm and struggled to regain her modesty.

'Teach Mummy new trick,' he said happily, 'for Mela. Undress women.'

Aditya reprimanded him severely, but Tara was now enjoying her game. Like a dirty old man with wandering hands, she moved towards another victim and explored her bottom with the tip of her trunk. I stopped her immediately. Although I had heard stories of amorous elephants, this was going too far. Not only was she of the same sex, her actions were both unchivalrous and coarse, quite unlike the elephants that Edward Topsell described in *The Historie of Foure-Footed Beastes*. 'At the sight of a beautiful woman,' he wrote, 'they leave off all rage and grow meeke and gentle.' He then describes how an elephant in Egypt was once passionately in love with the same woman as the poet Aristophanes. The elephant annoyed the poet by putting apples into the girl's bosom and dallying with her breasts. Another elephant loved a Syrian girl 'with whose aspect he was suddenly taken and in admiration of her face, stroked the same with his trunke'. Apparently the girl reciprocated his affections and made him 'amorous devices with Beads and Coral and Silver and such things as are grateful to these brute beastes'. When the girl died the elephant was overcome with grief and expired romantically at her side.

At Doohi, a dirty crossroad town, we turned off the Grand Trunk Road heading northwards for Bodh Gaya, Gaya, Nalanda and Rajgir, the great centres of Buddhism. The countryside was monotonous; little irrigated fields criss-crossed by narrow footpaths and rough roads leading to endless shabby villages. Few trees lined the road, and most were protected by barbed wire. When Bhim took Tara to drink in scummy pools, he would bend down and whisper in her ear. 'Walk careful, Mummy. Water dark. Maybe hurt feet.'

At each village, young boys set off fireworks and exploded crackers, prematurely celebrating Diwali, the festival of lights, which takes place on the darkest night of the year, when Laxmi, the goddess of wealth and prosperity, is worshipped. As it is the beginning of the New Year, Diwali is particularly auspicious for traders and businessmen. People flock to the shops and markets to stock up with new merchandise. A man with a brand new bicycle, a machine totally foreign to him, hopped past us with his right foot on the left pedal. Another man, more expert, his bicycle loaded with planks of new wood, hammers and nails, was on his way to his brother's home west of Patna, where, he told us, a huge earthquake had caused terrible destruction and death a month ago.

'Was your brother's house destroyed?' I asked him.

'Oh no, sir,' he replied cheerfully. 'Just turning round. Now better view.'

As we entered the outskirts of Bodh Gaya we were joined by a tall, fleshy, loquacious German girl. She exuded good health and strode along behind Tara with her enormous rucksack as if it were a handbag. I became more and more irritated by tales of her travels through India; of how she hated the filthy food, of the lack of good accommodation and particularly of 'ze dirty Indian men' who were always trying to molest her. They must have been very brave, I thought, staring in awe at the size of her red, meaty hands.

'Haw, haw, haw, haw, haw,' she suddenly guffawed loudly, pointing at Tara's rolling bottom. 'Eet looks zo zilly. Ya, like ze wears ze pantaloons.'

I had had enough of this Valkeryian chatterbox. Nobody insulted Tara. I saw red.

'Listen Fraulein,' I hissed, 'it might interest you to know that according to the Sanskrit scriptures women were supposed to emulate the walk of the elephant, because it was so sensual, and,' I added, pointing to her large, wobbling posterior encased in a pair of tight shorts, 'you could learn something from that.'

She stopped dead and went crimson in the face. For a moment I thought one of those great meaty hands would come crashing down on my head.

'Vell,' she spluttered. 'I have never been zo insulted in my life. You … you, focking Englishman,' and, with a swing of her pigtails, she stomped off.

I was still seething with anger as I rode into Bodh Gaya. The peace of the Buddha had not yet settled upon me, as I was confronted by a mass of Japanese tourists carrying white parasols, shuffling like anxious sheep in the wake of a shouting guide. A group of shaven-headed western Buddhists with sunburnt necks and arms, who wore their saffron robes self-consciously, were haggling with some enchanting Tibetan girls selling tourist knick-knacks from roadside stalls. As I came up quietly behind them, Tara reached out her trunk, tapping one of the devotees on his backside. He whirled around and uttered a strangled scream.

'Mon Dieu! Un éléphant …!' and hurrying to get out of the way, caught the hem of his robe in one of his heavy, leather sandals. The robe unfurled quickly, exposing a tight pair of 'Jockey' briefs, emblazoned with 'La Tour Eiffel'. 'Merde …!'

I smiled reprovingly at him from my lofty perch. Clasping my hands together and bowing my turbaned head, I said 'Bonjour and Hari Krishna,' while Tara moved serenely onwards.

As we moved through Bodh Gaya towards the hotel where I had arranged to meet Don McCullin, I saw a familiar figure approaching. He was elbowing his way through a mass of pedestrians, his head down, swinging it from side to side, suspiciously clutching his stomach as if in pain. But I knew better. He was zealously guarding his moneybelt.

'Watchya, cock,' I said. His head jerked up like a turtle. A pair of eyes rounded in disbelief under big, bushy eyebrows.

'Gordon Bennett,' he growled, shading his face against the sun. 'Shand! Is that you? Who the hell do you think you are – Jesus Christ? I've seen some strange things in my life, but this takes the biscuit.'

'Don,' I said dismounting, 'this is Aditya Patankar.' They shook hands.

'Congratulations, Aditya,' Don said. 'If you have managed to survive with this lunatic, you must be as mad as he is.'

Bhim and Gokul saluted smartly. Tara, her manners impeccable, raised her trunk and trumpeted loudly in greeting.

'Hop on board,' I said. 'I'll send the boys back in the jeep to fetch your gear.'

'If you don't mind, mate,' Don said as he eyed Tara suspiciously, 'I'd rather walk for a while.'

To avoid the congestion in the town of Gaya, we followed the course of the River Phalgu, sacred to the Hindus, and believed to be an embodiment of Vishnu himself. Once it was said to have flowed with milk. We made camp on the far side, in a grove of mango trees, looking across to the old town of Gaya, a façade of ancient, greyish ghats splashed with colour as devotees came to bathe under the shadow of the great Vishnupad Temple. Far to our right, the sound of traffic crossing a narrow iron bridge rolled across the river flats like distant summer thunder.

Leaving Don to sleep, Aditya and I took the jeep into Gaya to stock up on rum. We bought lights and fireworks to celebrate our Diwali, and paid a visit to the police station where it had been arranged for my visa to be renewed. Beneath us on the river banks as we crossed the bridge, a multi-coloured carpet stretched as far as the eye could see. Bathers had laid out their clothes there to dry in the sun. Beyond, just visible as a black glistening speck, Tara was taking her bath in the shallows.

At any time Gaya is a busy, thriving metropolis: now, only a few days before Diwali, its streets were almost impassable. Like the great Maratha chief, Baji Rao, who in the mid-eighteenth century had sacked and plundered the city with an army of fifty thousand horses, Aditya drove with aggression and total disregard. Scattering pedestrians, ignoring police signals and blowing the horn imperiously, he hurled the jeep around the labyrinth of crooked alleys, shut in by high old masonry houses, many of them still loop-holed for defence against the marauding hordes. Streets were lined with shops, outside which merchants were wheeling and dealing; cotton weavers, grain dealers, grocers, carpenters, tailors, shoe-makers, blacksmiths, brass workers, silver and gold merchants, all shouting and gesticulating to the endless ribbon of passersby.

To be honest, I had been concerned about Don's arrival. Although I had travelled with him on many occasions, it is always difficult when a newcomer joins an expedition and fills one's head with news of home. I had become so immersed in this pilgrimage, so much part of India, that I wondered if I would resent an intrusion from another world. I need not have worried. By the time we reached camp Don, with his ability to fit in anywhere, had already become a cog in the machine, as if he had travelled with us from the beginning. Curious and fascinated by his slightly eccentric character, the boys took to him immediately and unable to handle the word 'McCullin' called him affectionately Meester Macleen. We dined well, courtesy of Meester Macleen and British Airways on tins of pâté, washed down with half bottles of Château-Latour.

I sat up with Tara until the early hours, waiting for that moment when she would rock slightly and then, in a slow, silent movement go down. Elephants are like horses; they get most of their sleep standing up and will lie down only when they are sure that all the world is at rest. Being immensely cautious animals they are at their most vulnerable when in a prone position. I sat in front of her, staring at her intently, wondering if in my presence she would make an exception. But she continued standing. It was not until Bhim appeared, like a ghost, and motioned me to move away that she finally sank down with a long exhalation of content. 'Mummy shy,' he explained in a whisper. 'If not see you, she sleep.'

Her repose did not last long; nor did anybody else's. I was about to enter the tent when something stung me on my foot, burning me with such ferocity that for a moment I thought I had stumbled into the glowing embers of the fire. 'I'm dying, I'm dying,' I shouted wildly. 'I've been stung.'

Aditya's head shot out. 'It's the big black scorpion. Bihar is famous for them,' he stated authoritatively. 'Don't panic, I'll get the anti-venom.'

'Oh, God,' I moaned, panicking, 'I'm done for.'

I hopped from one foot to the other while Indrajit played the beam of the torch on the ground.

'Ants!' he shouted. 'Quick, I burn.'

Returning with a tin of kerosene, he sprayed it around liberally, lit a match and the offenders were executed in a puff of blue flame. Shamefacedly, I crawled into the tent, the pain quickly subsiding.

'I have never been in such agony,' I told Aditya, who was putting away a large, long needle with an expression of some regret.

'They're only fire ants,' he laughed. 'They must be attracted by your sweet English skin.'

A sleepy growl came from Don's tent. 'You never change, Shand. Bloody hypochondriac.'

The next night we celebrated our own Diwali beside a trickle of a river, under a dramatic backcloth of the Rajgir Hills, circumvented by an old, fortified wall on top of which glistening white in the moonlight stood a modern Buddhist stupa.

The boys surrounded the camp with little clay pots, in each of which flickered a candle. Tara was garlanded and fed bags of ludoos. We gorged ourselves on a young goat which Bhim had prepared. Sweets were eaten, sparklers lit, and we toasted the New Year with quantities of rum, after which a highly dangerous display of fireworks took place, engineered by Indrajit. We took refuge behind the jeep as rockets snaked at low level through the camp and mortars exploded deafeningly overhead. Long after Aditya, Don and I had retired, the festivities went on. They finally ended in a furious but good-natured contest between Khusto and Bhim to see who possessed the biggest penis. We heard them staggering around drunkenly as measurements were taken with a piece of string. According to Indrajit, it was won, unfairly, by Khusto. Being the kind of person who became excited at the sight of two beetles copulating, he managed to maintain a fleeting erection. It was a merry evening and the boys enjoyed themselves. They deserved it; we had come a long way together and soon it would all be over.

16

The Mighty Ganga

RAJGIR, OR RAJAGRIHA as it was known in the sixth century, was the ancient capital of Magadha, the nucleus of the first great empire in India. The fortified wall, which we had seen the night before, was the boundary of the city, almost thirty miles in circumference. Here the Buddha himself had passed many years living in different localities. His favourite place was the Vulture's Peak, a high rocky outcrop on which he spent most of his time in contemplation. Sacred to Buddhists, Jains, Hindus and Muslims alike, Rajgir was crowded with pilgrims who had come here to worship and to bathe in its famous hot springs. It was also full of scavenging dogs and little horses pulling tourists around in gaudily decorated traps.

It is difficult to explain why elephants should display such uneasiness towards dogs and horses, considering that neither is capable of inflicting on them the slightest injury. Tara was no exception. On seeing a dog, she stopped dead, rapped her trunk on the ground and squealed in terror. According to *The Wild Elephant* by Sir J. Emmerson Tennant, Bt. – a man who was regarded by other more reliable elephant experts as prone to exaggeration:

> One instance has certainly been attested to me by an eye witness in which the trunk of an elephant was seized in the teeth by a Scotch Terrier, and such was the alarm of the huge creature that it came at once to its knees. The dog repeated the attack and on every renewal of it the elephant retreated in terror, holding its trunk above its head and kicking out at the terrier with its forefeet. It would have turned to flight but for the interference of its keeper.

Horses threw Tara into an even bigger panic. At the mere sight of their droppings, she shied violently. The moment she heard the metallic ring of their hoofs, she bolted. If Bhim had not controlled her quickly with the ankush we would have arrived at Sonepur in no time. Afterwards she stood shaking, bending her front legs in rapid succession, the effect of which was like sitting in the epicentre of an earthquake.

'Horse eat Mummy when baby,' Bhim announced with the utmost pragmatism. 'No like!'

The belief, however, that an elephant is frightened of a mouse must be an old wives' tale, for Tara had come into contact with both rats and mice on the road and had shown no alarm. The legendary J. H. Williams, probably the greatest authority on elephants, wrote in his book *Elephant Bill*: 'the idea makes an obvious appeal to the human love of paradox. But if it is true I can see no reason for it. It certainly cannot be because the elephant is afraid of the mouse getting into his trunk, since, with one snort, he could eject it like a cork from a popgun.'

For the next three days we marched north – and marched is the right word – like a small army across a desperate, barren and poor rural wasteland which eventually would lead us to the Ganges. It was fortunate that we were travelling with an elephant – admittedly a benign one, but at least her size gave our pathetic party some semblance of authority. I envied the great King of Bliss who had marched at the head of a huge army of a thousand war elephants. Still, considering the difference in military might, I felt he would have been proud of us forming a tight phalanx around Tara, armed with an odd axe, ankush and spear, and Aditya's large, metal tripod that we pretended was a machine gun.

Jeering crowds greeted us at most villages, taunting us with insults. I was riding Tara through one of these villages, followed by the inevitable mocking crowd, which I had found it best to ignore. A rock whistled through the air, hitting me on my back. Another followed, and then a fusillade broke out, striking Tara on her back legs and backside. I whirled her around and charged them in a shuffling clumsy way. To my satisfaction they fled into the safety of their village. In moments the culprits, a group of teenagers, returned. Egged on by their leader, a young man with a pock-marked face and wall eye, another rock came whizzing past, dangerously close to my head.

'Right, that's enough!' Aditya yelled. 'Let's deal with the bastards.'

Leaving Tara with Bhim, Don and I joined forces with Aditya, who was dishing out some heavy Maratha treatment to the ringleader. We grabbed another young man, but slippery as an eel, he wriggled free and escaped.

In India an incident of any kind invariably draws a crowd quickly. We were soon surrounded by a group of village elders carrying long sticks. Although we prepared ourselves for the oncoming fracas, we were surprised to discover that they had simply come to apologise. Following old traditions, they revered the elephant, but the younger generation, they told us, had no respect. Politely, they asked Aditya to release the culprit. They would deal with him in their own way.

By the time we caught up with the jeep at a village called Kachra (or appropriately 'rubbish' in Hindi) it was already getting dark. An angry Indrajit and Khusto were keeping another large crowd at bay while arguing violently with a man who they had accused of throwing a stone, splintering part of the jeep's windscreen. Deciding that this place was unhealthy, we moved on and camped on a raised rocky road, shadowed by a solitary Peepul tree, and were quickly hemmed in on either side by unfriendly villagers, muttering amongst themselves, eyeing our paraphernalia greedily.

'I don't like this situation,' Aditya said warily. 'We'll keep all the stuff in the jeep and just sit it out.'

He told Indrajit to bring out the tripod. With great showmanship, Indrajit assembled the 'machine gun' and squatting behind it, traversed the 'barrel' (one of the telescopic legs) across the crowd. They moved, fractionally. Our ploy did not seem to be working. Tara was not helping matters either. She should have been trumpeting fiercely and rattling her chains. Instead she stood quietly greeting each villager with an affectionate exploration of her trunk.

Suddenly, the crowd parted. Two tall men, bearing obvious authority, strode through.

'The local landlord, the zamindar,' Aditya whispered.

'Can I be being of assistance?' the elder of the two men boomed fiercely.

Aditya replied, 'It's these people. We have already had a few bad experiences and we are a little nervous.'

The man turned to the crowd. 'Chale jao! Chale jao!' he shouted imperiously, dispersing the people with a dismissive wave. 'My name Sri Ram Chandra Prasad,' he said, introducing himself, 'and this my son Ram Singhar. I am Thakur of Dehra. My village over there.' He pointed to a few twinkling lights in the distance. 'You are guests in my country. I bring food tonight.'

True to his word, late that evening a posse of villagers, led by the admirable Thakur, made their way across the fields with fresh bread, vegetables and water. Before leaving he extended an invitation to us to breakfast with him the next morning at his village. He would prepare green pigeon in yoghurt, a speciality of his house.

I caught a glimpse of Don's face. It was as white as a sheet. He had never been an adventurous eater.

We rode to Dehra, an oasis of white-washed houses surrounded by a grove of date trees. The Thakur proudly showed us his cattle, after which we climbed the stairs of his large house, where a fine breakfast had been laid out; fresh naan, sour yoghurt and tea scented with ginger. Fortunately for Don, there was no pigeon. I thanked our host for his help, adding that I was overwhelmed by his kindness. He explained to me that hospitality was a tradition in his family, learnt from a good Muslim who had lived for many years in the village until partition came in 1947. 'Always make guests welcome,' the Muslim had advised. 'Even if you can only spare a cup of water, it will not make you any poorer.'

Our route from there was trouble free. Word, it seemed, had gone out. We stopped at a police station to watch the Test Match on television. The police had been informed that 'three angry men, eight foot tall, were travelling with a mad elephant'.

On the 13th of November we arrived at a main road. To the west, some fifteen miles away, lay Patna. In front of us, the holiest river in India, the mighty Ganges, lay glistening dully as the sun played on its vast caramel-coloured surface. We had travelled from the sea to the source. We may not have 'struck terror into the hearts of the people of Magadha', like the King of Bliss, but with the same pride we watched Tara drinking thirstily from the Ganges, as the King of Bliss had once watched his army of elephants and horses being watered.

It had been organised that in Patna we would stay in a magnificent mansion overlooking the river, a private museum that included among the exhibits Akbar's sword and Napoleon's bed. Lured by the majesty of the Ganges, Don hired a little sailing dhow and arranged to meet us later at the mansion.

As we approached the outskirts of old Patna, the narrow streets lined with tea-stalls, paan shops and endless bicycle repair outfits became congested. While Bhim and Gokul stopped to buy paan, I rode Tara on ahead, Aditya lolling behind in the howdah. Hearing an approaching horse cart, her huge body began to vibrate violently. Before I could do anything about it, she took off like a racehorse.

Over a short distance an elephant can achieve a high speed, and the sensation I was experiencing was aptly described by C. F. Holder in his book *Ivory King*: 'I have felt on the one or two occasions which I have been on a bolting elephant as a man must feel if bestriding a runaway locomotive and holding the funnel with the crook of his walking stick to hold it in.' Except in this case I did not have 'the crook of the walking stick', the ankush having fallen off.

'Stop her!' Aditya bellowed from behind, as we flashed past terrified pedestrians, who were scattering as all our pots, pans and kerosene lamps flew like missiles in all directions. 'I'm going to fall …' I heard a sort of thud behind me. Catching a quick glance back as I clung to the sides of the howdah, I saw Aditya rising shakily to his feet from an entanglement of tents and hammocks.

'Tara, Tara,' I yelled. 'Stop! Oh, bugger! What's the bloody word? Dit! Dat!' Finally I remembered it and screamed out the command. 'Dhuth!' Too late, I saw a bus approaching us. To avoid a headlong collision Tara suddenly swerved, snapping the posts of an empty tea-stall. We came to an abrupt halt amongst a cascading river of cups and tea-urns. Facing us, his dark face a mottled purple, was the enraged owner.

'Er … I'm frightfully sorry, sir,' I gasped, wiping tea from my chest and arms, trying at the same time to stop Tara, who was now helping herself liberally to a selection of cakes that lay on the ground. 'You see my …'

'You! you!' the man stuttered furiously. 'Everything gone, ruined, I take you to court. I am getting big damages.'

At that moment, Aditya turned up limping slightly, followed by Bhim and Gokul carrying a load of our possessions which they had recovered from the roadside.

'Now, sir,' Aditya said. 'There's no need for that. I am sure we can come to some financial agreement.' After the man had cooled down, they assessed the damage, compensation was paid and dignity restored.

'Why in the hell doesn't she behave like this with me?' I exclaimed to Aditya in exasperation as we sat on the re-packed howdah behind Bhim, watching him thread Tara expertly through the traffic. Quite suddenly the most ludicrous image floated into my mind and I began to shake with laughter.

'What's so bloody funny?' Aditya demanded angrily. 'You bloody nearly killed me …!'

'Forgive me, I'm not laughing at you, but I've just had this vision of us appearing in court with Tara.'

In his book *Elephants* Richard Carrington records that during the last century in Cleveland, Ohio, a famous trick elephant had been the star turn in a circus show. There was some argument about the elephant's maximum speed and his trainer had bet that Pikanniny could achieve three miles an hour. The matter was then put to the test. Pikanniny completed the first mile in only eight minutes. At this moment, the local Society for the Prevention of Cruelty to Animals intervened, accusing the trainer of using his ankush too much and drawing blood. When the case came up in court, the trainer subpoenaed Pikanniny for his defence. The elephant arrived at the appointed time but the court had not been built to accommodate so large a witness and he was unable to squeeze up the narrow staircase. Obligingly the magistrate agreed to take the case in the entrance hall. There Pikanniny duly took the stand. When the prosecutor asked him if he had been hurt, the elephant shook his head from side to side, and when asked if he was generally well treated, he nodded and made squeaks of assent. Whether the course of justice was altered by Pikanniny's testimony is unlikely, especially as the trainer seemed to be connected with the performance. Still, as the elephant was found to be in good health and quite unharmed, the trainer was discharged. Pikanniny was congratulated by everybody and, like a star witness, received every kind of delicacy for his loyal support.

Late in the afternoon, we reached our destination, the entrance to Quila House, built on the foundations of the fort that Sher Shah had constructed in 1541. The high, imposing iron gates were closed and remained closed, even after we explained to the old, argumentative and highly suspicious chowkidar that we were expected. But Tara had spotted a luscious grove of bamboo on the far side. She lowered her head, pushing against the gates until they sprang open, sending the indignant chowkidar flying, and trotted triumphantly through. As we rode under an impressive portico, flanked by romantic Italian stone statues and a pair of blue and white Chinese water jars standing in niches, a small, well-groomed, prosperous-looking man, wearing a smart suit, in the top pocket of which was a row of gold Cartier pens, came running out to meet us.

'Welcome to Quila House,' he said excitedly. 'I've been expecting you. I'm Bal Manohar Jalan, but my friends call me Bala.'

'Thank you,' I replied. 'But I must apologise for our discourteous arrival. My elephant is usually extremely well mannered, but she does on occasions show a certain impatience.'

'I should be the one to apologise,' he said, dismissing with a wave of a plump gold-ringed hand the angry chowkidar who had chased us up the drive. 'We do have to be careful whom we admit. As you know, Quila House is a private museum. Please choose a suitable place for your elephant.'

I nervously surveyed an immaculate sweeping lawn. In the centre was a stone fountain, surrounded by neat rosebeds, in which an army of gardeners were busily working. Beyond, more men laboured in a well cultivated vegetable plot.

'She really is a very large and greedy animal,' I said, remembering Seraikella. 'It's quite extraordinary the … er, damage that she can do.'

'It does not matter,' he said expansively. 'Plants and flowers and trees will grow again, and it is not often we have an elephant as a guest.'

Eventually Bhim found a suitable tree, covered in a bower of bougainvillaea. 'Mummy here. But flowers soon go,' he whispered nervously, looking around, overcome by the grandeur of the setting.

The jeep arrived, having collected Don from the river. Our baggage was unloaded and we followed Bala across the lawn, down some steps and through a covered walkway of flowering jasmine. In front of us stood an exquisite marble pavilion, surrounded by balconies carved like lace, by its side a large tank choked with white water lilies.

'I hope you will be comfortable here,' Bala announced anxiously, throwing open a pair of glass doors.

One could have been entering the home of an affluent Chinese gentleman in the nineteenth century. In the bedrooms, ornate opium beds, draped in mosquito nets, were strategically placed so that one could lie and gaze out at the Ganges. Polished rosewood and teak tables and chairs, elegant in their simplicity, filled the ante-rooms. Silk wallpaper printed with oriental court scenes lined the walls, and the doors were studded with blue and white Ming plaques.

'As you can see,' Bala laughed, noticing the expressions of astonishment on our faces, 'my grandfather was fond of Chinese works of art. But this is nothing. Later I will show you the main house and the collection. You will find that he really was a compulsive buyer. Come, let us have tea.'

On the main terrace overlooking the river, we reclined on charpoys covered in crisp, white linen as attendants served us tea from a silver service. We helped ourselves to cigarettes from heavy, green malachite boxes. Behind us, glowing pink and white in the setting sun, stood Quila House, a large, handsome two-storey mansion, built in the art deco style with a long, flat roof, its side elevation a series of tall bowed windows.

Sher Shah's fort was destroyed by a huge earthquake in 1934. Bala's grandfather, Dewan (Prime Minister) Bahadhur R. K. Jalan, built Quila House in this magnificent situation after acquiring the site from the Nawab of Gaya. It was by a quirk of chance that he had managed to purchase the land. He was travelling in the same compartment as the Nawab in a train going to Patna, when they struck up a conversation. It turned out that the Nawab was on his way to dispose of this property. At the station, the Nawab's carriage failed to show, so Bala's grandfather offered him a lift. When he delivered the Nawab to his destination he fell in love with the fort and made a deal to buy it there and then.

The next morning, after bathing Tara in the Ganges, we were shown round Quila House by Bala. I could not have imagined the scale and variety of the collection that spilled from one room to another in this wonderfully eccentric private museum. Bala told us that according to the last inventory over twenty thousand items had been listed. His grandfather had started his quest at the beginning of the century, buying in Kalimpong, Darjeeling and Calcutta, and moving on to the auction houses and art dealers in London and Paris during his visit to attend the Coronation of King George V.

Ancient Sanskrit scriptures lay in cabinets surrounded by the skins of cobras that had been killed in the house. Behind a pair of eighteenth-century Indian lacquer doors, which opened silently on oiled hinges, was displayed a complete George III Crown Derby dinner service, designed in its familiar bold pattern (as the King was short-sighted). We threaded our way through suites of Louis XV and Louis XVI furniture and towering display cabinets chock-a-block with nineteenth-century export Chinese porcelain. Smaller ones contained mutton fat and Imperial jade objects that glistened in the glow of the lights. Vast green celadon serving plates lay stacked up like common china in a soup kitchen. Propped up on an elegant Anglo-Indian table, was a set of Sèvres porcelain which had belonged to Marie Antoinette, hand-painted in an exquisite design of entwining roses and stamped with her cipher.

We sat on Napoleon's tiny four-poster mahogany bed, draped in heavy velvet curtains, and made cuts through the air with Akbar's curved sword, inlaid with gold and silver. Opening a strong safe, Bala pulled out the prize of the collection, a set of thirty-two solid silver Indian thalis, which belonged to Birbal, one of Akbar's nine 'jewels' or philosophers who advised him at his court. India's first Prime Minister, Nehru, was so overpowered with their magnificence that when he came to dine at Quila House he refused to eat off them. Somebody diplomatically whispered in Nehru's ear that other important statesmen and even royalty had done so, and the embarrassing moment passed.

Bala handed me the old visitors' books to leaf through. Viceregal guests, Wavell, Linlithgow, Dufferin and Ava; luminaries such as Mary Pickford and Aly Khan. The Maharajas of Dharbanga, Patiala, Jodhpur; Mrs Gandhi and the King of Nepal, whose brother is lucky enough to have the most romantic signature in the world – simply 'Himalaya' – all had passed through. In 1938 a British general had visited the house, his remarks typically brusque – 'Good show, bad taste.'

We were extremely fortunate to have arrived in Patna at this time, for the Chaat Festival of Bihar was about to take place. People gather from afar on the banks of the Ganges and, at the exact moment of the setting sun, immerse themselves in the holy waters, spreading their offerings on its smooth surface. The same ritual is repeated the following morning at sunrise. The belief is that the sun is harmful and its effects immediate, causing skin cancer, leprosy and other diseases. By making this puja, the sun's terrible wrath is appeased. For a state that has the worst reputation in India for violence and lawlessness, it is interesting to note that during the two days of the Chaat the crime rate drops so dramatically that the local newspapers have to work hard to fill their pages.

The terrace of Quila House, sitting high above the river, was the perfect vantage point from which to watch the ceremony. But Bala suggested that we should hire a boat for the evening and float slowly down the river past the ghats which line the banks of old Patna. As we drove to where we would board the boat, the streets were thronged with processions of people carrying offerings. The city was clean and the tarmac glistened from the water trucks that had preceded us. Above, a canopy of tinsel and fairy-lights formed a glittering tunnel. Brass bands of old men in red and khaki uniforms marched proudly, blowing curled highly polished silver horns. At moments, traffic would come to a grinding stop, enabling devotees to cross the road repeatedly prostrating themselves in their laborious pilgrimage to the river.

We boarded a large motor launch and slowly began to edge down river. A continuous stream of colour, like the flowing molten lava of an exploding volcano, ran thickly downwards as the masses descended the steps of the ghats carrying flowers, grain, little candlelit terracotta pots and garlands. On reaching the water's edge lit by the last rays of the setting sun, they made their puja, immersing themselves and spreading their offerings on the dancing waves. Their faces serene, there was no rush, no pushing or shoving, just a completeness, a sense of contentment and peace.

Looking up at the crumbling oriental façades of former palaces and opium factories and the massive wall and buttresses of the old fort, entangled with overhanging trees, the stains of history were indelibly painted on the worn surface of this city, one of the most ancient capitals in the world. It was founded in 600 BC when King Ajatasatru built a fort which later became the capital of Magadha. It was there that the might of the Mundas compelled Alexander and his legions to retreat back home. In 304 BC in the reign of the great Emperor Chandra Gupta Maurya after his defeat of the Nunda Empire, it came into its full glory. By then he commanded a vast empire stretching from Kabul in the north to Mysore in the south, from Saurashtra in the west to parts of Bengal in the east. The Greek ambassador Megathesnes described the scene:

> The public appearances of the Emperor Chandra Gupta were occasions of pageantry and grandeur. The Emperor was carried in a golden litter adorned with strings of pearls hanging on all sides. His linen robe was embroidered in gold and purple and before him marched attendants, carrying silver incense pans. The Emperor was followed by armed men and his immediate bodyguard was comprised of armed women. He rode in a chariot drawn by elephants. The King had a guard of twenty-four elephants and when he went forth to do justice, the first elephant was trained to make obeisance. In the King's pay, there was a standing army of six hundred thousand foot soldiers, thirty thousand cavalry and nine thousand elephants.

Later, the great Emperor Akbar lived in what is now Quila House, from where he conducted his battle against the Afghan rule of North Bihar. Akbar was acknowledged as the greatest elephant rider of all time. In the *Ain-I-Akbari*, the record of Akbar's reign, is written:

> His Majesty, the royal rider of the plain of auspiciousness, mounts every kind of elephant from the first to the last class, making them notwithstanding their almost supernatural strength, obedient to his command. His Majesty will put his foot on the tusks and mount them, even when they are in the rutting season (musth) and astonishes experienced people.

Early the next morning, feeling a little like the Emperor Akbar, I rode Tara down from Quila House through a continuous procession of delighted devotees. We passed a line of sodium lamps which glowed eerily through the mists rolling off the Ganges, like a gas-lit street in Victorian England. As the sun rose over the horizon, we stood looking down upon a crowd of three hundred thousand people, spread out like some endless richly brocaded carpet which undulated softly as the saris and dhotis of the bathing devotees danced on the surface of the water. Leaving Tara with Gokul, Indrajit and I waded far out into the river through a sea of floating flowers. Indrajit performed a small puja for Sri Ram Naik, the resin collector who had been killed by the tiger in the Simplipals. Wrapping rose petals into his blood-stained lunghi we attached his sandals and watched the little bundle float gently away, taken by the eddies, to mix with the other offerings of the festival.

The following dawn we returned to the river. In a few hours we would enter the Sonepur Mela. We worked hard on Tara until she shone like obsidian. Bhim anointed her forehead vivid crimson with the sign of Shiva. After oiling her head and toenails, we loaded her up and bade farewell to Khusto, who was driving home to Orissa. The jeep was now due back.

Indrajit was staying on for the Mela as our driver, since Bala had kindly lent us a small minibus to ferry provisions back and forth, and for use if there was any emergency. Don would accompany Indrajit in the minibus. Aditya and I climbed on to Tara, flanked by Bhim and Gokul in their smartest dark-green khaki outfits. I lifted my hand upwards and forwards, like some American cavalry officer at the head of his troop, shouting 'Challo' and we trundled through the gates of Quila House towards Sonepur and the great elephant mela.

17

The Haathi Bazaar

WE SHOULD HAVE been imbued with a sense of excitement and fulfilment, and moved accordingly through the quiet streets of Patna in anticipation of the end of our pilgrimage. Instead we moved almost reluctantly, knowing that each of Tara's steps was bringing us closer to the moment when we would finally have to part. No one spoke, each of us lost in our own thoughts, lulled by the quiet sound of Tara's soft shuffle. The view from my lofty perch had become so familiar, so natural, that I found it hard to imagine any other way of life. I gazed vacantly at the top of her broad head, at the little white patch of criss-cross healed scars, where the point of the ankush had been used, and I ran my toes through the sparse, springy hair of which I knew there were two hundred and ninety-seven separate strands. I felt the heavy thump of her large ears against my legs, a sensation that had once annoyed me, but which I now enjoyed. My hands caressed the sweat-stained wood of the howdah, and I wiggled my backside deeper into the old faded red cushion, wanting never to dismount.

We circled on to the approach road leading to the Mahatma Gandhi bridge, one of the longest in the world, a masterpiece of engineering, simple and elegant, spanning the vast reaches of the Ganges. A long tailback of modern conveyances – buses, trucks, tractors, taxis, cars and scooters – were waiting to pay the toll, revving their engines impatiently and belching out blue exhaust fumes. We passed them slowly, waved on cheerfully by the toll-keeper, for such an ancient mode of travel was untaxed.

At Hajipur we joined up with a group of elephants. Two or three of the large females – we discovered from their mahouts – were owned by a local landlord hoping to purchase a big tusker. Veterans of the mela, they were capable, quiet old men, with faces that had seen it all. They rode proudly with straight backs, becoming wildly enthusiastic about the firinghee mahout, asking me if I would do them the honour of leading the cavalcade into Sonepur. As we cut through back streets I heard them talking eagerly with Bhim. Breaking into elephant language unintelligible to the outsider, they were enjoying the chance to advise a newcomer, and, no doubt, cleverly trying to extract the parameter of Tara's price which would then spread like a bushfire across the elephant market.

Although Aditya and I had decided earlier that we would not sell Tara to anyone unless we were convinced they would provide her with a good home, secretly I did not want to sell her at all. To cut down this risk I would make her the most expensive elephant of the mela. I had the feeling, though, that Tara would attract a lot of attention. Apart from her obvious cachet – fame – she was a beautiful elephant.

Sonepur is similar in shape to an isosceles triangle. It is flanked by two great rivers; the Ganges from the south and the Gandak from the north-east which begins its journey in the snow-capped peaks of the Himalayas, thundering down to its confluence with the Ganges. The fair takes place on the right bank of the Gandak. On the auspicious day of Kartik Purnima, hundreds and thousands of people line the ghats to take a ceremonial dip in its holy waters.

The Sonepur Mela has a special significance for Hindus, owing to the temple of Hari Nath Mandir where uniquely the gods Vishnu and Shiva are worshipped together. Near to the temple a mythological battle between a crocodile and an elephant took place.

According to legend, there once lived two brothers, Jai and Vijay, devotees of the Lord Krishna who were asked one day by their king to perform a puja, and he was so pleased with their devotion that he showered them with gifts. The two brothers argued about the distribution. Jai thought they should be divided equally, but Vijay disagreed, saying that as he had performed a better puja, he should be entitled to more. Hurt by his brother's greed, Jai cursed him, saying he would become a crocodile in his next life. Vijay retaliated and said Jai would turn into an elephant. After some time they made up their differences and asked Lord Krishna to break the evil spell they had cast on one another. He was helpless to do so and in due course the brothers became a crocodile and an elephant. One day, on Kartik Purnima, the day of the full moon, the elephant was bathing in the river when the crocodile grabbed him by the leg. A fierce battle raged, continuing for thousands of years. The elephant, finally tiring, was about to drown and he cried out to Lord Krishna for help. The god appeared on his Garuda (eagle) and killed the crocodile with the Sudershan Chakra (wheel).

From that day on devotees have flocked to this place every year, paying their obeisance to Lord Krishna after bathing in the river.

Over the centuries the position of the fair changed. Sonepur, however, must have been the original site. According to old records, Raja Man Singh, one of Akbar's Mogul generals, camped there while advancing on Patna. The Haathi Bazaar is to this day still called the 'Garden of Raja Man Singh', and further records show that during Aurangzeb's reign, traders from far flung Tartar Desh and from Arabia used to come to the fair to sell horses.

Over the last forty years or so, Sonepur has been known as a cattle fair, but for thousands of years it was primarily a place for the sale of elephants, like three other smaller fairs in northern Bihar. For centuries these fairs were fed by elephant-catchers from the jungles of Assam, Bengal and Orissa, and must have been the main markets for the sale of war elephants to Pataliputra, the ancient capital of Chandra Gupta Maurya, whose vast army relied so heavily on these animals.

We approached the bridge spanning the Gandak. It was considered too narrow to accommodate the increasing volume of trains that stopped at Sonepur, an important junction on the north-eastern railway which, until 1950, boasted the longest platform in the world. Now a new parallel bridge takes the rail traffic across.

The cavalcade came to an abrupt halt. In front of us stretched a mile of mela traffic, waiting for the signal to proceed, as the oncoming vehicles inched across the narrow bridge. Bellowing cattle stamped impatiently against the wooden floors of their trucks. More were filled with horses neighing nervously, poking their heads out of the slatted sides. Some vehicles were unrecognisable under gigantic mounds of fodder, spilling over the back, the front and the sides. Business was brisk for the hawkers. They patrolled up and down the armies of bicyclists, selling fruit, ice-cream, newspapers and bags of sticky ludoos. We gained a few yards as the traffic was stopped on the far side and with a crunching of gears and hiss of air brakes, the procession would move forward. Tara was becoming impossible. One moment she would be swiping food from the hawkers, the next vibrating in panic at the horses, forcing me to use the ankush. Aditya swung down impatiently from Tara's back.

'We'll be here all day. I'll see what I can sort out.'

Half an hour later I caught sight of him signalling to me frantically to come forward. I bulldozed my way through, closely followed by the other elephants who were not going to miss this chance. At the entrance Aditya was standing with a smiling policeman who saluted smartly and waved us on to an empty bridge.

'How on earth did you manage that?' I asked Aditya incredulously, as we lumbered across.

'I told him you were related to the Queen of England and that royalty did not expect to be kept waiting.'

'Really?' I said, impressed by his ingenuity.

'No, of course I didn't,' he replied. 'I gave him a hundred rupees.'

To our right, a steam engine clanked across the new railway bridge. To our left, a vast shady grove of mango trees stretched out parallel with the river, under which I could see a few elephants standing. 'Haathi Bazaar!' shouted one of the old mahouts.

Urging Tara into a lumbering trot, with Bhim and Gokul running alongside, we reached the end of the bridge and, swinging left, thundered down into the 'Garden of Raja Man Singh'. We jumped off Tara, and to the amazement of incredulous onlookers the four of us danced a jig around her. Opening a bottle of rum, I poured half the contents down her throat. Each of us then took a swig and yelled 'Jai Mata Sonepur!' We had made it.

It was as well that we had arrived early. As newcomers, we needed to check the lie of the land and to learn the rules. The area between each mango tree, in front of which the elephants would be staked, belonged to a different landlord. We made our way slowly through the orchard, passing fodder stacked like giant teepees. Each landlord tried to interest us in his plot, offering discounts and special favours, knowing that Tara would almost certainly attract a large crowd. We settled on a site at the far end of the orchard which gave easy access to the Gandak some fifty yards behind and close to one of the main bathing ghats. Situated amongst the nearest row of trees to the river we would not be hemmed in. Elephants would stand in front and to the side of us, but not behind.

Our landlord, Lallan Singh, a delightful, wise old man, a veteran of fifty melas, took us under his wing, bustling and fussing over us like a kindly matron on our first day at school. I paid him 100 rupees, the traditional mela rent for the use of his land. (If the elephant was sold, the buyer reimbursed this amount.) Two large wooden stakes were driven deep into the ground and one of Tara's front and back legs were chained to each. An 'account' was opened with the fodder and firewood suppliers, who delivered in the morning and the evening of each day. To ensure some kind of privacy, Lallan Singh organised a large colourful 'kanat' (a rectangular canvas wall) to surround our camp. Between the two mango trees we draped Tara's caparison, the Union Jack, which hung grandly like a war standard. Tables and chairs were produced and by the time the tents were erected and a fire lit, we could have been guests in some Maharaja's grand shikar camp, lacking only uniformed attendants, popping corks from champagne bottles and a floor covered in richly embroidered carpets.

To ensure good luck and a good sale, our landlord performed the 'Aarti', a special puja. He circled our camp holding a terracotta bowl in which a holy flare burned. Then, standing in front of Tara, he raised the flame to her like a toast-master, chanting a few solemn prayers.

Lallan Singh then sat down with us and explained mela etiquette. 'When your elephant is sold, everything on the back legs belongs to the seller, the chain, ropes etc. It is customary to give the buyer the gudda [the saddle], the girth ropes, the bell, and any other decoration on the elephant, like silk cords and tassels. It is most important that your elephant is never unattended at any time, during the day or night. Accidents can and have happened frequently at the mela and a loose elephant can cause terrible carnage amongst "five lakhs" of people. Be very careful,' he warned us, 'to keep your money hidden, as the mela will be full of thieves. When your deal takes place, it must be done quietly, out of the sight of prying eyes and, if possible, in the presence of a few members of your entourage. A showing of people,' he explained, 'means power and wealth,' as we were to discover when approached by the local zamindars, who never went anywhere without a large armed bodyguard.

E. O. Shebbeare gives an ingenious description of how he dealt with this situation, in his book *Soondar Mooni*:

> I have assumed a companion because to go elephant-buying alone is a miserable business. Two heads are better than one when deciding what to buy and how much to pay; they are very much better than one when it comes to justifying your purchases and their prices before a critical audience when you get them home. There is another, more practical reason for hunting in couples; a proverb even more apt than 'two heads', is the one about 'safety in numbers'. As any policeman in the India of those days could have told you, a *mela* attracted more than just buyers and sellers, pilgrims and merry-makers; it was a magnet for every 'bad hat' in northern India. The reason was simple: since cheques were not accepted, a buyer before a sale or a seller after one was an object which no serious evil-doer could afford to overlook. My own security measures were simple. There was then, and may be still, a

practice in India of cutting currency notes in half. If a large sum was to be sent by post, one half of each note was sent first and not until these had been acknowledged were the second halves dispatched. Before going to a *mela* all the money that would be required was drawn from the treasury in notes of high denominations – hundreds, five hundreds, and a thousand rupees each. Each was cut in two and each half put into a separate pack clipped together in their right order. The packs were then slipped into the corresponding pockets of a pair of linen belts which my companion and I wore round our waists next to the skin. This ensured that the prospective robbers would at least be put to the trouble of committing a double murder.

By now a few more elephants had arrived. In front of us was a large tusker. To our right, attended by two mahouts, stood an old female with two terrible wounds in her flanks oozing a greenish pus. The owner, an overly helpful man from Orissa, explained that she had received these injuries while working in his cement factory. He was here to sell or exchange her for another. Looking at the suffering of this friendly, docile elephant I vowed again that I would never let Tara be maltreated.

Behind us, carpenters and builders were busily erecting marquees, fenced in by impregnable bamboo enclosures. These were for the different sects of religious saddhus who would soon be arriving. Our little set-up was somewhat dwarfed by the opulence of these encampments, particularly the kitchen facilities. Huge cauldrons and stacks of tin platters were being unloaded and carried inside, in readiness for the great feast on Kartik Purnima, which would feed thousands of devotees.

Further down the Haathi Bazaar rich zamindars had been allocated the prime sites, where entire canvas villages had been set up, in front of which stood their richly caparisoned elephants. Behind, surrounded by armed chauffeurs, their cars were parked, highly polished vehicles with blacked out windows; so the arrival of Don and Indrajit in the minibus added a certain cachet to our humble enclosure.

Already our presence had caused a stir and groups of people had started to gather outside. It was easy to discern between those who were merely curious and the professionals. The curious, straining on tiptoes, peered over the 'kanat' to catch a glimpse of the firinghee mahout. The professionals, tough, bow-legged men with sun-blackened faces and shrewd eyes, sauntered casually past Tara inspecting her with a well-assumed air of indifference. They would stop to have a few words with Bhim, hoping to glean a few titbits of information on pedigree and price. They would then report back to their bosses. These momentary inspections would take place continuously over the next few days. Unlike the hustling West, where fast decisions are the name of the game, a hasty deal is considered undignified in the East, and a strict etiquette is adhered to.

Aditya and I were worried about Bhim. He was not his usual pragmatic, cheerful self. His spirit had left him and he wandered around lackadaisically. Worst of all, he seemed to have lost all interest in Tara. Perhaps it was due to exhaustion or to thinking that once he had reached the mela his duties would be less arduous and he would have time to enjoy the fun. In fact, we eventually realised, he was simply overawed. Used to the relative quietness and routine of a zoo, he had suddenly been thrown into the lions' den, the 'Newmarket' of the elephant world, where true professionalism counted and one's knowledge was put to the ultimate test and carefully scrutinised. He was out of his depth and had lost his confidence.

Tara, too, was affected. Whereas she should have been in her element, as carts drawn by white bullocks continuously replenished her larder, she stood listlessly, a look of total resignation on her face. I began to think this was all too familiar to her. She had been here before, I realised, and my heart stopped.

At Gau-Dhuli (the hour of the cow dust), that quiet magic moment just after sunset, when the sky shimmered gold between the branches of the mango trees through the dust thrown up by the elephants, a group of men entered our encampment. Their faces showed a certain relief as they spotted me. The spokesman stepped forward and formally introduced himself.

'Mr Shand,' he said, 'we are the proprietors of the Shoba Nautanki [the folk theatre]. Thanking goodnews we have found you in time. Would you do us the honour of inaugurating our first show tomorrow? Already we have sent out this gentleman in a jeep to find you' – he pointed to a man who looked both exhausted and exasperated – 'and he has been travelling for five days. You will enjoy the show. There are many girls. Our theatre,' he continued proudly, 'has the reputation of the most beautiful women. But first we would like you to garland the statue of our local freedom fighter and then we will proceed to the theatre. Our last guest of honour was a famous dacoit. Now it is appropriate that the first English mahout should open the show. We will collect you tomorrow afternoon.'

That evening, when the muddy water was turning crimson from the rays of the setting sun, we bathed Tara in the Gandak, approached from a steep muddy bank, down which she slid on her bottom, like a child on a toboggan. She then proceeded to queue-barge into the elephant-filled shallows, much to the annoyance of the other mahouts, who were waiting their turn patiently. It was dark by the time Tara had finished her ablutions. Beneath us, elephants lay motionless, like giant prehistoric boulders. Then, as if infused suddenly by some unseen force, they erupted out of the water and lumbered towards the bank. Under the stars, we joined a silent cavalcade of returning elephants, this silence only broken by the soft shuffle of their feet, the swish of their tails and the flapping of their ears. An old mahout, riding the lead tusker, broke into song, swelling louder and louder as others joined in, then echoing quietly away into the blackness of the Gandak running swiftly beside us. I was by now so much part of this ancient brotherhood that my other world seemed like a dream as I felt the coolness of Tara's back beneath me.

Indrajit had built a blazing fire against the chill of the November night. We huddled round it, drinking with the owner of a big tusker. He was a landowner, but unlike most of the other zamindars, he himself rode and looked after his elephants. He was an honest straightforward man whom I felt we could trust, with a vast knowledge and love of elephants that bordered on passion. His family had always kept elephants. He remembered, as a child, coming to the mela with his father and counting over a thousand. The bridge is always closed on the day of Kartik Purnima and he remembered the latecomers trying to swim across the river. Due to the strong current, they had been washed away, mahouts and elephants drowning.

He admitted quite openly that his tusker was dangerous and only he could control it. However, unlike almost all the owners in the mela, he did not use drugs to quieten his elephant. There were now over a hundred elephants here, but he told us that Tara was the best he had seen so far. To an expert, she was obviously naturally fed and of a good temperament. He was not surprised that we were thinking of asking two lakhs for her.

'Bide your time,' he advised us, 'for her that is not an exorbitant price' – adding that if we needed any assistance he would be glad to give it.

In the middle of the night I was woken by the fierce shouts of 'Mahout!! mahout!!' – and running outside our encampment I found Tara, her stakes uprooted, about to escape. Bhim, who was supposed to be on watch, was fast asleep in a pile of sugar cane at the side of the kanat. I shook and reprimanded him. He apologised sheepishly and promised it would not happen again. But it was too late, the incident had been noticed. An unattended elephant, as we had been told, is an unforgivable crime in the strict mahout law of the mela and we had, as it were, lost face.

18

Mela Madness

AWOKEN EARLY BY the urgent shouts of mahouts and the chanting of saddhus, I walked to the side of the kanat and peered over. Though relatively empty last night, it was now as if an army had moved in quietly during the night and surrounded our encampment. The orchard was alive with elephants, swaying, feeding and dusting, while mahouts, wrapped in blankets, squatted beside fires, watching them carefully over rims of little terracotta bowls containing their morning tea. Arcades of hastily constructed stalls, like mini-bazaars, had mysteriously sprung up, selling paan, spices, food, cheap jewellery, clothing and medicines.

Behind us, like flowers in a desert, huddled little groups of families. When the sun rose, the women stretched languidly, turning bejewelled arms, ankles and tips of noses and ears bright gold as the first rays filtered through the smoke-filled air. Elephants ridden proudly by young well-muscled mahouts, their teeth a brilliant white against the black of their faces, raced each other down to the river. Like picadors, holding an ankush in both hands behind their elephants' ears, they showed off their skills and their mounts to the best effect. To the casual observer it would seem like a game but it was, in fact, in deadly earnest. Prospective buyers would be watching carefully.

Lallan Singh arrived with an electrician who ran a cable up one of the trees in our camp to connect a large high-wattage bulb. At night it would effectively illuminate Tara and, we hoped, keep the boys awake. I watched shamefacedly, but Lallan Singh consoled me. Three other elephants, he told me, had escaped during the night. It was only a precaution.

Our first buyer offered 70,000 rupees for Tara. This man, a magnificent actor, almost brought tears to my eyes. He told me of the wonderful elephant he had owned for thirty years, which he only rented out on very auspicious occasions. Just last week, tragedy struck when he was away on business. He had instructed his mahout to take the elephant to one of these very special occasions. The mahout, a lazy man, did not carry out his orders and when he returned he gave the mahout a sound beating. A week later the mahout disappeared, not before he had poisoned the elephant, which had just died. I declined his offer.

After Tara returned from her bath, I went shopping. From one of the many stalls specialising in elephant decorations, I bought her a beautiful brass neck bell attached to a bright crimson silken cord. Anklets made of bells and strips of silken material to hang from ears and tusks were also available, but I wanted to keep her looking simple, elegant, like a beautiful woman at a ball, wearing a plain dress, unadorned, except for one astonishing piece of jewellery. She did not need decoration.

I employed a specialist in elephant painting. After drawing a line that sharply demarcated the blackness of her oiled crown from the natural grey of her skin, he created with simple coloured chalks of purple, yellow, white and blue, a series of flowers and lotuses on her ears, face and trunk. In the centre, between her eyes, he traced a dazzling star. Taking down the Union Jack, we draped it over Tara's shoulders and when prospective buyers approached, Bhim and Gokul would dramatically draw it back.

As Don and Aditya had disappeared earlier to take photographs, I set off through the Haathi Bazaar, leaving Tara with the boys. My nostrils were instantly filled with the evocative smells of India – spices, incense, the heavy scent of the tribal women, mixed with the more pungent odour of urine and excrement, and I found myself thinking I never wanted to leave. Passing down the elephant lines, mahouts and owners alike called me over – not out of curiosity but because I was part of them, an elephant man, inexorably entwined with their way of life. I sat cross-legged by little fires and shared bowls of tea and littis, small balls of hot dough roasted over the ashes. I inspected their elephants, checking their backs for tell-tale sores and scars, and chuckled disapprovingly when, opening their mouths, I found patches of black on their pink tongues.

Easily now, I mounted the elephants by way of their trunks and tusks. I sat caressing their ears, and barked commands to make them sit. I watched a big male having part of its tusk sawn off, for a legal sale of ivory. The mahout first carefully measured the distance from eye to lip. After marking a spot which avoided cutting into the nerve, he sawed through it quickly. In India ivory fetches about 5,000 rupees a kilo. Magically, the tusk will grow back, just like a finger nail.

At one encampment stood a huge tusker, excessive in its ornamentation. Richly caparisoned in red brocade, bells hung round its neck and feet, yellow and red silken scarves dangled from its ears and tusks and its tail was braided with silver tinsel. The beast swayed from side to side continuously, its piggy little eyes transfixing everyone who passed, with a stare of pure venom. An old mahout warned me to keep my distance. This was a dangerous elephant, he told me. In the last ten days it had killed three people.

I counted a hundred and ninety elephants; last year there had been more than three hundred and next year probably there would be even fewer. It is inevitable that this way of life will, in time, die out.

Leaving the Haathi Bazaar I moved on to the other animal markets. For the first time, the sheer size of the great mela struck me. At the horse lines I watched a small snow-white arab, its pink eyes heavily kohled to highlight their dullness, its tail dyed the colours of the rainbow, being put through its paces. The rider urged him along at a furious pace, then suddenly pulled him dead on his hocks, whirling him about to perform a kind of 'pas' or, in military terms, 'marking time'. The horses were even more elaborately decorated than the elephants. Some sported headbands worked in gold thread, others had their legs encircled with brass bangles. One wore a necklace of silver and gold, containing verses from the Koran. They came from Rajasthan, the Punjab, Afghanistan and even Australia, watched over carefully by their dealers, old men with faces creased like parchment paper, shrewd all-knowing eyes wrinkled against the glare of the sun.

Beyond the horses, stretching for almost two miles, were paddocks crowded with cows, bullocks and buffaloes. Finally, I reached the bull pens, known locally as the 'jewel market'. Apart from the elephants, the bulls fetch the highest prices.

Making my way back to Tara I entered the shopping centres, a maze of streets lined with booths, overshadowed by the giant Ferris wheel of the fun fair and the Big Top of the circus arena. A crowd surrounded a pair of chained, moth-eaten bears. Goaded by their keeper, they shuffled miserably from paw to paw in time to a disco song. For five rupees you could dance with them.

A discordant screeching announced the bird market. Hyacinthine blue macaws from South America sat quietly on their perches, their feathers ruffled, swivelling their heads suddenly, blinking their baleful eyes. Nepalese mynahs chuckled and laughed, and a cage of little rice birds, so gaudy in colour that the owner admitted they had been dyed, hopped nervously from side to side. Outside, a shiny black mynah loaded and fired a miniature cannon, and for ten rupees would play cards.

The inevitable snake-charmers squatted at the sides of the streets, playing their flutes tunelessly to serpents swaying from wicker baskets. One snake-charmer, more enterprising than the rest, advertised 'a fight to the death' between a mongoose and a cobra. I hoped he had an unending supply of cobras, for inevitably the mongoose would win. Or perhaps he waited until he had attracted a large enough crowd to make it worthwhile.

Jugglers ferried their way through the crowds performing with extraordinary skill considering all the pushing and shoving. As I pushed and shoved I noticed an exceptionally tall man with piercing eyes bearing down on me. I tried to move, but it was as if I was hypnotised. Dipping a long large finger in a small jar of vermilion, he stabbed it against my forehead and demanded five rupees. I christened him 'dot man' and over the next few days, whatever preventative measures I took, he always managed to get me. Once, seeing him approach I slipped behind Aditya as the great finger shot out like a sword. I thought I had escaped. Aditya, obviously a seasoned mela veteran, simply ducked and I received it on the end of my nose.

'Your teeth pulled for only 20 rupees. Get a new set. A new look.' Dentists did a roaring trade from padded chairs operating foot drills. Naive patients writhed in agony as the dentists dug into mouths with what looked like pairs of pliers. In intervals between the shops bold placards hung advertising eating houses, their cuisine varied to suit the tastes of every caste and creed. The smell reminded me of the observation of the old planter who wrote in his *Reminiscences of Behar*: 'I cannot say the dishes look tempting while the smell of bad ghee makes you wish you had put a little extra eau-de-Cologne on your handkerchief before you left your tent.'

Passing brassière shops and signs advertising 'Genuine Siamese Twins' I entered the Bombay Bazaar. The smell of bad ghee disappeared in a wave of perfume. Here was everything for the lady. Women, young and old, queued up at scent booths, in which men sat cross-legged behind a thousand different bottles. After twirling cotton-wool on to long silver sticks, they dipped them in and dabbed them on the backs of waiting hands. Glass-bangle sellers displayed their incandescent wares on long tall poles. They fought a losing battle to prevent their eager clients from shattering fragile merchandise as the women pulled and pushed them up and down their arms.

In large mirrors, the ladies coquettishly painted on different hues of cosmetics and lipstick and applied kohl to their eyes, while others tried on gold nose and ear ornaments. Baskets filled with brilliant hues of sindoor (the powder used to make the 'tikka') sat in rows of tiny coloured mountains and gorgeous bolts of gauze, silk and cotton to be made into saris, fluttered like butterfly wings as they were gently unfurled.

As I moved on, persistent salesmen pressed me to buy their products; brasswork from Benares, inlaid boxes and trays and miniature Taj Mahals from Agra, enamel objects from Jaipur, beautifully embroidered shawls from Kashmir, and in one rather modern shop a Hell's Angel's leather biker's jacket and a pair of co-respondent brogues.

The ingenuity of the beggars knew no bounds. Beside a man sitting near the temple lay upright in the dust what appeared to be a human head – and it was just that. He had buried his colleague up to the neck and rubbed his face with paste to give it the colour of a corpse. Another simply walked around naked from the waist down, with a large padlock clamped through the end of his penis. Yet another had buried himself head downwards to the waist and was managing to breathe through the open ends of two bamboo tubes that just broke the surface of the ground. Unfortunately, he had neglected to hire an assistant. Passersby liberally helped themselves to his begging bowl.

On the other side of the temple, I came across the Naga Saddhus, who are fiercely ascetic and protect their privacy zealously. Trained in all forms of fighting they are treated with great respect. Their naked bodies daubed in ash, their faces painted white and vermilion, they resent any intrusion from outsiders, and woe betide anyone stupid enough to try and photograph them. I managed a short conversation with one of them. As a penance, he had not sat down for six years and supported his stiffened and deformed legs by leaning on a kind of wooden swing. He was most indignant when I told him that an elephant belonging to King Louis XIV did not lie down for the last ten years of its life and had worn two holes in the stone buttress with its tusks, on which it supported itself. I beat a hasty retreat.

There were the usual abominable sights of the poor unfortunate cripples. One was more terrifying and heartrending than anything I had ever seen. It was a young boy – or rather what was left of a young boy – just a small torso supporting a head, twisted and contorted by some hideous disease. He was pushed around in a little cart. On it perched a parrot, which took your money in its beak.

As I re-entered the Haathi Bazaar, I witnessed two extraordinary fights. Both had been caused by theft, and both were not without humour. The first was a clash of titans between two female elephants, staked next to one another. One of the females had stolen the other's sugar cane. She turned quickly on the thief and instead of using her head as a battering ram, she tried in the most ludicrous fashion to bite off the other one's tail. They whirled around trumpeting and squealing in a cloud of dust, looking like squabbling schoolgirls pulling each other's hair. Three or four mahouts, armed with spears, waded in quickly and put an end to this farce.

The second fight was decidedly one-sided until an unusual intervention stopped it. A thief had been caught and was being punished in typical local fashion. His hands had been tied behind his back and his feet bound together. Two hefty men wielding long bamboo sticks proceeded to give him a sound beating on his head and the soles of his feet until he was a crying, bleeding wreck. The women, I noticed, particularly enjoyed this spectacle and joined in enthusiastically kicking the unfortunate man's ribs with sturdy feet, their toes encircled by gold rings, like knuckle-dusters. He would have been killed but for the sudden arrival of a tall, pale, sweating Englishman, a camera slung around his neck, wearing a floppy sun hat. I looked more closely. It was a friend of mine, a travel editor for a glossy London magazine. He waded bravely into the mêlée holding his hands above his head shouting 'Bas, bas,' the only word he knew in Hindi. When this had no effect, he clasped his hands fervently together as in prayer, fell to his knees and cried 'por favore, por favore!!' Immediately the beating stopped and the crowd became silent. He called the police, who took the bleeding man away.

There was great excitement in the camp when I returned. Tara's price had gone shooting up, from 70 to 90,000 rupees. This offer had come from a man, Aditya told me, who had a dishonest face and apparently owned a hotel in Delhi. The man had said his elephants were well looked after and simply took tourists for rides once a day. Unfortunately, one of them had been hit by a bus.

19

Swept Away

OUR PROCESSION INTO Sonepur town to garland the statue of the freedom fighter was most impressive. The grandees of the Shoba Theatre supplied us with a bodyguard and I felt terribly important. Forming a phalanx around us, they spearheaded a path through the gaping onlookers. Our entourage, however, did not quite match that of the Prime Minister of Nepal who arrived in Sonepur in 1871 with a bodyguard of three hundred Gurkhas and a harem of pretty, lively Nepalese princesses.

My self-importance now blown out of all proportion, I expected a tumultuous welcome to greet me. Instead, there was an infuriated, sweating policeman, trying vainly to control the traffic, roaring uncontrollably around the monument, and a madman juggling ludoos. One of the grandees placed a garland of marigolds in my hand. Self-consciously I climbed over the fence protecting the statue, looped the garland over the marble head, and feeling I should somehow justify this honour that had been bestowed upon me, bowed deeply. As I climbed out, the madman dropped his ludoos, grabbing me fiercely in a sticky embrace.

Again cocooned by our bodyguard, we soon reached a large building like a warehouse, constructed from wood and corrugated iron. Its front façade was painted gaudily with ladies cavorting in various stages of undress. Tannoys noisily advertised the delights of the show to an eagerly waiting crowd, pushing and shoving to get nearer an entrance controlled by four large policemen wielding large lead-topped bamboo canes with clinical efficiency.

'Welcome to the Shoba Theatre, Mr Shand,' the spokesman shouted. 'As you can see it is very popular. Come. We will go through the back.'

Inside it resembled an aircraft hangar. At one end, shrouded by a gauzy curtain, was the stage, the backdrop a grove of palm trees set against a starry night. Below, in the pit, fenced off by large iron palings, sat the orchestra tuning their instruments in a cacophony of discordant notes. Behind the pit were the best seats, costing 25 rupees, and separated from them by a triple-stranded barrier of barbed wire, was standing room only, at five rupees per person. The theatre put on three shows daily and could hold a crowd of eighteen thousand people.

We sat sipping tea and eating cakes in the wings. Aditya and I were introduced to the artistes – highly painted, plumpish ladies in sequinned outfits, their male partners squeezed into tightly fitting jumpsuits, brocaded like matadors' costumes. The building vibrated suddenly, as the gates were opened and a surge of people fought their way in.

Behind the curtain, a row of chairs had been placed beyond a large red ribbon. A barrage of arc lights hit us as we sat down. I felt inordinately self-conscious and nervous. Sweat began to trickle down my back. The star of the show, Miss Shoba, whose appearance caused a roar of excitement from the crowd, blessed and garlanded us. Long speeches followed. The Master of Ceremonies, wearing a smart, navy blue blazer with shiny gold buttons and white bell-bottomed trousers, introduced me as the famous English mahout and gave a lengthy account of my adventures. The crowd became instantly restless, longing for the show to start.

The band struck up, the gauzy curtains lifted and a pair of scissors were thrust into my hands. I stood up, sawed through the ribbon and stammered a few appropriate words, which Aditya then translated. Miss Shoba reappeared and led me off the stage to a small smattering of applause. I wanted to leave immediately to see Tara but Aditya insisted it would be impolite. We must stay to watch at least one act.

I'm glad we did. A seductive girl dressed in a black, transparent sari worked the crowd into a frenzy. The origins of the dancing girl go back to the Gandharva women, renowned for their beauty and skill in dancing and singing. In the old days when the fair was a meeting place for Rajas, zamindars, big agriculturists and businessmen, the girls made a good harvest. Fees of 500 or 1,000 rupees were a common feature for a few dances. On some of the more noted dancing girls, lakhs of rupees used to be spent for more personal services.

The seductress of the Shoba Theatre undulated across the stage, singing a ballad of obviously erotic content. She was singing about her lover, with whom she was in bed, complaining he would not make love to her. Aditya translated: 'Why do you not come to me, my darling? My breasts are young and firm.' There was a groan from the crowd behind us. 'My thighs are as soft as satin, my crop green and young, ready to be irrigated.' This brought the house down. Turning around I saw the barbed wire bulging outwards as the crowd pressed against it, frantic to reach her, followed by the whacks of the police sticks as they rained down on unprotected heads.

It was a relief to be back in the relative peace of the Haathi Bazaar. Smoke rose in eddies through the rich foliage of the mango orchard from the fires round which mahouts were huddled, their animated faces illuminated in the ruddy glow, as they traded tales and secrets of their ancient craft. To reach our camp we had to thread our way carefully across a carpet of sleeping people. Inside, feet and arms protruded from under the kanat.

Relieving Gokul, I took the next watch over Tara. She still was not her old self. There was something else, an uneasiness about her, which immediately transmitted itself to me. I felt that sick feeling in the pit of my stomach that precedes impending disaster. She seemed to be trying to communicate with me. When I started to feed her sugar cane, she suddenly grabbed my arm and held it firmly in her mouth. She pulled me even closer and we rested against one another, like lovers in a long embrace. Eventually, she released me and lay down.

All down the orchard, in night air hazy from the smoking fires, elephants lay sleeping. Disturbed by something, one would silently rise up like a monstrous spirit and then settle down again as it realised that all was well. Surrounded by six hundred tons of these huge animals, soothed by their snoring, like a ward of asthmatic old men, I felt for the first time a sense of vulnerability. I had never really given it a thought before, but as I looked back on the journey, I realised how much I had taken for granted. At any stage Tara could have killed me. Or any of us for that matter, as simply as swatting a fly. Now I understood that she had always been in control. My destiny had been in her hands. With that realisation, once again, she had taught me respect.

The day before Kartik Purnima, we took Tara down to the Gandak for her bath. We passed the saddhu encampment. Its entrance was guarded by two wild creatures carrying tridents. Inside the saddhus were busily preparing food, churning great vats of stew in readiness for the feast the next day. Among their dark skins, I noticed an old pale woman with long grey hair, dressed in a sari, sitting quietly in the back of the marquee. At first I thought she was an albino, but looking closer I saw she was a white woman, a firinghee, and I waved to her gaily. There was no response. She sat like a stone, staring blankly. Later I found out she was deaf, dumb and blind. Fifty years ago she had been accepted by this sect, which had looked after her ever since.

As we stood patiently in line with the other elephants, waiting for a space in the river, a fight broke out between a large tusker and a female bathing side by side. Throwing off the mahouts washing him, the tusker lumbered to his feet and charged the female who was being ridden by her mahout out of the water. His tusks, even blunted (as they have to be by law), gouged a great rip in her side. She toppled over, squealing, blood bursting from the wound, in the process crushing her mahout. The tusker charged again, enlarging the wound, then turned as if to run up the bank. Tara and the other elephants scattered in alarm. Immediately, mahouts rushed into the river. Surrounding the tusker, they stuck their spears viciously into its legs, flanks and trunk, forcing it back into the water where they managed to chain both its back and front legs. It was then led away. The poor female, badly gored, struggled to her feet, blood streaming down her flanks. From underneath the mahout emerged, miraculously unhurt.

Disturbed by the excitement, we had neglected to chain Tara's front feet together. As she entered the water she flipped me off and swam out about twenty yards. There she started to perform her dolphin act, plunging in and out before turning on her back to float for a few seconds, like an old lady in a swimming bath. Indrajit and I struck out towards Tara but we were unable to reach her. The current was far too strong and we struggled back to the bank. We watched helplessly as she was being swept away. Unless we could somehow cut her off, she might easily drown.

Bhim and Gokul rushed back to the camp. Immediately Aditya arranged a posse of mahouts led by a large, unpleasant individual with a scar running down his face. He demanded, before he did anything, a fee of 600 rupees. Everyone thought this an exorbitant sum but I would gladly have paid anything to get Tara back. Two boats were arranged. Splitting into two groups, we pushed the boats out of the shallows and were at once swept down by the current. Excited crowds ran up and down the river bank, desperate not to miss the action. We caught up with Tara a mile down the river, where she was struggling, whirling round and round in a strong eddy. I dived in, followed by two mahouts. In a second we were pushed back and just managed to catch hold of our boat. Panicking, Tara lurched towards the bank and somehow extracted herself from the current.

She sat blowing in the shallows. From the other boat, a mahout jumped into the water. Crooning gently, he approached cautiously and patted her backside to soothe her. Then he crawled up her back and sat astride her. She surged off again trying to throw him off, shaking her head and rolling. Like a champion rodeo rider, he managed to cling on, steering her to the bank.

He was the same man who had painted Tara. When I thanked him, he told me with a smile that 'the little one' was only playing and he would come later to decorate her again, since most of his handiwork had been washed off in the river. I rode her back to camp, followed by a phalanx of mahouts carrying raised spears. Feeling again that unpleasant coldness in the pit of my stomach, I was convinced that this time she was not playing. It was as if she had sensed some bad omen and had made a desperate attempt to escape.

20

Elephant Trading

AT LAST IT was Kartik Purnima. From three o'clock in the morning a continuous wave of people surged past, and sometimes through, our encampment, on their way to the bathing ghats. The eastern horizon started to show a hint of red. As the visibility increased I saw it would have been difficult to insert a stick between the solid mass of people stretching down from our camp.

I was deeply impressed by the orderliness of the proceedings. Again there was no jostling, pushing or shoving. When a child fell from its mother's arms – a frequent occurrence – the crowd instantly withdrew like a wave, opening a small gap from which it was plucked to safety. As the sun rose battalions of different sects of saddhus marched to the river, carrying their holiest men on flower-decked palanquins, heralding their arrival with the blowing of trumpets. The first elephants started to trundle down, and the crowd again parted magically to let them pass. Convinced that Tara wanted to escape, I waited until the crowds had thinned out before taking her for the ritual bath. While we waited, we were entertained by a troupe of transvestites, whose performance was brazenly suggestive. One was totally outrageous. Wearing a long black wig, and a gold-threaded tribal dress which when he pirouetted revealed his long black hairy legs, he winked and blew continuous kisses through thickly rouged lips that barely camouflaged his heavy moustache. Recognising a good portrait, Don photographed him. The transvestite took this zealous interest to be of the romantic kind, and each time Don left the camp he had to take evasive action to avoid his advances.

Just after midday, preparations for the cremation of an old woman took place at the side of the river. Her body lay on a bamboo pallet, cocooned in a simple white sheet, scattered with marigolds and rose petals. Her neck was wrapped in a blood red silk gumcha, her face in death, serene. As the sharp rays of the sun lanced downwards, illuminating her composed features, she almost seemed to smile. The pallet was then lifted and placed on a funeral pyre. Before 'the dom' (the undertaker) lit it, a young boy, her grandson, came forward and placed a single red rose in her gnarled, clasped hands. The fire ignited in a burst of yellow flame and a thick black plume spiralled slowly upwards, for a moment blacking out the orb of the sun. Gathering her ashes, the family spread them on the smooth, fast surface of the Gandak, transporting her to rest in the holy Ganges.

We bathed Tara in the mid-afternoon. The multitudes of people had largely dispersed by then, but space was still cramped. Elephants and devotees bathed side by side, in complete harmony amongst a floating carpet of droppings and rose petals. I felt weary and oddly depressed, and could not find the energy to scrub her. As she lay in the water, I stood by her head idly stroking her trunk. Perhaps it was because I realised that this was one of the last times that I would be bathing her, or perhaps it was because I knew that I had failed in my role as her protector. As I rode her up the bank towards the camp, under a tunnel of gently flapping saris in yellows, reds, saffrons, vermilions and greens, where the women had draped them in the trees to dry, not even the riot of colour could lift my gloom.

Kartik Purnima was the day when elephant trading began in earnest. Groups of powerful zamindars wearing 'Jawahar jackets' (coarse handwoven silk waistcoats) and dhotis were waiting to see me. Each one was surrounded by a posse of armed guards carrying ancient shotguns. Like Mexican bandits, they wore bandoliers filled with cartridges.

One of them offered a lakh, which he said was the highest price ever paid for a female elephant. He had just sold his elephant for 75,000 rupees, he informed us, and she was undoubtedly the best elephant of the fair. He promised that his elephants were only kept for prestige. After all he was a rich man. Why should he need to rent her out? Another zamindar offered one lakh, 5,000 rupees, and whispered urgently in Aditya's ear. It was a bribe – of any woman I desired, to be delivered anywhere, any time, at my convenience. They all left disconsolately. One group stopped at the next camp, to talk with the owner of the injured elephant. He listened to them and then nodded reassuringly in my direction.

'What's he up to?' I asked Aditya.

'He's managed to sell his elephant, somehow, for 40,000 rupees. He's already pestered me about selling Tara. He's acting as middle man for that zamindar on a commission basis. We will have to be careful. I don't trust him. I've asked our friend who owns the tusker to keep an eye on things. If we have any trouble, he will come over immediately.'

Further down the orchard, I watched a deal being negotiated in the traditional way. The prospective buyer and seller sat side by side, with a blanket covering their hands. The joints of the fingers represent different amounts of money. The buyer presses the first two joints of the first finger of the right hand which, for instance, represents 5,000 rupees. The vendor in reply squeezes the same, but also pinches the first joint of the purchaser's next finger, raising the price to say 5,500, and so on. A bargain was struck almost immediately. The two men got to their feet smiling, and clasped their hands together. The beauty of this lies in its secrecy and simplicity. The vendor may sell well below what he had asked, but no one but the purchaser would know.

Later, Aditya drove Don into Patna as he was leaving for Delhi, and then for London the next day. Suddenly I was alone. The mela seemed to close in on me, and feeling adrift on this sea of alienness I crawled into the haven of my tent. I was sitting quietly when, a few moments later, Indrajit, looking anxious, poked his head around the flap. I noticed he was carrying a spear.

'Come quickly,' he said, 'people make trouble with Tara. Bring ankush.'

I hurried outside. Surrounding Tara, Bhim and Gokul was a large group of unruly ruffians led by the scar-faced man who had organised Tara's rescue. One ruffian was carrying a knife. I noticed him edging slowly around her hindquarters towards the rope that tethered her back legs. Scarface stared at me insolently and pointed to Tara, then back to himself, as if announcing he was taking her. I realised they must have been employed by one of the zamindars. They had bided their time until Aditya, whose presence gave us some kind of authority, had left the mela, leaving me virtually defenceless, unable to speak the language.

Heavily outnumbered, I looked towards the camp of our friend who owned the tusker and was alarmed to see he was not there. Bluff seemed the only alternative. I was about to try to charm Scarface when, suddenly, a vicious, uncontrolled anger exploded inside me. I didn't care any more. I had had enough. The pressure had become too great. I lunged at him with the ankush, knocking him backwards.

'Listen, you shithead!!' I hissed. 'Nobody takes my elephant. Not even over my dead body. If I catch you near her again I'll kill you.'

He had no idea what I was saying, but understood the intonation. I must have looked like one of the Naga saddhus – naked apart from a lunghi, my hair knotted and wild and my mouth drawn back in a rictus of hate. We stared at each other for a moment, eyeball to eyeball. With a forced laugh, trying to save face in front of his cronies, he turned and walked away. He stopped suddenly and shouted something at me.

'What did he say?' I asked Indrajit, shaking with emotion.

'Fat man warn you. He come back later.'

It was midnight before I heard the sound of the minibus. I pulled Aditya into the tent.

'You know what happened while you were away?' I said through clenched teeth. 'We got threatened by those bastards. They said they're coming back later. We'll have to go to the police.'

'We'll go first thing in the morning,' Aditya said. 'But now get some sleep.'

At first I couldn't. I sat at the entrance of our tent. Above the kanat Tara's trunk reached up and over, and she stared at me with sad eyes.

The police station was in the English Bazaar. Aditya had an introduction to the Superintendent of Police who, surprisingly, turned out to be a woman. To my knowledge, only three women in India hold this exalted position. As we approached the police lines, situated opposite the pig market, I was still in a deep rage. I imagined myself dealing with a masculine, humourless, domineering lady, characteristics with which I, as an Englishman, was only too familiar in the highest echelons of our government. We walked up a red gravel path bordered by a sweeping lawn that was surrounded by neat flower beds. It was like entering another world. Gone was the stink, the noise and the confusion of the mela, as we entered an opulent canvas oasis. Smart candy-striped marquees were pitched neatly, their sides draped in floating mosquito nets. Butterflies and birds played in the trees, and the air was filled with the sound of droning bees.

We were ushered into the coolness of the largest tent by a smart sergeant wearing highly polished brown boots. The floor was covered in clean white linen and I winced as I left a trail of dirty footprints. We sat down on a luxurious velour sofa. In minutes, we had been served hot coffee from a silver pot and I helped myself to a cigarette from the box on the polished teak table.

'Mem-sahib will be with you shortly,' the sergeant announced, saluting smartly.

As I gazed out into the garden I began to feel strangely at home. Up until Partition this whole area was known as the English Bazaar. I found myself torn between two worlds – the real India of the mela – and here, where my western upbringing reasserted itself. When the Superintendent of Police arrived I found myself automatically adopting the manners of a guest at an English country weekend, leaping to my feet politely. I couldn't have failed to do so anyway, for she was quite unlike any other police officer I had ever encountered.

'I am so sorry I have kept you waiting. I am Kumud Choudhury. Please sit down.' She held out her hand, shaking a thick mane of freshly washed hair. 'This bloody dust gets everywhere,' she complained, 'I have to wash my hair at least twice a day. How on earth are you surviving? If you need to take a bath, feel free to come here.'

Aditya explained the situation. She rang a bell. Immediately two officers appeared and saluted. With a quiet authority, she ordered them to take us back to the Haathi Bazaar and deal with the problem. She even offered us a policeman to guard our camp, adding that, if she had time, she would love to come and see Tara.

'I'm sorry about your floor,' I said as I got into her green Suzuki jeep, which flew a smart stiff pennant.

'Don't worry about that,' she replied, laughing. 'A fresh one is laid down every day. But are you sure you would not like a bath? Apart from your accent, I cannot tell whether you are Indian or a foreigner.'

'That's my problem,' I replied. Thanking her, we drove off.

21

God's Will

IN FORMER YEARS, the Sonepur Mela was the occasion for a large sporting and social gathering of Europeans. Where we were driving now, horse racing, polo, gymkhanas, cricket matches and lavish balls had taken place in the past.

We slowed down as we passed the encampments, so that the zamindars could clearly see that we were now under protection of the Superintendent of Police. As I breathed in the evocative smells of the elephant camps, the reality of the situation bore in on me once again and I found my emotions being torn one way and then the other. Inside our tent I asked Aditya, helplessly, 'What do we do now?'

'I'm afraid you're going to have to sell, Mark,' he said quietly, 'and you'll have to find a buyer here.'

'NO!' I shouted. 'I just can't sell her ...'

'You have no alternative. What are you going to do with her? Take her to England? The wheeling and dealing here is nearly over. Due to the poor quality of elephants, only a few have been sold. When I was driving back last night, elephants were already moving out of the mela. Please be reasonable. I know I am being brutal, but she is, after all, only an elephant.'

'She is more than that,' I yelled angrily. 'How can you say that after all we've been through together?'

'You have completed an extraordinary journey, Mark. You have become a mahout. The boys feel you are one of them, and consider you a brother. But your western side is now showing. You're too emotional. India is a hard place. Here, people have to survive. Life has to go on. If you can't face it, let me deal with it.'

I couldn't face it. Sitting in the tent in despair, I could hear the commotion outside as the zamindars bid furiously against one another. They had returned in force. I covered my ears. I did not want to know, and as the dread and panic churned my stomach, I almost vomited. I pulled down the flap of the tent, blotting out the colour of the crowds, and Tara herself. A wind had blown up, pushing dust into every nook and crevice of the tent. I sat despondently and found myself writing her name in the dust on my pillow.

Aditya poked his head into the tent. 'The best price we are going to get is one lakh, 15,000 rupees,' he said wearily. 'The prospective buyer has given me his word that he only wants Tara for prestige and good fortune. She will not even be used at weddings. He's given me his address and you will be free to visit her at any time.'

'Just hang on a little longer,' I implored, trying to buy non-existent time. He shrugged and left the tent. Praying for a reprieve, I thought I was dreaming the very English voice calling my name. I clambered out and stood bewildered in the middle of the encampment before two English women who were old friends of mine. We stared at each other in astonishment.

'Anne! Belinda!' I shouted. 'What on earth are you doing here?'

'I might ask you the same question, Mark,' Anne replied, looking in amazement at my appearance. 'We've come to buy an elephant – what else? Bob wants one.' (Bob is Anne's husband, Belinda their daughter.)

'Why does he want an elephant? What about the golf course?' I pictured Tara straying on to those immaculate greens and rampaging up and down the fairways. 'And what about your horses? They'll go berserk.'

'No, no, no,' she replied in exasperation. 'Not for the Tolleygunge Club. For Kipling – our jungle camp in the buffer zone of Kanha National Park in Madhya Pradesh. Bob wants an elephant to take the guests for rides.'

'Bob wants an elephant,' I repeated parrot-fashion.

'Are you all right, Mark?' Anne said, looking at me oddly. 'You haven't gone deaf or something? Yes, an elephant.'

'Well,' I heard myself saying, in a distant echo, 'I've got an elephant. You can have her. I'll give her to you. She's the best elephant here, or anywhere for that matter.'

'You've got an elephant!? I can't believe it. What on earth are you doing with an elephant?'

I told her briefly of our journey. 'Go and see for yourselves. She's a princess.' A crowd of zamindars was still gathered around Tara, inspecting her carefully. 'Tara,' I said. 'Bowl, bowl.'

As if she sensed my happiness, her little brown eyes lit up and she blew a long, shrill trumpet. I hugged her fiercely and she wrapped her trunk tightly around me.

Anne and Belinda took no more than five minutes to make up their minds.

'She's beautiful,' Anne kept repeating. 'She's so pretty, and she's got such lovely kind eyes. Are you sure, Mark? I mean, this is not exactly an ordinary present. Of course we will always regard her as yours.'

'Absolutely convinced,' I replied. 'She'll be so happy with you and thoroughly spoiled. You have no idea how extraordinary this is. I can't begin to tell you how relieved I am.'

The zamindars, altogether confused on hearing that Tara was no longer for sale, became highly aggressive, and Aditya had to call the police again.

'I think you should take her as soon as possible,' Aditya advised. 'I'll arrange another truck and we'll find you a new mahout. Unfortunately Bhim has to return to his job in Bhubaneshwar.'

An elephant mela is full of mahouts looking for jobs, but first we asked Gokul. He thought it over but declined. It was too big a move for him and he had to think of his family. The man who owned the tusker offered his assistance and introduced four candidates. By now I could spot a mahout immediately, by his carriage, straight-backed and proud and by his build; sinewy, slight and bow-legged. However, picking a good mahout is an instinct inbred, a knowledge only gained or handed down from a lifetime of experience. I turned to Bhim.

'Mahouts ride,' he said. 'Mummy choose.'

Each one, in turn, rode Tara, their styles and commands differing, yet all clearly experts.

'Well?' I said.

'Him,' Bhim replied, unhesitatingly, pointing to a middle-aged man with gentle eyes, a Muslim called Mujeem.

'Why him?' I was fascinated. We all were.

'When mahout finish ride, Mummy kiss. Others Mummy not kiss. Also Mussalman,' he added with a grin. 'Not drinking like Bhim.'

Everything was arranged. A truck would arrive early next morning and Indrajit volunteered to accompany Tara to Kipling. Aditya and I would go down there in a couple of days' time to meet up with Bob. I said goodbye to Anne and Belinda who had to return to Calcutta.

'How can we ever thank you enough,' Anne said. 'Bob will be so thrilled.'

'I should thank you. I now know that she will be in good hands – with friends. Look at her,' I said happily, 'it's as if she already knows.' Tara was stamping her feet impatiently, ordering Bhim with urgent signals of her trunk, to bring her some more sugar cane.

'Well! How about that!' I exclaimed to Aditya excitedly. 'What luck! Let's get really drunk!'

Exhausted from the pressures of high level negotiation, we sat around a small fire reflecting on the day.

'Right, Aditya. I'm going to teach you the famous drinking song from the time when we ran the Sonepur Mela.'

Aditya sighed wearily. 'Oh God. Not another childish English ...'

'No, you idiot,' I interrupted. 'This was written by Mr Hodgson, a very handsome man, who by the way, ran off with the wife of an Indian Army Officer. He also made Hodgson's Beer, known in the English Bazaar as "rare good stingo".' Raising my voice in military style I sang:

Who has not tasted of Hodgson's pale beer
With its flavour the finest hops ever gave?
It drives away sadness – it vanishes fear
And imparts a glad feeling of joy to the grave.

O to drink it at morning, when just from our bed
We rise unrefreshed, and to breakfast sit down,
The froth crested brimmer we raise to our head
And in swigging off Hodgson, our sorrows we drown.

Or to drink it at tiffin when thirsty and warm,
We say to the khidmutgar 'bring me some beer',
Soon, soon do we feel its most magical charm,
And quickly the eatables all disappear.

Or at ev'ning when, home from our ride we return,
And jaded and weary we sit down to dine,
We ask but for Hodgson and willingly spurn
The choicest – the dearest – the rarest of wine.

Then hail to thee, Hodgson! of brewers the head,
Thy loss we in India would sadly bewail;
May you live long and happy and when you are dead,
I will think of you daily whilst drinking your ale.

Raising his empty glass for a refill, Aditya roared in lusty Maratha fashion, 'Then hail to thee, Hodgson! of ...' when with a crack like a pistol-shot, the chair on which he was sitting collapsed. In the process of trying to break his fall, Aditya buried his arm in the red hot embers of the fire. He was wearing a long-sleeved nylon shirt which promptly burst into flames. For a moment, Indrajit and I were too stunned to do anything. Then we leapt forward to pull him free. As gently as possible, we patted out the still smouldering shirt. The air was filled with the smell of burning flesh, and something glistened white in the charred skin. It was bone.

'I seem to have burnt myself,' Aditya said, gazing at the hideous wound in fascination. Being obsessed with medical matters, I knew that if the wound was not covered immediately, infection would set in quickly, particularly here in the filth of the mela. Aditya could lose his arm.

Indrajit and I bundled him into the bus and drove like lunatics to Hajipur, where we found a hospital. In the emergency room an overworked doctor was dealing with the victims of a bad car accident. The floor was awash with blood. A man lay with a leg half amputated. Another man was sitting quietly, smiling strangely, his glistening eyeball hanging by a thread against his cheek-bone. Shards of sharp glass were embedded in his head, like arrows.

The doctor took a quick look at the burn and gave me some dressings. 'Put these on and go immediately to the main hospital in Patna. I am sorry. I cannot dress the wound myself, sir. As you can see I am most busy.'

With amateurish clumsiness I bound up Aditya's burn. Not once did he complain or show any sign of pain. He was extraordinarily brave. If it had been me, I would have been screaming, demanding a helicopter to fly me out. In Patna, the wound was cleaned and dressed properly and he was pumped full of morphine. They wanted to keep him in, but he insisted on leaving. At five o'clock in the morning, we reached the camp, where he collapsed.

The sunrise turned the Gandak into a smooth carpet of gold as Bhim and I took Tara down for her last bath. The journey was over. Today we would go our separate ways. As I scrubbed Tara, Bhim sat on her neck, rubbing her head, talking to her quietly. Tara's trunk lifted up to touch his wise old face. I realised he was saying goodbye so I waded back to the bank, to leave them together. As he rode her towards me, they were silhouetted against the huge rising sun. The sharp rays reflected off the droplets of water on Tara's skin, and she could have been wearing a cape of pearls.

I held out a lump of gur. Her manners now impeccable, she stretched out her trunk, plucked the gur delicately from my hand, rolled it into a more suitable shape and popped it into her mouth. She then rumbled softly to say 'thank you'.

'You see Raja-sahib, Mummy no longer beggar. Now royal princess.'

We struck camp, rolled up the tents and packed up our belongings. Bhim formally presented me with the ankush, an object I had once so hated. Now its smooth cold surface was as familiar as my own hands. In a few days, I thought sadly, I would have to hand it over to the new mahout.

The truck arrived. There was now only one last obstacle to overcome – getting Tara on to it. Bhim climbed on top of her for the last time. Whispering encouragement into her ear, he moved her slowly forwards. She put one foot inside, checked the wooden structure carefully with her trunk. Then, with a suspicious squeal, she backed out hurriedly, her head held low. A phalanx of mahouts carrying spears rushed at her from behind, jabbing her in her backside and legs. She whirled round trumpeting in rage, flaying the mahouts with her trunk. They fell back. She then rapped her trunk hard on the ground and stood defiantly, her sides heaving, blood dripping down her legs. I could hardly bear to watch her pain, even though I was determined she would get on this vehicle which would carry her to a happy new life.

'Wait! wait!' Bhim shouted suddenly to the mahouts. 'If Mummy see, not go. Maybe go backwards.'

With strong feet movements against her neck Bhim urged her backwards into the truck. Cautiously Tara planted one back leg inside, then the other. She was now half in and half out.

'Now,' Bhim shouted, 'come with spears.'

A solid wall of sharp points rushed towards her. Squealing in terror she reversed hurriedly into the truck and the big steel-lined doors were slammed behind her.

Encased in this foreign wooden prison, Tara went berserk stamping her feet, swaying from side to side. Her trunk curled around the top edges of the open box, as if trying to pull herself up. The truck lurched alarmingly and, in her fear, a continuous gush of urine and runny excrement poured through the floor-boards. The mahouts clambered up the sides of the truck. Using their ropes like lassoes they trussed her tightly. Bhim and I climbed up and peered inside. Tara's eyes rolled in terror and she squealed, reaching out desperately to us with her trunk.

There was one last rope to tie, the most dangerous, the one that would secure her back legs. From the top of the truck Bhim shouted down to Gokul who was standing on the ground looking miserable.

'You go my son. Mummy not hurt you. Then you proper mahout.' It was his final test for the young man – Bhim's last lesson. Gokul lithely clambered up the side of the truck and dropped in beside her. Rubbing her ears to soothe her, he moved quickly underneath her legs. Tara became still, obediently lifting one leg and then the other, to step into the open nooses. Bhim bent forward and kissed her once on her forehead. As he climbed down, tears were streaming down his face.

The taxi arrived to take Bhim and Gokul to the station. I embraced them both tightly and thanked them. I couldn't face a prolonged farewell. I had become so close to them. Now they would disappear from my life for ever. Bhim saluted smartly. As he got into the car, he wound down the window.

'Bhim happy now. Mummy go good place. But remember Raja-sahib, Mummy miss you. Haathi do forget. See her by six months. Not forget,' he called as the car drove away.

When the truck moved slowly through the Haathi Bazaar, all the mahouts scrambled to their feet, clasping their hands together and shouting – 'Go safely, little one. Our blessings are with you.'

As we reached the road leading to the bridge, a police escort was waiting – a last kind gesture from the Superintendent. The truck joined the queue of vehicles inching down the road. Tara lifted her trunk and let out one last shrill trumpet, but the sound was drowned by the roar of the traffic.

Epilogue

ADITYA AND I flew to Delhi. Three days later we left for Kipling Camp. I tried to dissuade Aditya from coming. His burn was giving him great pain, his usually sun-blackened face had turned pale and was covered in a permanent sheen of sweat. But he insisted on accompanying me, to see that Tara was happy.

Kipling Camp nestled in a grove of trees, rows of little white-washed bungalows, surrounded by luxuriant forest, where Tara could gather her fodder. Near by, a clean river flowed, spilling into deep rock pools. Tara could not have found a better home. It was wonderfully peaceful. Bob was there to greet us, a kind man, his gentleness camouflaged by a brusque manner. He was enthralled by Tara, and had already made plans to build her a proper stone stable, and quarters for Mujeem.

Indrajit and Aditya left the next day. I would see Aditya again in Delhi, but Indrajit was going back to Bhubaneshwar. We shook hands formally. Indrajit's fierce eyes softened for a moment and I realised how fond I had become of this loyal man, as he told me of how the journey had changed his life: of how much he had learned and benefited. I would never forget him.

I spent two idyllic days with Tara. Everybody left us alone, respectful of my feelings. She was still a little shaky, not quite her old self, affected by the long truck ride. Her neck was a mass of sores and abrasions where the ropes had cut into her. We explored her new territory together – going for long rides in the quiet forest – wallowing and playing in the rock pools. In the afternoons, she would stretch out in the lengthening shadows and I would lie on top of her and write my diary. In the evenings I would watch her feeding on a new delicacy prepared by Mujeem – large doughy chapatees, as big as serving dishes, which she would chew slowly, her eyes squeezed tight, in total bliss.

On the evening of my last night, my stomach started to churn with the dread of having to say goodbye. I needed something to numb my feelings. I needed to get drunk and leave with a hangover. Bob kindly gave me a bottle of whisky and after dinner I joined her.

Tara was already lying down. I settled comfortably between her legs, my head propped up on her stomach. However, she wasn't going to let me drink alone. As we shared the whisky, I told her of my home, the land that I lived in and why she would not be happy there. In reply, she occasionally rumbled. Before I passed out I vaguely remembered feeling something long and warm encircle my neck and draw me closer.

I awoke with a start in the early hours. The mist was heavy on the ground. Something was poking me urgently on my backside. I rolled over, my head throbbing. She was standing over me, looking disapproving, signalling towards a pile of sugar cane. I fed her for the last time.

As the car was taking me out of the camp later that morning, I asked the driver to stop. I walked slowly towards Tara, my mind detached, floating. Holding her tail, I clipped off three long springy hairs, the only memento I would take with me. It was then that Tara gave me my last lesson: elephants do weep. When I kissed her on her eye, one hot salty tear fell, staining my cheek. I walked quickly back to the car. We moved slowly away. I forced myself to look stonily ahead. But, as we rounded the corner, I turned and caught one last glimpse of her standing quietly, looking at me. Then she was gone, swallowed up in India's dust.

Afterword

'WITH ONE HIND leg crossed over the other she was leaning nonchalantly against a tree, the charms of her perfectly rounded posterior in full view, like a prostitute on a street corner. I knew then that I had to have her. Suddenly, nothing else mattered and I realised with some surprise that I had fallen in love with a female Asian elephant.'

Twenty-five years have passed since this meeting with an elephant whom I called Tara. It was a meeting that was to change my life – a life which, although filled with adventure and fun, had been going nowhere. Through Tara, I found a real purpose, more than that – a passion. For the last 10 years I've been heading up one of the most successful elephant conservation charities in the world, and if it hadn't been for my love affair with Tara, God knows where I'd be.

* * *

But how did it happen? How did a posh, privileged, fat, little boy with a fiendish temper end up one steamy, Indian monsoon night, deep in the jungles of Orissa, buying an elephant? It was a circuitous 35-year route, detouring through the respectable and the disreputable, the fast, the furious and the far reaches of adventurousness.

A love of animals developed early on. Spending my childhood holidays in the English countryside, often with an old gamekeeper, I developed my natural affinity with, and love of, nature and the indigenous wildlife. And at the same time, during lengthy shopping trips to Harrods, I would give my mother the slip and escape into the pet department, a deafening and exotic emporium that smelled of hay, birdseed and fur. I spent some of my happiest times there, wandering through the bewildering and magical labyrinth of cages that squawked, squealed, chirped, grunted, roared, growled and dazzled with myriad exotic species that conjured up for me the mysteries of far-flung lands. It was here that I bought 'Charlie', much to my mother's horror – a glossy mynah bird that woke me up every morning saying 'I love you' in a broad Irish accent. It was here, to my mother's even greater horror, that I took possession of 'Tiki', my cunning and swift Indian mongoose which nearly gave an elderly lady a heart attack in an Italian restaurant by climbing up her stockinged leg, on to her lap and on to the table, to help her open the clams of her *spaghetti alla vongole.* And it was here, perhaps, that a passion to discover the mysteries of those distant places was awakened in my child's mind.

Expelled from public school at the height of the swinging sixties for smoking dope, and excelling only in History of Art, I was sent by my father, who thought it 'might put some spine in the little bugger', to Australia. I spent a year down under, working on sheep and cattle stations, and as a guard on an Opal mine in Cooper Pedy, bang in the desolate and blistering heat of central Australia. I travelled round the country with two friends in an old car and even made some money by investing in the booming mining market. But, I could have made more. I still kick myself at the wasted opportunities, but considering my character, I can well understand my father's hesitation in sending more money. In those days, I was offered beach-front property, for a dollar a mile, in Northern Queensland. It is now the Gold Coast.

But it was India, where I stopped on the way to Australia, that awoke a passion and love that has and will remain with me for the rest of my life. I was supposed to stay a few days. I stayed a month. I don't know what it was, but I believe you can fall in love with a country with the same passion that you can fall in love with a person or, in my case, an elephant. I felt immediately at home. I had lived there in another life, at another time. It was that smell – the smell of incense, cow-dung, smoke, shit, sweat, burning fires, Chamoli and Champa blossoms, sandalwood, disinfectant, frying curry leaves, chilli, chai and moth balls. It is a fragrance so heady that I've always thought if a great parfumier could bottle it, the scent would be the most intoxicating in the world.

Returning to the West, after a number of false starts in business I founded Obsidian in London with a friend, Harry Fane, selling objets d'art and jewellery by the great jewellers of the Art Deco period, such as Cartier, Van Cleef and Arpels and Boucheron. It was perfect for me, combining travel and art. We were both good salesmen, and Harry took care of the finances, which were not my strong suit. Like posh swagmen in linen suits, with sacks of beautiful booty over our shoulders, we hit the rich and famous, the old and new wealth in the money-drenched capitals of the Americas: Caracas, New York, Dallas, Houston, Los Angeles, Palm Beach and Miami. In the mid '70s, New York became the party capital of the world with the advent of the infamous nightclub, Studio 54. It was hedonistic, decadent, glamorous and fuelled by the drug of the moment – cocaine. Although this period remains a complete haze I made many good friends.

Every year, to escape the partying, socialising and selling, Harry and I set off for the magical island of Bali for two months. There, a friend designed and built us a beautiful Robinson Crusoe house on a surfer's beach. We lived a bohemian life, chilled-out and very anti-social. We had a sign on the door to the property - *'If you are a friend of a friend fuck off'*. This didn't endear us to the growing expat community, but it was an effective deterrent against 'friends of friends' who thought it was perfectly normal to come and visit us or, even worse, stay.

I had a boat, a 20ft local *prahu*, a kind of outrigger used for transporting horses and cows between Bali, Lombok and Borneo. I named it the *Gin Pahit,* an Anglo-Malay term for 'gin and bitters'. We made many fantastic journeys through the pristine islands of the beautiful Indonesian archipelago. If anything, these trips to Bali and the Far East just increased my passion to seek adventure and travel. The moment we became successful and opened an office in Jermyn Street, and I found myself in a suit going to work every day, I quit. I felt bad about leaving Harry. But I think he understood, and he went on to make a major success of the business.

My experience on the *Gin Pahit* inspired me to think of sailing round the world. Financing the trip was not going to be easy. Sailing can be one of the most expensive occupations, likened to tearing up ten pound notes while standing under a shower. But perhaps I could follow in the footsteps, of rather the wake, of my intrepid ancestor Admiral of the Fleet Sir Henry Keppel, and write a bestselling book? My maternal grandmother, who was immensely proud of her sailing ancestors and had written a book about them herself, might act as a secret weapon in helping me persuade my parents to release the last funds I possessed in the world. As soon as I'd secured the minimum necessary, I set off for Thailand to stay with friends, find a boat and plan my journey.

An amazing tale, told to me in the early hours of the morning in a bar in Bangkok, gave me the bestselling angle I'd been looking for. I should have remembered never to believe a story told under the influence of too much drink. Apparently, during the Second World War, a very young Catalina flying-boat captain used to fly regular missions from Sydney to Bougainville on Papua New

Guinea, to supply the allies against the invading Japanese. His flight path took him over a beautiful island called Rennell, with a large volcanic cobalt blue lake at its centre. As he swept low over the lake, he saw hundreds of canoes, paddled by beautiful, topless girls with flowers in their long oiled hair. They would wave at him longingly and blow him kisses. He would wave back longingly and return the kisses. It all became too much for him. He landed the flying boat on the lake, sunk it and entered paradise. My friend paused for a moment, took a long gulp of beer, before uttering the words that would seal my fate. 'Apparently,' he said 'He is still there. He has many wives and many children. His name is Sexy Tyler.' How could I resist? I was going to sail to Rennell, find this elusive character living in paradise and write his story.

I bought a boat, found a more experienced sailing companion, Tim, and eventually we set off from Fiji. Although it was the hurricane season, I was determined to haul anchor. We'd lost too much time restoring the 28-foot, eight-ton, twin-keeled yacht and I was terrified that Sexy Tyler would die before I arrived. But we never made it to Rennell.

It was sunrise on a glorious Friday morning as we motored quietly out of the lagoon into the vast Pacific Ocean and headed due west to our first port of call, the New Hebrides, or as they are known now, Vanuatu.

In our rush to get going I had forgotten to buy a sextant, but Tim did not seem concerned. 'Don't worry,' he reassured me. 'I'll navigate by dead reckoning. Vanuatu is due west. We'll follow the sun. I know a bit about astrology. I'll set the course on auto pilot.' I gulped. 'Dead reckoning'. I didn't like the sound of this.

I was right to be concerned. We nearly died on that first passage. It usually takes a maximum of four days to reach the New Hebrides from Fiji. You really can't miss these islands. There are around twenty in the archipelago and the majority are very large. Somehow it took us fourteen days. We ran out of food and more importantly water. We were forced to drink distilled seawater. I had also run out of cigarettes. In desperation, I started cutting up rope and rolling it in newspaper to smoke. And it was here that my love-hate relationship with sharks intensified.

I've always admired them, but facing starvation I also came to hate them. I'd sit with my legs hanging over the stern, holding a long line stretching out about a hundred metres or so into the wake. Fish were abundant in those days and every few minutes I'd feel a tug and pull the line in as quickly as possible. As I reeled in, there would be another tug, a more violent one and the line went limp. The sharks had taken not only the fish, but the lure and the hook as well.

We eventually made land at Port Vila, the capital of Vanuatu on the island of Efate. I remember cheers of derision from the locals in the port bar as we limped in, and they toasted us with ice-cold Fosters. I could taste the drops of condensation on the tins as I looked at them. Never had a cold beer tasted so good. As we took our first long gulps an earthquake hit the island. Clutching our tins of beer, we ran out as the bar disintegrated around us. An ominous sign, perhaps?

We re-victualled, cleaned up the boat and headed north-west to the capital of the Soloman Islands, Honaira. We anchored about half a mile offshore, opposite the yacht club. We heard that a hurricane was approaching, put down storm anchors and waited nervously. Then news came that the hurricane would miss Honiara, but that we should expect strong winds. Tim decided it would be better to head for open sea, rather than be near land. I was not convinced, but respected my captain's experience. I went to start the engine. It would not start. It had totally seized up. If the hurricane was to hit us we were sitting ducks. It was April Fool's Day – April 1st 1982.

Hurricanes are fickle, and this one turned round and hit us at full force. Everything happened so fast. Wind speeds soared to 60 knots onshore. This is why Tim had tried to get out into the open sea. Yachts are designed, when hit sideways, to roll 360 degrees, to capsize and right themselves again. You lose your masts and most of your deck structure, but you can survive. If you're hit head on, the boat will pitchpole – flip backwards and break in half. The waves were now seven metres, crashing over the stern and sweeping onto the deck. The boat was like a bucking bronco – one moment sitting on her stern, the next burying her prow in the waves.

Tim and I were being hurled around in the main cabin, trying to grab anything to hold on to. Then the galley stove came off its hinges and hit Tim on the side of his head, opening a deep wound. I decided we had to get off, otherwise we were dead. I managed to tie Tim to one of the 20 litre plastic jerry cans used for storing water and I literally flung him overboard. I quickly followed. I don't remember anything else. The next thing I knew, strong hands were pulling me out of the massive pounding surf. We found ourselves huddled in the yacht club holding cups of hot tea. We were both cut to pieces, lacerated by the coral while being swept ashore.

I will never forget those wonderful people. They saved our lives. One of them was a doctor who stitched up Tim's head and did his best to patch us up. They told me to sleep. I couldn't. I burst into tears and cried all night as

I watched my beloved boat fighting for her life, illuminated by the headlights of the many vehicles lining the shore. Winds had now hit 80-85 knots (about a hundred miles an hour). Palm trees were uprooted and crashed against the yacht club. The waves were up to twelve meters. The boat had no chance. Early in the morning, I saw her rise up once more, topple backwards and snap in two like a matchstick. I was numb. My dream had ended. I had lost everything.

After several months sitting in total depression in Bali, I received a letter – one of my father's very special letters – which read: 'I think it's about time you stopped feeling sorry for yourself, contemplating your navel under the bodhi tree, and got back home'. Shortly afterwards a friend introduced me to one of my heroes, the legendary war photographer Don McCullin. I'd always been in awe of and fascinated by Don. He seemed such a complex man and came across as incredibly depressed and very grumpy. I love grumpy people. But I also felt an enormous compassion, lying under his gloomy exterior. Don had given up covering wars. He had a row with the editor of the *Sunday Times*, a newspaper he had risked his life for so many years. He now wanted, as he put it, 'To get rid of the rubbish in my mind and record the disappearing tribes of the world, before it's too late.' He asked me to accompany him to Indonesia, as I knew the area well.

We made many fantastic journeys, particularly to the Mentawai Islands, off the west coast of Sumatra where Don took stunning photographs of the Sakkudei people, who have now been wiped out. In 1986, joined by my friend Harry Fane, we set out on expedition to the remote Asmat area of South Irian Jaya – Indonesia's largest island. It was here in the 1960s that Michael Rockefeller was supposed to have been eaten by cannibals. We went to find out.

In 1987, I proudly published my first book, *Skulduggery*, an account of that journey. It got one review in a free property magazine. It read something like:

'This book should be called *Carry-on up the Jungle* – a farcical attempt at travel-writing.'

This was not encouraging. However, I was lucky enough to have the late great Abner Stein as my agent and the late great Tony Colwell as my editor at Jonathan Cape. With their support and perhaps because my publishers needed to recoup their losses, they gave me another chance to write.

* * *

I had long wanted to write a book about India, the country that fascinated me most. I felt my soul was in India. So in 1988, I set off and came face to rump with Tara.

During that journey, through Tara I got my first inkling of the dangers facing her wild Asian cousins. I remember that in rural Orissa I was approached by a local teacher who was convinced that Tara and I had been sent by the Gods to catch a rogue elephant which had decimated his village's crops and already killed eleven people. This was but one of many similar situations that I would encounter, exposing the growing imbalance in India between rural man and the natural life of the elephants. Both are blameless and both are victims of greed, greed caused by a desire for timber and space, and the consequent massive deforestation. Elephants are creatures of habit and have for centuries followed the same migratory routes in search of food. When they arrive and find that their larder has been cut down, in desperation they turn to raiding the crops on which the villagers' livelihoods depend.

Over one hundred years ago, the American naturalist Charles Frederick Holder had recognized the inevitable. He wrote, '*The Asiatic elephant is said to be holding its own. But the rapid advance of the British in the East cannot fail to have a fatal effect and extermination is only a matter of time. They are the last of a powerful race worthy of earnest efforts of preservation. The question of their extinction rests with the rising generation*'.

Unfortunately, the rising – or should I say exploding – generations (India's population alone is over 1.2 billion) have failed to address this urgent problem. It was only on returning home from my journey with Tara that the full impact of the experience began to take effect. Elephants, like India herself, move slowly and subtly to educate humans, and Tara had been a clever and instructive teacher.

What had started as a whim soon turned into a passion. I came to realise that Asian elephants had once roamed in their millions from Syria to China, but that now they were reduced to pathetic little herds in equally reduced forest fragments. Today it is doubtful if as many as forty thousand elephants survive in the whole of Asia. Africa's elephant population is over half a million.

Unlike the larger, mammoth-tusked African elephant, the Asian elephant does not suffer to the same extent from poaching because only certain males carry ivory. Ironically however, and I say this with no prejudice because I adore all elephants, the African elephant has benefited from a highly emotional public outrage at their bloody slaughter for ivory. Appeals to help fund this fight have been so lucrative, positive and widespread that the Asian elephant, like the proverbial poor relation, has remained in the background waiting patiently for some crumbs. It seemed to me that the world had forgotten there was another elephant.

So I became what is now socially fashionable in western capitals, a person with a cause. But – to borrow an Indian expression – 'what to do?' I had no qualifications or scientific knowledge and, as I was to find out, the closed and rather arrogant coven of Asian elephant experts and NGOs did not take a mad Englishman's journey on an elephant across India seriously. They thought it was a publicity stunt. If I was to be taken seriously, I needed credentials. I needed to get out to Asia and really understand the problem. My old mahout, Bhim, had told me 'Rajah-Sahib there is only one way to learn about Haathi – be with them.'

Fortunately my book, due to Tara, was beginning to make waves and I was soon approached by independent documentary film-makers to write and present films on the Asian elephant. The first was with the Hollywood actress Goldie Hawn. Others followed and I wrote another book on my experiences with elephants. But what was most important was that the Asian elephant was finally getting some exposure in the West, and I was getting real hands-on field experience.

In the early nineties, I was approached by Fauna and Flora International, founded in 1903 and the oldest and most prestigious conservation society in the world. I was made a vice-president alongside the legendary Sir David Attenborough and David Bellamy. Perhaps I was finally being taken seriously. Fauna and Flora International had started to support Asian elephant conservation, particularly in Sumatra, Indonesia. It was a real learning curve for me. I spent a lot of time in the field, studying conservation and seeing how a charity works. But for my purposes, Fauna and Flora was too diverse. I wanted to concentrate only on the survival of the Asian elephant. To my knowledge such a charity did not exist. So on 1st September 2002, under the patronage of the late Rajmata of Jaipur, Sir Evelyn De Rothschild and five friends with the same passion, Elephant Family was born.

* * *

We began as a welfare organisation, concentrating on improving the life of captive elephants in Jaipur and Sumatra. But soon we realised that every elephant in captivity reflects a failure of conservation efforts. It is like sticking on a plaster. There are many welfare organisations doing great work, but Elephant Family's mission is to save the *wild* Asian elephant from extinction, before it is too late. We had to look at the bigger picture.

And we had to move fast. Ninety percent of the Asian elephant population had been wiped out in the previous hundred years. Ninety-five percent of their forest homes had been destroyed to make way for plantations, farms, mines, roads, railways and villages. And the situation was getting worse each year. The boom in the economy and in the human population had been catastrophic for the region's wild places. The last remaining elephants were forced into tiny pockets of forest where they were competing with their human neighbours for food, water and space.

When they don't have enough space and food, elephants can cause chaos. When stressed, disorientated elephants clash with poor subsistence farmers and villagers, causing deaths on both sides. In India alone, a person kills an elephant and an elephant kills a person every single day of the year. By corralling them into ever smaller areas, we have changed the psyche of this peaceful herbivore into that of a dangerous, paranoid animal that will seek revenge. Elephants are the only species that are intelligent and big enough to take on humankind. And they won't go quietly.

Elephant Family is dedicated to ending this daily battle between people and elephants. We are saving vital stretches of forest while we can, and reuniting isolated groups of elephants by reconnecting pockets of forest with 'elephant corridors'. These corridors of protected land act as elephant highways, joining up forest fragments and allowing all wildlife – including tigers and orangutans – to roam freely, to find new sources of food and, crucially, to breed successfully. We are giving elephants the space they need. And we are helping poor rural communities protect their livelihoods so that their families can live safely in the last remaining elephant habitats.

There are over eighty-eight identified elephant corridors in India alone. Four years ago, in partnership with the Wildlife Trust of India, we set out to save the most important corridor of all, linking Tirunelli and Begur Forest Reserves in Kerala, South India. It is a lifeline for 6,500 elephants, the largest population of elephants in Asia.

Just six kilometres long by a kilometre wide, the corridor was home to fifty-four human families in five settlements. Four of these settlements have been relocated to brand new safe homes where they are now able to grow crops without the fear of raiding and dangerous elephants. We are just in the process of relocating the last settlement. Already, there have been sightings of other wildlife including tigers, leopards and spotted deer using the corridor. This is another reason why it is so important to save the Asian elephant. It is the apex species. Elephants are the guardians of the forests as they need the maximum amount of space. If you save them, you save all the other species that share their habitat.

* * *

To start a charity from scratch is not an easy task. It takes real graft and belief. One person who has stayed with me from the beginning of this roller-coaster ride, Ruth Powys, is now the Director of Elephant Family. She instilled into the young and inexperienced team a passion and commitment that has made Elephant Family the success it is today. And a little later, we were joined by a kharmic beauty called Carla Vincent, whose Zen-like calm spread to us all.

Funding is always a problem. I have spent most of the last ten years with a begging bowl. On reflection, I realised that my past life hadn't been such a disaster. I had made so many friends, many of whom have supported me with the utmost generosity. But you can't just rely on major donors again and again. Donor fatigue sets in. The charity sector is highly competitive. You have to think out of the box and find other ways to raise funds and awareness. And you have to make it fun!

Initially, we took the traditional route by holding a grand dinner and auction called the 'Elephant Durbar'. Its success was partly due to the fact that the event was held in a beautiful private garden in Richmond. In addition, in 2006 my sister Camilla married The Prince of Wales. Overnight, the demented young brother, the black sheep of the family, became a little more respectable, perhaps. Both have been long and loyal supporters of Elephant Family and kindly attended the event. In The Prince of Wales, I am lucky to have as a brother-in-law a truly brilliant ally, a legend who has contributed massively himself to conservation and the environment. But those traditional ways of raising funds are no longer sufficient.

Apart from her extraordinary work ethic and her refusal to fail, Ruth Powys possesses that rare ability to think out of the box. In 2005, we got involved with the fashion photographer, Bruce Weber, an avid elephant nut. He created a group of life-size metal elephant frames and dressed them in Haute Couture fashion for a shoot for *W Magazine*. The elephant frames were built by an eccentric and brilliant topiary artist from the States, Topiary Joe.

We never looked back. Elephant Family began to hit the headlines starting with 'Elephants in the Park' – a herd of ten beautiful life-size willow elephants covered by elephant blankets designed by top fashion designers. It was also the year that 'Date an Elephant' was launched. It's a charming and much more personal adaptation of 'Adopt an Elephant'. On Valentine's Day, elephant daters receive personalised photographs and love poems from special elephants with different characters, chosen from our welfare projects, written painstakingly and beautifully by one of our team.

In 2008, the Survival Tour rocked off – thirteen life-size topiary elephants created by Topiary Joe, Ruth's twin sister, Mary, and her husband, Derek, in a barn near their home in Clonakilty, Ireland. They travelled right across the UK and Ireland and were showcased in spectacular locations. Audiences from these two exhibitions had now reached thirteen million and significant funds had been raised from the sale of the elephants and the blankets. Most importantly Elephant Family was growing a reputation as the charity that did things differently.

In 2010, we staged the largest outdoor art exhibition to date, in London. Two hundred and sixty elephant sculptures were placed across London, all painted by top artists, fashion designers and architects. It caused a sensation. At the auctions, conducted by Sotheby's and online, we raised over £4 million from the sale of the elephants. The top price – £155,000 – was paid for a fantastic elephant creation by the Scottish artist Jack Vettriano.

In 2011, Ruth dreamed up 'Jungle City'. One of the objectives of this new exhibition was to unite the conservation movement in Asia. We partnered with six other charities working in Asia with different species. A hundred and thirty elephant, tiger, orangutan, crocodile and hornbill sculptures, again painted by fantastic artists, were hidden across Edinburgh and raised over a million pounds.

This year we changed shape. Elephant Family, in partnership with Action for Children put on the largest egg hunt ever, sponsored by the jeweller, Fabergé. For forty days and forty nights, two hundred and ten giant eggs designed and created by top artists were hidden across London. We broke two Guinness World Records - for the most expensive chocolate egg ever sold, and for the most entrants in an egg hunt competition. We raised over one million pounds for the different charities and artists such as Zaha Hadid, The Chapman Brothers, Marc Quinn, Sir Peter Blake, Bruce Oldfield, Sir Nicholas Grimshaw and Nicky Haslam headlined the event with others.

Elephant Family has grown. We now have thirteen projects in four countries: India, Thailand, Malaysia and Indonesia. Campaigning is a high priority. If you can't encourage conservation, or put pressure on the governments and major companies, you're hitting a brick wall. I am deeply proud to have played a role in this wonderful charity – probably more proud than of anything else I have done in my life. We are now the UK's biggest funder of the endangered Asian elephant. To date we have raised £9.7 million for their conservation. Not bad for a charity that celebrates its tenth anniversary this year.

* * *

It's fitting to end with Tara, who is the true founder of Elephant Family. Over the years, I've visited her regularly at her home in Kipling Camp, Madhya Pradesh, where she lives like a pampered princess. She wakes up, eats, sleeps, swims, has a massage, eats and then goes back to bed – day in, day out. I would swap her life for mine any time. If I ever feel the need for motivation, all it takes is a few days with her to relieve the stress and fill me with hope again.

People ask me all the time how old she is. I know it is impolite to ask a lady her age. However, I will disclose that we celebrated my sixtieth and her fiftieth birthday last year when she consumed a cake which took four strong men to carry. I hope she does not read this. She, like most vain women, has always lied about her age.

Though she is getting older, she is just as beautiful. The tops of her ears are curling over, and she has lost two sets of molars. But this has not affected her appetite. And she is in better shape than me, with my two replaced hips. She doesn't frolic so much now in her private swimming pool in the local river. She sits quietly, her eyes (fringed by lashes long enough to suggest that they are false) closed contentedly. Occasionally, she will flick her trunk out of the water, spraying us with cooling water as I rest my head against her back – two old friends, enjoying the evening of their lives together.

I remember when I had finished my journey, the old elephant hands of Assam told me that I could now retire. 'You have performed Haathi Dhun,' they said. 'You have given life back to an elephant. From now on your life will be gilded in gold.' How could I think of retiring? I did not save her. She saved me.

Mark Shand
London 2012

ELEPHANT FAMILY

Protecting Asian elephants and their habitat

To find out more about Elephant Family's work, or to donate to the charity, please visit www.elephantfamily.org

Bibliography

NOTE: I have referred to some of these books in the text and they have all provided helpful background information.

Harry Abbot, *Reminiscences of Sonepore*, Star Press, Calcutta, 1896.

Salim Ali, *The Book of Indian Birds*, Bombay Natural Society, Bombay, 1979.

George Franklin Atkinson, *Curry and Rice: The Ingredients of Social Life at 'Our Station' in India*, Day and Day, London.

R. D. Banerji, *History of Orissa*, vols 1 & 2, Calcutta, 1931.

A. L. Basham, *The Wonder that was India*, Sidgwick & Jackson, London, 1954.

Hilaire Belloc, *The Bad Child's Book of Beasts*, Duckworth, London, 1938.

J. Moray Brown, *Shikar Sketches with Notes on Indian Field Sports*, Hurst & Blackett, London, 1887.

Richard Carrington, *Elephants*, Chatto & Windus, London, 1958.

Jane Dunbar (ed.), *Tigers, Durbars and Kings: Fanny Eden's Indian Journals 1837–1838*, John Murray, London, 1988.

Gerald Durrell, *Rosie is my Relative*, William Collins, London, 1968.

Emily Eden, *Up the Country: Letters from India*, Curzon Press, London, 1978.

Franklin Edgerton (tr.), *The Elephant-Lore of the Hindus: The Elephant Sport (Matanga-Lila) of Nilakantha*, Yale University Press, 1931.

Abu 'L-Fazl, *Ain-I-Akbari*, translated by H. Blochmann, Calcutta-Asiatic Society of Bengal, Bengal, 1927.

Robert Fermor-Hesketh, *Architecture of the British Empire*, The Vendome Press, New York, 1986.

Bamber Gascoigne, *The Great Moghuls*, Jonathan Cape, London, 1971.

C. F. Holder, *Ivory King*, Samson, Low, Marston Searle & Rivington, London, 1886.

Samuel Israel and Bikram Grewal (eds), *Insight Guides: India*, Harrap, London, 1985.

Ramchandra Jain (ed.), *McCrindle's Ancient India as described by Megasthenes and Arrian*, Today & Tomorrow's, New Delhi, 1972.

Anne Morrow, *Highness: The Maharajahs of India*, Grafton Books, London, 1986.

Cynthia Moss, *Elephant Memoirs: Thirteen Years in the Life of an Elephant Family*, Elm Tree Books, London, 1988.

Naveen Patnaik, *A Second Paradise: Indian Courtly Life 1590–1947*, Sidgwick & Jackson, London, 1985.

An Old Planter, *Reminiscences of Behar by an old Planter*, Thacker, Spink, Calcutta, 1887.

Louis Rousselet, *India and Its Native Princes: Travels in Central India and in the Presidencies of Bombay and Bengal*, revised and edited by Lieutenant-Colonel Buckle, Scribner Armstrong, New York, 1876.

G. P. Sanderson, *Pack Gear for Elephants*, Calcutta, 1887.

G. P. Sanderson, *Thirteen Years Among the Wild Beasts of India*, W. H. Allen, London, 1890.

Ivan T. Sanderson, *The Dynasty of Abu*, Cassell, London, 1963.

E. O. Shebbeare, *Soondar Mooni*, Victor Gollancz, London, 1958.

P. D. Stracey, *Elephant Gold*, Weidenfeld & Nicolson, London, 1963.

Sir J. Emmerson Tennant, Bt., *The Wild Elephant*, Longmans Green, London, 1867.

Edward Topsell, *The History of Foure-Footed Beastes, describing the True and Lively Figure of Every Beast ... Collected out of all the Volumes of C. Gesner and all other Writers of the Present Day*, W. Jaggard, London, 1607.

Leonardo da Vinci, *The Notebooks of Leonardo da Vinci*, arranged and translated by Edward MacCurdy, George Braziller, New York, 1954.

Francis Watson, *A Concise History of India*, Thames & Hudson, London, 1974.

J. H. Williams, *Big Charlie*, Rupert Hart-Davis, London, 1950.

J. H. Williams, *Elephant Bill*, Rupert Hart-Davis, London, 1959.

Colonel Henry Yule and A. C. Burnell, *Hobson-Jobson*, John Murray, London, 1903.

GAZETTEERS

Bengal District Gazetteer – Gaya, 1906.

Bengal District Gazetteers – Saran, 1908.

Bengal District Gazetteers – Singhbum, Sareikela and Kharsawan – Calcutta, 1910.

Bihar and Orissa District Gazetteers – Saran, 1930.

Bihar and Orissa District Gazetteers – Cuttack, 1933.

Bihar District Gazetteer – Singhbum/Patna – Bishar, 1958.

Bihar District Gazetteer – Saran, 1960.

Bihar District Gazetteer – Ranchi, 1970.

Bihar District Gazetteer – Patna, 1970.

Hazaribagh Old Records (1761–1878), 1957.

Orissa District Gazetteers – Puri District.

Acknowledgements

ABOVE ALL, I would like to thank Naveen Patnaik and Aditya Patankar, whose friendship, support and patience really made this all possible.

Foremost, for unending generosity with their time, knowledge and resources my sincerest gratitude is due to: Sri Bijoyananda Patnaik, Sri Martand Singh, Ajai Singh of Maksudpur, Maharaj Kumar Anang Udai Singh Deo and Maharaj Kumarani Vijay Lakshmi Devi of Patna, Maharaj Kumar Ranjit Singh of Wankaner, Sri Bal Manohar Jalan, Tavleen Singh and Pepita Seth.

I am deeply grateful to the following people, all of whom in many different ways contributed so much:

In India Rajmata Gayatri Devi of Jaipur, Maharaja Gaj Singh of Jodhpur, Maharani Vasundhara Raje of Dholpur, Maharaja Pradeep Chandra Bhanj Deo of Mayurbhanj, The Raja of Seraikella, Mahijit Singh Jhala, Rani Sunita Pitamber, Sri Bijoy Sorangi, Sri Brijendra Singh, Mrs June Lal, Sanjiv Lal, Rajkumar Braja Bhannu Singh Deo, Bheem and Reeta Dev Varma, Hershad Kumari of Jamnagar, Amita Beg, Sri H. S. Jassal, Bittu Saghal, Doctor Duke Chawla, the late Sri Babla Senapathy, Sri S. K. Patnaik, Sri Nand Kishore Singh, Sri Arun Pathak, Sri Ashok Singh, Sri Nilmandhab Mohanty, Sri N. K. Panda, Kumud Choudhury, Sri B. C. Verma, Peter Carter, Toby Sinclair, Gudu and Christina Patnaik, D. K. Lahiri Choudhury, Doctor Kumar Suresh Singh, Pramod Kasliwal, Kumar Ashok Singh Diggi, Deepak Rana, Sita Ram Singh, Bishwanath Singh, Ranjivoy Singh, S. P. Singh, U. P. Singh and the people of McCluskiegunge. For their generous hospitality and impeccable service I would like to acknowledge Mr P. R. S. Oberoi and the managers and staff of the Oberoi hotels in Delhi, Bombay and Calcutta.

In England Belinda Burton, Mariuska Chalmers, Mitchell Crites, Simon Elliot. H. E. The Deputy High Commissioner for India, Mr Salman Haidar, Sir Geoffrey

Howe, Sir Owain Jenkins, Harry Marshall, Don Munson, Marjorie Naisbitt, Doctor John Price, Joan Phillips and the staff of Sussex Secretarial Services, John Hatt, Abner Stein and Beverley Sturdy. From my publishers Jonathan Cape: Georgina Capel, Jenny Cottom, Rachael Kerr, Hilary Turner, Sarah Wherry, and in particular my editor Tony Colwell whose care and erudition is legendary.

I can never begin to thank Gita Mehta for giving me so selflessly her guidance, knowledge, encouragement and time; my mother and father for their total support and allowing me to use their home to write this book; Don McCullin for being as always an indefatigable travelling companion and friend and Bob, Anne and Belinda Wright for giving Tara such a wonderful home at Kipling Camp where I know she will enjoy a long and very happy life.

Finally, I would like to thank the many unnamed people who I encountered in Orissa and Bihar, whose welcome, spontaneity and sense of humour made this journey so memorable for me. I shall never forget them.

M. S.
London
October, 1990